The Best of Defoe's Review

THE BEST OF Defoe's REVIEW

AN ANTHOLOGY

Compiled and Edited by
WILLIAM L. PAYNE

Essay Index Reprint Series

BOOKS FOR LIBRARIES PRESS
FREEPORT, NEW YORK

INTERNATIONAL STANDARD BOOK NUMBER:
0-8369-1873-8

LIBRARY OF CONGRESS CATALOG CARD NUMBER:
73-128233

PRINTED IN THE UNITED STATES OF AMERICA

DEDICATED TO

E. C. P.

Preface

Naturally, I think that not enough of the *Review* has been included here—that other interesting and pertinent essays should have been included; but I console myself with the thought that the *Review* "fan" can satiate his appetite with the fifteen hundred essays which comprise the complete *Review* as published in twenty-two volumes by the Facsimile Text Society in 1938.

While making my *Index to Defoe's Review* I found myself wishing that a representative selection were available to the general reader so that those who today read its contemporary, the *Spectator*, might get a glimpse of another England. Accordingly, I have tried to select essays which show the variety and range of the journal. Essays upon the social scene are included not as rivaling those in the *Spectator*, which Defoe "venerates," but to reveal the man Defoe. For the same reason I have included a number of autobiographical essays. If it appears that the bulk of the essays concern themselves with impending legislation, projected treaties, and national credit, we can only conclude that the Englishman of 1711 is the true-born ancestor of the Englishman of 1951.

I have nowhere changed Defoe's wording, and where additions have been necessary the word or letter has been put in square brackets. I have ventured to modernize the punctuation, spelling, and paragraphing. However, Defoe's sentences sometimes defy one who would diagram them. Since I would not meddle with his words, I was constrained to break up some long, hard-to-understand sentences into shorter ones. But punctuation alone could not of itself always correct the syntax, make clean-cut English sentences. I can only say that in my punctuation I have been scrupulously careful not to alter Defoe's meaning as I have understood it.

As originally published, the separate *Reviews* had no subject titles. I have given each essay a title which tries to point up its central thought or spirit. I have added notes only where I thought them necessary to an adequate understanding of the matter in hand; volumes have been written on the War of the Spanish Succession, and Defoe himself wrote a large book on the history of the union of Scotland and England. Where I have not been able to cite chapter and verse I trust my friends will believe I made an honest search, and that my correctors (first having taken an honest lick at my slothfulness) will generously share with me the fruits of their own industry.

Miriam Bergamini of the Columbia University Press has been a vigilant and faithful editor.

W. L. P.

New York
May 1, 1951

Introduction

The reader who knows the eighteenth-century periodical only through the *Tatler* and the *Spectator* may well feel some bewilderment as he leafs through the pages of these selections from Defoe's *Review*. He will find no casual and charming comment upon the passing scene of court and coffee-house, of lovely (if slightly ludicrous) ladies, no periwigged dandies at the opera or theatre, no sense of a world at leisure with infinite time for brilliant chatter. He will seek in vain for amusing reflections upon beaux's heads and coquettes' hearts or for quiet ponderings on the tombs in Westminster Abbey. But it is possible that if he goes on to read the essays, he will find something that strikes him as more "modern" than the charmingly artificial world of Mr. Spectator. In the essays of Mr. Review he will discover another side of the eighteenth century, will learn how earlier men faced political, social, and economic problems which we sometimes think peculiar to our own times. It is possible too that he will turn from these pages to reread *Robinson Crusoe* or *Moll Flanders* with new eyes and new understanding.

In an age famous for its periodicals (more than three hundred were published during the first sixteen years of the eighteenth century) Defoe's *Review* was remarkable for its longevity. The *Spectator* lived only into its second year, as did the *Tatler* and the *Guardian*. The *Rehearsal* maintained its hold on life for four years, the *Observator* only a little longer. But the *Review* held its course for nine years, from February 19, 1704, until June 11, 1713. On occasion it changed its format, its days of publication, its long-title, but whatever it was officially called, it remained what it had been from the beginning, the *Review*.

Various explanations have been offered for its unusually long life, the most probable of which is that the periodical was subsidized by an influential member of the government, well aware of the importance of periodicals in what we now call "propaganda." Defoe himself has left us only one cryptic statement about the origin of the magazine: he said that it "had its birth *in tenebris*." For many years modern scholars believed that its origin was to be found in the dark period when Defoe was in prison as a result of his inflammatory pamphlet, *The Shortest Way with the Dissenters*. While that theory has been disproved, authorities seem in general agreement that there was some connection between Defoe's imprisonment and the genesis of the *Review*. Defoe's release from prison seems to have been a result of intercession on the part of Robert Harley, Secretary of State, to whom Defoe wrote that he stood "ready to dedicate my life and all my possible powers to the interest of so generous and so bountiful benefactors." We know that Defoe wrote Harley, begging him to "appoint me a convenient private allowance on which I might comfortably depend and continue to be serviceable in a private capacity." Certainly, as modern biographers have pointed out, there was a remarkable coincidence between the policies of the *Review* and those of Harley. Some of Defoe's contemporaries took for granted that his periodical was an organ for the government. "Review," wrote one of them, "you are a damned rascal; do you think to persuade us that you are not writing for the ministry, because you're writing upon trade?" Defoe's denials were not convincing then nor are they now, particularly when we read his veiled references at the end of the first and the beginning of the second volumes to unidentified benefactors "who have it in their power to sink it with their breath; and by withdrawing the influence which now supports it, cause it to receive its death from the same hands it had . . . life." In the closing pages of the last volume, too, he expressed his appreciation of "the few friends I have left; who from the beginning have been benefactors to the work, and without them I could not have supported the expense of it."

Whether Defoe's statement that the origin of the *Review* lay *"in tenebris"* referred to prison or poverty makes little difference. The charges of his contemporaries that he was in the pay of one party or another were not unusual; they were hurled at many contemporary editors. Leslie of the *Rehearsal* was labeled a "High Flyer" (that is, a High Churchman). Tutchin of the *Observator* was branded a Whig; Swift of the *Examiner* was a Tory, as was Maynwaring of the *Medley*. All possible epithets were applied to Defoe: he was first a Whig, then a Tory, variously a High Flyer and a Papist, in addition a stupid dog, a canting rascal, and—vehemently on the part of an adversary—one who "deserves not only the correction of the gallows, but the personal correction of every man that meets you, and 'twill be no more sin to cut your throat, than to kill a dog."

We who live in a world in which party politics are reflected in many of the newspapers we read and many of the radio commentators to whom we listen need not linger over the controversy of the extent to which the *Review* was subsidized by governmental officers. Other eighteenth-century periodicals were subsidized, yet their histories were short. There was one primary reason for the long life of the *Review:* the pertinacity and assiduity of its editor. On this there is no disagreement among scholars. In sickness or in health, from English inns or Scottish taverns, no matter where he was or how he was, Defoe continued to send his copy to the printer for nine years. Replying to malicious gossips who doubted the authenticity of the authorship of certain numbers of the *Review*, published while he was in Scotland, Defoe said: "The papers are wrote with his own hand, and the originals may be seen at the printers." We have external evidence in plenty to prove the truth of Defoe's statement, but even if we had none, we would still have the internal evidence of Defoe's style and characteristic point of view, echoing everywhere to ears accustomed to the peculiarities of Defoe's vocabulary, rhythm, moods in his novels, pamphlets, or occasional papers.

The periodical of the eighteenth century was neither a newspaper nor a magazine, in our modern sense. Newspapers of somewhat the sort we know today were familiar in England, where they began to appear at least as early as 1621—"corantos," they were called, single-sheet, two-column publications containing foreign news. In 1622 had appeared a "news book," the *Weekely News*, edited by Nicholas Bourne and Thomas Archer. This averaged twenty-two pages to the issue and, in addition to foreign news, offered its readers accounts of murders, witches, monsters, miracles, and other "wonders." In 1666 appeared England's first "official" newspaper, the *London Gazette*, a news organ that was supposed to carry only authenticated reports of political events, intended as an antidote to ignorant and unfounded reports that made up the material of other newspapers. The Restoration government was fully aware that political news was a power either to arouse or allay the fears of the people. Other newspapers and news-letters flourished during this period,[1] but the "periodical," as most of us know it, really began in the first years of the eighteenth century.

We must not think of these early periodicals as newspapers in our sense. A closer parallel may be found in the contributions of modern "columnists," syndicated today in many newspapers. Addison, Steele, Defoe and others did not offer their contemporaries "news," which they could learn from many other sources; they offered opinion, commentary, prejudice. The principal feature of most of their issues was a single essay, which interpreted current news and gossip or commented upon the passing scene of manners and morals and which frequently affected readers' opinions as do our columnists and radio commentators today. But before we consider Defoe's commentaries in his main essays, we may stop for a moment over other "features" (the word is even more familiar today than in the eighteenth century) of the *Review.*

One important "feature" of the eighteenth-century periodical was the "advertisement." Defoe wrote in 1705, "The principal support of all the public papers now on foot depends upon the advertisements," and indeed advertisements might have kept the *Review* alive, with or without patronage, if Defoe had been more interested in them than he evidently was. At times his advertisements took up as much room as two of the eight columns; sometimes there were none at all; often there were only one or two. Modern scholars who have examined hundreds of eighteenth-century periodicals say that the prevailing advertisements of the day were for cures of venereal disease, cosmetics, and books, approximately in that order. An occasional periodical—Leslie's *Rehearsal,* for example—limited its advertising to books, but most of them, including the *Tatler* and the *Spectator,* allowed wide latitude. In the case of the *Review,* advertisements of books led the field (there were 168 among a total of 361 advertisements in the first three vol-

[1] The number of newspapers and newsletters in circulation at any one time during the seventeenth century can only be approximated; but some idea may be gained from Andrews' statement that seventy different journals were begun between 1661 and 1668, and that twenty-six were begun between 1688 and 1692. Defoe and other writers mention nine newspapers in the year 1704/5. An anonymous writer of the period gives their estimated circulation, running from a low of 400 to the high of the *London Gazette,* 6,000. Defoe, arguing in 1711 against a tax on newspapers, estimated the total weekly circulation in the nation at 200,000. His figures were probably greatly exaggerated.

umes), but cures and cosmetics also had their place.[2] The "warty" individual of the day might well have been attracted by such an advertisement as this: "An excellent secret to take away warts; being a noble mineral tincture, which safely and without trouble takes away the largest and most ugly warts from the hands or other parts of the body so as never to return again, rendering the places on which they grew as smooth and fair as if no such excrescence had ever been." The dandy would have read of "the royal essence for the head and periwigs, being the most delicate and charming perfume in nature, and the greatest preserver of hair in the world. . . . By its incomparable odour and fragrancy it strengthens the brain, revives the spirits, quickens the memory and makes the heart cheerful, never raises the vapours in ladies, &c. . . ." Parents then as now proved eager buyers of "purging sugar-plums for children, and others, to whom physic is irksome." The eighteenth-century editors of periodicals had none of our modern "display techniques," but they knew their buying public.

That Defoe was not so dependent upon advertisers as some of his descendants may be seen from his whimsical attitude toward such subsidy. He seems to have been both casual and prejudiced about those he included and those he omitted. Apparently he had a standing agreement with his advertisers that he would give them space only when he did not need it himself. So far as we can tell, "copy" must have been accepted "at the pleasure of the editor," who ran it for the required number of entries when he had room for it. If Mr. Review, the columnist, happened to be ardently engaged on one of his programs in regard to High Flyers, peace, moderation, or the economic problems of the kingdom, he left out all advertisement in the issue.

Another "feature" of the *Review* may well have kept on the subscription list some readers who would have been bored with Defoe's political and economic essays. In the early issues Defoe included a "department" which he entitled "*Mercure Scandale:* or, Advice from the Scandalous Club. (Translated out of the French.)" The parenthesis suggests, as so often in the period, the added weight in readers' minds

[2] Mr. Payne, who has examined the 361 advertisements that appear in Volumes I, II, III, finds the distribution as follows: books, 167; announcements, 77; cures for various diseases (including many other than venereal), 48; "patent medicines," 41; cosmetics, 28.

given to anything French. The subtitle of the department might well have sold out the first issue: "Being a Weekly History of Nonsense, Impertinence, Vice and Debauchery." Later the title was shortened to "Advice from the Scandalous Club." Probably Defoe borrowed the idea of this "feature" from an earlier journal with which he seems to have been temporarily associated, *The Athenian Mercury*, edited by John Dunton from 1691 until 1697. Dunton was the ancestor of our modern radio "quiz programs," the most famous "answer man" of the late seventeenth century. Then as now, the public seems to have had unlimited time and inclination for writing letters and inquiries to popular commentators. No query was too insignificant for Dunton, who took on all comers and replied to high and low alike (though not in the order in which he received inquiries, since his periodical abounded in apologies for procrastination in replying to a neglected letter that he had just unearthed from the mountain-piles on his editorial desk). Through his early experience with Dunton, Defoe seems to have discovered—what our modern newspapers and radio "quizzers" know very well—that adults are as curious as children, that, as Aristotle said, "Man by nature desires to know."

The "Scandalous Club," like the "Spectator Club" of which Sir Roger de Coverley was a member, had no existence other than in the imagination of its creator. It was a journalist's fiction, yet it became an object of belief to readers. The "*Mercure Scandale*" differed in one important way from the earlier *Athenian Mercury*, and the difference is significant of Daniel Defoe himself. "Ask-me-another" Dunton had prided himself on his ability to answer any question, no matter how absurd, and the official program of his journal—that of "informing" and "correcting"—often gave way to the most trivial chitchat. Mr. Review, however, took seriously the program of his "Scandalous Club." "The Society's main battery," he wrote, "was always erected against vice and folly." Serious questions were answered seriously; "merry" quips and queries were included only when the editor believed his answers would benefit readers in general and the querist in particular. "Our Society," he said, "openly declare, they publish nothing in the most diverting manner, but what they design for a serious improvement." Implicit in the policies of these early journals is an extension of the old basic opposition between two schools as to the function of literature, one holding its primary purpose was to "delight," the other insisting that it was to "teach." The "Scandalous Club" did not object to "diversion" in so far as diversion was compatible with instruction. Here as always the author of *Robinson Crusoe* considered himself primarily as a counselor and guide.

The themes that bulked largest among the letters Defoe printed were the perennial ones of love and marriage. "Mr. Review," a young woman wrote sadly, "I am a servant maid, living near Boo church. . . . I thought I should long ago have had a sweetheart, but I have missed my expectations." A gentleman wants to know "whether I may have any hopes from a lady who is far beyond me in fortune, but has given me some encouragement." But there were other problems than domestic. "Gentlemen, your opinion is humbly desired . . . whether a person being born deaf and dumb, is capable of learning to write." Readers wrote to Mr. Review about talking dogs, about lending money, about magistrates who swore in the very act of sentencing a prisoner for the very same offense, about preachers who used the Scripture as a point of departure for political discourse, about the conductor of the Club himself, who dared pass judgment upon other mortals. Profound or frivolous, the questions, if answered at all, were always answered seriously by Defoe.

Undoubtedly here lay Defoe's weakness as a popular journalist in an age that liked both its learning and its scandals handled lightly. The "Scandalous Club" lived only a little over a year, from February, 1704, to April, 1705. It was succeeded by other "features" that grew increasingly serious.[3] Defoe's comments show that from the first he had

[3] In May, 1705, the material appeared as a separate publication in "The Little Review" and continued twice a week until the end of August. From September, 1704, to January, 1705, Defoe issued five monthly numbers entitled "A Supplement to the Advice from the Scandal. Club." By way of compromise with readers who apparently had protested the discontinuance of the Scandalous Club, Defoe announced in the introduction to the 1706 volume: "I purpose certain 'Miscellanea' at the end of this paper as a just alleviation to the tedious vein of other matter, and as a handle to introduce anything useful and advantageous either to the reader or myself." He added that the "Miscellanea" would contain nothing improper or impertinent, nor would it be allowed to interfere with the main essay. The "Miscellanea" was a soberer "feature" than the "*Mercure Scandale.*" It did not print letters on marital problems, on foolish lovers, on talking dogs. Ordinarily a single inquiry from a reader was followed by an essay of 400 to 1,000 words. The "Miscellanea" appeared irregularly, sometimes omitted for weeks at a time.

found the "Scandalous Club" an intrusion upon space which might be better used for serious essays, a drain too upon his time and energy. "I am letter-baited by querists," he wrote impatiently, "and think my trouble to write civil, private answers to teasing and querulous epistles has been equal, if not more troublesome than all the rest of the work." The historical importance of the *"Mercure Scandale"* lies less in itself than in its posterity. It was from this feature that Steele and Addison probably picked up the idea of a club of commentators on vice and folly, which they handled with the lightness and literary skill lacking in Defoe, who bequeathed his creation to his successors with relief for the cessation of his own uncongenial labors, and with bitter invective against the level of a popular audience that demanded a frivolity against which his own sense of decency revolted. "Tired with the mass of filth, the stench of which was hardly to be endured," he wrote savagely, "I laid aside the Herculean labour for a while, and am glad to see the Society honoured by the succession (in those just endeavours) of the venerable Isaac Bickerstaff, Esq., who, vouchsafing to rake in your beloved lay-stall may, perhaps, contrary to nature, bring you to smell your own stink, and have a just notion of your follies."

Defoe's attitude toward the *"Mercure Scandale"* gives us a clue to the *Review* as a whole. From the first, he intended his periodical to be a "star that scatters light." His purpose was "to open the eyes of the deluded people, and set them to rights in the things in which they are imposed upon." To this aim he remained faithful during his nine years of editorship. His interest was not in the "social scene," in the sense in which Addison and Steele described it to the delighted eyes of men and women who would have liked to be a part of it, as well as to those who already were. Defoe had no entrée to the high places of society, nor did he desire one. His interest in "society" was much more akin to our own: he was concerned (in more modern parlance) not with the Four Hundred but with the Four Million; his approach was what we today would call "sociological." Actually, however, he was less interested in sociological problems than in political and economic questions of the day. The appeal of the *Review* was not to the dandy, the fop, the "gentleman" or the "ladies." On more than one occasion Defoe made clear to the aristocracy that he, a mere Grub Street scribbler, was not trying to instruct *them*. On the other hand Defoe was not—as various modern critics say—writing to "the common man," "the masses." [4]

The *Review* was made of sterner stuff than would have interested either the fop or "the masses." No editor then or now, writing for either extreme, would devote the first eighty numbers of a new periodical to consideration of the war with France and abstract points of strategy—and this almost without relief for forty weeks. It was not "the masses" in England who needed lectures on the duties and responsibilities of members of the House of Commons, not "the masses" Defoe was addressing when he pointed out the errors of the clergy of the Church of England. Even today, when universal education has gone so much farther than in Defoe's time, it is doubtful whether "the masses" would appreciate a periodical that specialized in essays on the true nature of money and what it symbolizes in terms of wealth; on the nature of credit and its importance in a nation's trade. Defoe was writing less to either extreme of society than to the great middle group of "freeholders" and "electors" who, if he could arouse them to the dangers in which their country stood from foes abroad and at home, might become partakers of his own high moral purpose as a defender of English liberties and an exponent of what was most important for England's economy. His own function, as he sincerely believed it to be, he expressed vigorously: "I saw a parcel of people caballing together to ruin property, corrupt the laws, invade the government, debauch the people and in short, enslave and embroil the nation; and I cried, 'Fire!' "

We will not expect to find in Defoe's pages, then, attitudes and sub-

[4] Secord in his prefatory notes to the facsimile edition of 1938 says that the periodical "taught the masses in Queen Anne's reign what to think upon important political and social questions." Sutherland, the most recent biographer, quotes one of Ned Ward's couplets to indicate that the *Review* was "read most by cobblers and by porters." Defoe's competitor, Leslie of the *Rehearsal*, justified the first appearance of his periodical on the ground that it might tend to counteract the subversive teachings of the *Review*, whose readers—or, rather, listeners—could not read for themselves but "will gather together about one that can read and listen . . . (as I have seen them in the streets)." To be sure, Defoe himself sometimes furthered such an impression by insisting that he was not writing to the aristocracy. He was writing, as he said, "to enlighten the stupid understandings of the meaner and more thoughtless of the freeholders and electors." But "freeholders" and "electors" denoted men who were property owners, certainly not "the masses" in our modern use of the term.

ject matter familiar to us in the periodicals of Steele and Addison. To be sure, most of the periodical writers of the eighteenth century, like most of the satirists, paid lip service to the program of "exposing vice and folly." So too Defoe: one of his main purposes was "to exalt virtue, expose vice, promote truth and help men to serious reflection." Defoe really meant what he said, and he took his high office more seriously than did his more aristocratic competitors. The *Review* had as high a moral purpose as did *Robinson Crusoe* or *Moll Flanders.* Those more familiar works live in our memories today, perhaps in spite of rather than because of the express purpose for which they were written; the *Review* must live, if at all, *because* of its purpose.

And indeed there is every reason that the *Review* should interest modern readers, and perhaps seem more "modern" if less charming than the *Spectator* and the *Tatler.* The times in which Mr. Review lived were serious times, from his point of view, beset by problems no intelligent citizen had the right to avoid. He turned impatiently from the frivolous amusements of his day to confront real problems of real people in a world much too busy to worry about Italian tenors and party patches, about beaux's heads and coquettes' hearts. Like our own generation Defoe lived with war and the aftermath of war. The problems with which he was concerned are on a lesser scale our own problems today. Indeed his vocabulary is very familiar to us: he has much to say of inflation and deflation, of taxation, of the changing values of money, of consumer credit, of monopolies. He gives cogent reasons for a "ceiling price" on coal; he demands that seamen be assured an annual wage and that that wage be "frozen"; he declares that high wages make for high consumption and thus for national prosperity. He insists that in the war with France England came not as "oppressor" but as "deliverer," that it was a "holy" and a "righteous" war. His many essays on the troublesome question of "refugees" are as modern as the problem they involve, even though the scale of his problem was smaller than ours today. And if Defoe did not foresee a United Nations, he was fully aware of the difficulties of establishing a United Nation in the British Isles.

The *Review* has suffered from the persistent tendency of modern critics to compare it with the *Tatler* and the *Spectator* always to its disadvantage, merely because it was a "periodical" and because on some few occasions Defoe handled similar themes. We find, for instance, essays in the *Review* on the opening of a new theatre, on the use of cosmetics, on the "Mohocks," on the existence of witches, on female politicians. But the differences are so much more striking than any similarities that comparison is almost impossible.

Mr. Spectator, for instance, mildly shakes his powdered head at the use of cosmetics. Mr. Review attacks the practice as indecent, as a deliberate falsehood, remembering that vain indulgence in cosmetics caused the painful death of one of his own acquaintance. Faced with the serious problem of the "Mohocks," Addison with true rationality delicately suggests that good breeding will shame them into desisting from their nightly forays. Defoe vehemently recommends the use of the Protestant Flail and offers to join any group that will use it. Even the "serious Addison"—the important critic and aesthetician—is entirely different from the always serious Defoe, who had no interest in literary and critical problems. There are book reviews in the *Review,* to be sure, but the books Defoe selected dealt with economic and political problems, not with *belles lettres.* The complete difference between Defoe and Addison may be seen in a moment if the reader turns to the essay in the *Review* called by our editor "Mr. Spectator, Mr. Review, and Mr. Milton." We may think that we have discovered a Defoe who was a literary critic. "If anything could heighten the imagination, or move the passions and affections in the subject which Milton wrote upon, more than reading Milton himself," wrote Defoe, "I should think the world beholden to the Spectator for his extraordinary notes upon that sublime work." But Mr. Review has praised Mr. Spectator only to cavil at his limitations. Though Defoe declares *Paradise Lost* "beyond all praise," he is not interested in Milton the artist, but in Milton the theologian and Milton the Puritan teacher, and he goes on at once to grapple with certain problems of theological dogma which he considers far more important than literary sublimity. So too if we turn to Defoe's essays on the theatre and the stage—perennials of periodicals—we find the Puritan and the teacher everywhere. In the essay our editor has called "Hamlet Repairs a Church" we hear an echo of earlier puritanical men who sold Shakespearean folios as "baggage books." When Defoe learned that in order to repair a chapel in Russell Court, a special performance of Hamlet was to be given at the Theatre

Royal, he wrote: "See, *tempora mutantur*, times are finely changed; in the late reigns the church built the playhouses; and now the playhouse builds the church; from whence I cannot but prophesy the time will come, either the church will pull down the playhouse, or the playhouse will pull down the church."

The *Review* may well serve as a corrective for modern readers who see the eighteenth century through the rosy spectacles of Sir Roger de Coverley. Defoe's was a different eighteenth century, and one much closer to our own. And Mr. Review will explain to us much that we now lose in *Robinson Crusoe* and the other novels. He is well worth knowing for himself. His personality is everywhere in these essays. No one who knows him well can miss his characteristic voice and mood. Forcefully, vigorously, he thrusts himself into nearly every sentence. His is not the remote cool sophistication of Mr. Spectator who "never espoused any party with violence." Defoe is opinionated, because he has opinions in which he firmly believes and he expresses them courageously without fear or favor. Subsidized or not, the opinions of Mr. Review on a united Britain, on disgraceful election practices, on refugees, on morals, are not those of a hireling. They are the firm convictions of Daniel Defoe. He could not smile or chuckle over follies that he really believed vices, bad for the individual, bad for the country. He wrote no part of his periodical for the sheer pleasure of writing, included no essay merely for the joy of the contemplative man. Each essay had its purpose, and that purpose was the improvement of life and society in England.

The death of the *Review* came about, in part at least, as a result of one of the "abuses" of government against which Defoe had often inveighed. On August 1, 1713, a tax of a halfpenny was levied on half-sheet news magazines, a penny tax on whole sheets, with a tax of twelvepence on advertisements. "This is the day on which many eminent authors will probably publish their last words," Addison wrote in *Spectator*, Number 445. "I am afraid that few of our weekly historians . . . will be able to subsist under the weight of the stamp." Perhaps the *Review* had outlived its usefulness, as modern critics surmise; perhaps the temper of the times reflected in the newer periodicals was such that readers no longer desired Defoe's economics and his overserious warnings. The stamp tax added one more straw to difficulties Defoe was facing. In May, 1713, he was jailed for maligning the court while being tried on a trumped-up charge. His political connections secured his freedom, but it was clear that the days of the *Review* were over. Defoe announced the end of the journal in characteristically moral tones: "To give others an example of a dutiful subject to [the laws], I willingly impose a silence upon myself." After the last issue of June 11, 1713, Mr. Review laid down his editorial pen, to take a "voluntary recess." "None," said the proud fighter, "can say I was forced to desist."

MARJORIE NICOLSON

Northampton, Massachusetts
July, 1951

Contents

ECONOMICS AND TRADE: BRITAIN'S MYSTERY AND BULWARK

POLITICS: BRITAIN'S GLORY AND SHAME

CURIOSA: BRITAIN'S MANNERS, MORALS, AND WONDERS

Portrait of the True-born Englishman

THE AIM, PURPOSE, AND MANNER OF THE *Review*[1]

WHEN AUTHORS present their works to the world, like a thief at the gallows, they make a speech to the people. The author indeed has something like this to say too, good people all take warning by me—I have studied to inform and to direct the world, and what have I had for my labour, profit, the press would not allow. And therein I am not deceived, for I expected none. But good manners and good language I thought I might expect, because I gave no other; and it was but just to treat mankind as they would be treated by them. But neither has this been paid me, in debt to custom and civility. How often have my ears, my hands, and my head been to be pulled off! Impotent bullies that, attacked by truth, and their vices stormed, filled the air with rhodomontades and indecencies, but never showed their faces to the resentment truth had a just cause to entertain for them. I have passed through clouds of clamour, cavil, raillery, and objection, and have this satisfaction, that truth being the design, *finis coronat.* I am never forward to value my own performances: "Let another man's mouth praise thee," said the wise man; but I cannot but own myself infinitely pleased, and more than satisfied that wise men read this paper with pleasure, own the just observations in it, and have voted it useful.

The first design [2] I allow is not yet pursued, and indeed I must own, the field is so large, the design so vast, and the necessary preliminaries so many, that though I cannot yet pass for an old man,[3] I must be so, if I live to go through with it.

This volume has passed through my description of the French grandeur, with its influence on the affairs of Poland, Sweden, and

[1] The preface to each volume was written after the volume was completed. See his remarks to that effect, below, pp. 39 and 47.

[2] Defoe declared that the *Review* was to be a history of France, with whom England was then at war.

[3] Accepting Defoe's year of birth as 1660, he was forty-five at the writing of the Preface, which was prepared after Volume I was completed.

Hungary. What assaults I have met with from the impatience of the readers, what uneasiness of friends lest I was turned about to the enemy, I leave to their reading the sheets to discover. How is this age unqualified to bear feeling truth; how unwilling to hear what we do not like, though never so necessary to know! And yet if this French monarchy was not very powerful, vastly strong, its power terrible, its increasing encroaching measures formidable, why do we, and justly too, applaud, extol, congratulate, and dignify the victorious Duke of Marlborough at such a rate? If it had been a mean and contemptible enemy, how shall we justify the English army's march through so many hazards, the nation's vast charge, the daily just concern in every article of this war; and as I have frequently hinted, why not beat them all this while? They who have made or may make an ill use of the true plan of French greatness which I have laid down must place it to the account of their own corrupted, prejudiced thoughts. My design is plain: to tell you the strength of your enemy that you may fortify yourselves in due proportion, and not go out with your ten thousands against his twenties.

In like manner I think myself very oddly handled in the case of the Swedes and Hungarians [4]—how many complaints of ambassadors for one, and fellow Protestants for the other! And yet after the whole story is finished, I have this felicity, than which no author can desire a greater, viz., not one thing I ever affirmed but was exactly true. Not one conjecture I have made but has appeared to be rational; not one inference drawn but the consequences have proved just; and not one thing guessed at but what has come to pass.

I am now come home to England and entered a little into our own affairs. Indeed, I have advanced some things as to trade, navies, seamen, &c., which some may think a little arrogant because perfectly new.

[4] Twice during the nine years of the *Review* Defoe was in the bad graces of the then Swedish ambassador. The first time, here referred to, Defoe had commented acidly upon the Swedish-directed "election" of a king for Poland. Again, in October, 1707, he had been complained against.

Followers of Jan Hus, the Hungarian Protestants were pawns in a power politics struggle. Though deploring their religious persecution, which they hoped to lighten by siding with the rebel Francis II Rakoczi against the Emperor, Defoe would not urge their relief lest it add to the power of Catholic Louis XIV and thereby weaken the position of all European Protestants. His readers did not applaud his coldly logical stand.

But as I have offered nothing but what I am always ready to make appear practicable, I finish my apology with saying to the world, "Bring me to the test, and the rest I leave to time."

In the bringing the story of France down to the matter of trade, I confess myself surprisingly drawn into a vast wilderness of a subject so large that I know not where it will end—the misfortune of which is that thinking to have finished it with this volume, I found myself strangely deceived, and indeed amazed, when I found the story of it intended to be the end of this volume and hardly enough of it entered upon to say it begun.

However, the volume being of necessity to be closed, I am obliged to content myself with taking what is here as an introduction to the next volume, and to give this notice, that the matter of our English trade appears to be a thing of such consequence to be treated of, so much pretended to, and so little understood, that nothing could be more profitable to the readers, more advantageous to the public interest of this nation, or more suitable to the greatness of this undertaking than to make an essay at the evils, causes, and remedies of our general negoce. I have been confirmed in my opinion of the consequences and benefit of this undertaking by a crowd of entreaties from persons of the best judgment, and some of extraordinary genius in these affairs, whose letters are my authority for this clause [claim?] and whose arguments are too forcible for me to resist. And this is to me a sufficient apology for a vast digression from the affairs of France, which were really in my first design, and to which my title at first too straightly bound me.

Whoever shall live to see this undertaking finished, if the author or some better pen after him shall bring twenty or thirty volumes of this work on the stage, it will not look so preposterous as it seems now to have one whole volume be employed on the most delightful as well as profitable subject of the English trade. Things at short distances look large, and public patience is generally very short; but when remote, the case alters, and people see the reason of things in themselves. 'Tis this remote prospect of affairs which I have before me. And this makes me not so much regard the uneasiness people show at the story being frequently broken abruptly and running great lengths before it revolves upon itself again; but as time and the course of things will bring all about again and make the whole be of a piece with itself, I am content to wait the approbation of the readers till such time as the thing itself forces it from the at present impatient readers.

Readers are strange judges when they see but part of the design. 'Tis a new thing for an author to lay down his thoughts piecemeal. Importunate cavils assault him every day who claim to be answered to day before tomorrow, and are so far from staying till the story is finished that they can hardly stay till their letters come to hand, but follow the first with a second—that with clamour and this sometimes with threatening scoffs, banters, and raillery. Thus I am letter-baited by querists, and think my trouble to write civil, private answers to teasing and querulous epistles has been equal, if not more troublesome, than all the rest of this work. Through these difficulties I steer with as much temper and steadiness as I can. I still hope to give satisfaction in the conclusion; and 'tis this alone that makes continuing the work tolerable to me. If I cannot, I have made my essay. If those that know these things better than I, would bless the world with farther instructions, I shall be glad to see them and very far from interrupting or discouraging them as these do me. Let not those gentlemen who are critics in style, in method or manner, be angry that I have never pulled off my cap to them in humble excuse for my loose way of treating the world as to language, expressions, and politeness of phrase. Matters of this nature differ from most things a man can write. When I am busied writing essays and matters of science, I shall address them for their aid and take as much care to avoid their displeasure as becomes me; but when I am upon the subjects of trade, and the variety of casual story, I think myself a little loose from the bonds of cadence and perfections of style, and satisfy myself in my study to be explicit, easy, free, and very plain. And for all the rest, *nec careo, nec curo*.

I had a design to say something on the entertaining part of this paper, but I have so often explained myself on that head that I shall not trouble the world much about it. When I first found the design of this paper, which had its birth *in tenebris*, I considered it would be a thing very historical, very long; and though it could be much better performed than ever I was like to do it, this age had such a natural aversion to a solemn and tedious affair that, however profitable, it would never be diverting, and the world would never read it. To get over this difficulty, that secret hand I make no doubt that directed this birth into the world dictated to make some sort of entertainment or amusement at the end of every paper [5] upon the immediate subject then on the tongues of the town, which innocent diversion would hand on the more weighty and more serious part of the design into the heads and thoughts of those to whom it might be useful. I take this opportunity to assure the world that receiving or answering letters of doubts, difficulties, cases, and questions, as it is a work I think myself very meanly qualified for, so it was the remotest thing from my first design of anything in the world. And I could be heartily glad the readers of this paper would excuse me from it yet. But I see it cannot be, and the world will have it done. I have therefore done my best to oblige them; but as I have not one word to say for my performance that way, so I leave it where I found it—a mere circumstance casually and undesignedly annexed to the work and [a] curiosity, though honestly endeavoured to be complied with.

If the method I have taken in answering questions has pleased some wiser men than I expected it would, I confess 'tis one of the chief reasons why I was induced to continue it. I have constantly adhered to this rule in all my answers, and I refer my reader to his observation for the proof that from the loosest and lightest questions I endeavoured to draw some useful inferences, and if possible to introduce something solid, and something solemn in applying it. The custom of the ancients in writing fables is my very laudable pattern for this; and my firm resolution in all I write to exalt virtue, expose vice, promote truth, and help men to serious reflection, is my first moving cause and last directed end. If any shall make ill use of, wrest, wrongly interpret, wilfully or otherwise mistake the honest design of this work, let such wait for the end, when I doubt not the author will be cleared by their own vote, their want of charity appear, and they be self-condemned till they come to acknowledge their error and openly to justify

Their humble servant,

D. F.

[5] The "Scandalous Club" was a "department" of the amusing, the fanciful, or just of lighter subject matter. Often it was devoted to answering readers' questions, or scolding public immoralities and irresponsible journalists. It was superseded in May, 1705, by "Miscellanea," an occasional feature much more sedate and sober.

Vol. VIII, No. 105 Saturday, November 24, 1711

A SHORT DIGRESSION UPON THE CONSEQUENCES OF TRUTH[1]

I ASK my readers leave to make a short digression relating to myself as pleading a cause which some cannot receive. He that will serve honest men must not promise himself that he shall not anger them, must be content, while he [is] pushing on their interest, to be out of their favour, and must run the venture of their doing him right when their rectified judgments come at long run to be farther enlightened. I have been early exercised with this usage from honest blinded men, even from a youth, which I am obliged to expose—not to charge them, but to defend myself. I had their reproaches when I blamed their credulity and confidence in the flatteries and caresses of popery under King James, and when I protested openly against the addresses of thanks to him,[2] for his illegal liberty of conscience founded upon the dispensing power.

I had their anger again when, in print, I opposed at the utmost hazard the taking off the penal laws and Test, and had the discouragement to be told by some grave but weak good men that I was a young man and did not understand the Dissenters' interest but was doing them harm instead of good. To which, when time undeceived them, I only returned the words of Eliphas to Job, for which God never reproved him—"Old men are not always wise, neither do the aged understand wisdom." . . .

I had their utmost displeasure again at the first coming out of *The Shortest Way with the Dissenters,* when they run away with it as they do now, without giving themselves leave to search into things, that

[1] This "digression" occurs in an essay on the strengthening of the Protestant interest in Europe. The first five paragraphs of the number have been omitted.

[2] In 1687 James II issued a Declaration of Indulgence, whereby all religious sects were given full toleration and excused from conforming to the Test Act. Some corporate groups hailed this tolerance, but dissenter Defoe argued that it was a two-edged weapon.

the book was really a plot to destroy all the Dissenters; [3] when honest Col—— W——ll undertook to be the hangman rather than the author should want a pass out of the world; and Mr. S—— at the head of a whole club at ——— declared if he could find me, he would deliver me up and abate the government the 50£ promised.

Yet in all these things, the gentlemen have done me justice in their turn: that is, time and truth has vindicated me and convinced them; and they have lived to own themselves mistaken in them all, and so they will do now. He that will follow principle and espouse truth must prepare to disoblige those he serves and, however discouraging, must be content to be condemned unheard, censured unconfuted, and have all the reproach which prejudice, backed with ignorance, can invent. And I am prepared for this, nor shall I ever abate speaking open truth, what power or party soever I provoke or displease, if I am but first satisfied and convinced that I am right. He that dares not own truth is unworthy to be owned by the God of truth. Therefore, and because I am convinced, I not only speak truth but am defending the interest not of Britain only, but of all the Protestant nations in Europe. Therefore, I say, I go on despising the opposition of those whose interest I am sure I serve in it. . . .

I ask the readers pardon for this digression, and shall make amends for it by making no more. . . .

Vol. I [IX], No. 1 Saturday, August 2, 1712

MR. REVIEW TAKES A STAND

I HAVE DONE making apologies; I shall trouble myself no more who like or dislike, who approve or who reproach. I shall endeavour to speak truth and reason, and with the utmost impartiality, and neither give myself or the reader any more trouble about the rage or disquiet of the enemies of this paper. For this reason, the Introduction

[3] An ironical pamphlet (1702) which dissenter Defoe patently designed to out-Tory the Tory arguments against the dissenters. He urged the government to root out,

to this new part will be very short. The tax laid upon papers of this kind [1] has made the rate and expense to the reader higher than before; the first use every writer ought to make of this, I think, is to take the more heed to avoid trifling, and make what he writes more effectual, more substantial, and more worth the time and the expense of those that read. And as I give this hint to others, I shall endeavour to make it a rule to myself.

I appear in a less compass than I did before; but the reader will have a full compensation for that by the letter being smaller, the paper better, and the printing part better performed; and he will soon find that there is as many words in a *Review,* though less in compass, than before. As the price of this paper is advanced by the tax, so at first, lest the expense be too great to those who take it in, I shall publish it but twice a week, viz., Tuesdays and Saturdays, so that it costs them just as much as it did before. If there appear room for it, and that it may be worth the expense, it shall come out oftener hereafter. I purposed to have begun it in a large octavo, so to have been the better bound up in volumes, but for divers reasons I have adjourned that design, at least for one year; and if I resolve on it, notice shall be given in time.

I recommend the work and its author to the charity of the unbiassed readers, who, if they please to read it with temper, may find it useful and instructing. As to those who read it with prejudice and partiality, resolving to dislike and condemn right or wrong, I bid them DEFIANCE, and assure them they shall not want occasion to rail because they shall not fail to find occasion enough of self-conviction. I am fully prepared to meet with all that a prepossessed rage can throw upon me; but as

purge, and crucify the dissenters (about one third of the population). But the irony backfired, and Defoe was jailed for threatening the peace. Together with *The True-Born Englishman* (1701), this work made his name a household word.

[1] Effective July 28, 1712, all periodicals and pamphlets were taxed a halfpenny if on half sheets, or a penny if on full sheets. Swift, writing to Stella on August 7, says, "Do you know that Grub Street is dead and gone last week? . . . The *Observator* is fallen; the *Medleys* are jumbled together with the *Flying Post;* the *Examiner* is deadly sick; the *Spectator* keeps up and doubles its price." The *Review,* previously issued thrice weekly in four pages and selling for a penny, was reduced to two pages twice a week. It still sold for a penny plus a halfpenny tax. In January, however, it resumed thrice-a-week appearance, which it maintained until its conclusion in June, 1713. See below, p. 44.

I adhere steadily to *principle* and to *truth of fact;* that truth and I, against all the devils in Hell, and all the knaves on earth, I fear none of them. . . .

Vol. V, No. 37 Tuesday, June 22, 1708

DEFOE'S ALTER EGO [1]

AND NOW, gentlemen, to divert you with a little variety shall I give you a new scene and tell you a story—whether it be history or a parable, let the issue discover. Walking along your streets not long ago near an old tenement of Satan's called Westminster Hall,[2] I saw two men standing together who looked earnestly at me; and one of them, who it seems knew me by face, having told the other who I was, he comes after me and desires to speak with me.

"Sir," says he, "are you such a man?"—naming my name. "Yes sir," quoth I, "at your service." "Who, D.F.," says he again, "the author of the *True-Born Englishman?*" "Yes sir," quoth I again, very mannerly. "What," says he again, "the same man that writes the *Review?*" "The same, sir," quoth I again. Says he, "Here's the key of my chamber, sir"—putting his hand in his pocket and fumbling, but did not bring it out. "What must I have the key of your chamber for," says I, "sir, I do not want a lodging." "As good as you have, sir," says he, "it was my good will to you, however, sir: you might have accepted it." "I thank you, sir," quoth I, "but pray, what sort of a lodging is yours, sir, that you are so free to part with it?" "It is a very good chamber, sir, in Bethlehem. I assure you it is one of the best in the house." "But, sir, perhaps you may want it yourself; pray do not part with it upon any account." "Truly, sir, I want it enough, and perhaps as much as any man alive but yourself—for I have been mad a

[1] From the department entitled "Miscellanea," an occasional feature following the main essay of an issue (see above, p. 7).

[2] One of the Parliament buildings.

great while, and am so still, except now and then a lucid interval—but I think you are so much madder than myself that I thought I ought to lend you my key." "That may be because you are mad that you think me so," quoth I, "for they say madmen think all the world mad but themselves."

"Aye, sir, that is your case exactly," says the lunatic. "I thought I should catch you now. And are not you a right madman, for do you not tell all the world they are mad? Today the High Flyers [3] are mad, tomorrow the Whigs are mad; then the French are mad, and everybody has their turns of lunacy with you; and what is the reason of all this now but only because you are mad yourself? Here, here, take the key of my chamber, sir; pray take it, pray take, Mr. Review, pray take it."

Review. Well, well, patience, patience, stay a little; you have almost persuaded me that I am mad. But will you hear me a little?

Madman. Why, there again now, did ever anything act madder than you to bid a madman have patience, and hear you, and stay a little, and such things as that? I told you you were mad. Will you take my key, I tell you?

Review. You are not so mad as I, for aught I see; and I am, sure, not so mad as you would have me to be. But pray, why am I to be concluded mad about the High Flyers, &c.?

Madman. Why, if they were all as mad as you say they are, is it not a mad thing for you to tell them so? If they were really mad, what must you be that talk to them? Did ever talking cure a madman? It must be physic and art must cure lunatics. Talking to men makes them mad; it never cures them.

Review. Well, but when I talk to them, though it will not recover them, it may prevent others falling mad with them and falling in with their cause.

Madman. Nay, now you are wrong again. For they that have the use of their reason can never turn High Flyers, or Jacobites,[4] or malcontents, under this government; and they that have not, what good

[3] Members of the Tory party, High Churchmen.

[4] Adherents to the claims of the house of Stuart to the throne of Great Britain after 1688. Especially numerous in the north of England, and in Scotland, they included Roman Catholic and extreme Tory groups who believed in the doctrine of nonresistance and in the divine right of kings.

will your talking do to men out of their wits? I tell you, you are mad. Come, brother madman, you had better for the future talk with me. Who knows what two madmen may do, and how our discourse may work upon the world! Besides, as they are all lunatics they are fitter for our conversation.

Review. With all heart, quoth I, and there we parted.

And thus you are to be entertained a while with the wise discourse of the *Review* and a madman. How it may please you, time must discover. I must tell you that at first sight this madman has been a shrewd fellow, and believe you will find he will not cross the proverb that fools never go mad. Whatever he is now, he has been no fool; and you will find many a shrewd rub from him. Let all our modern self-wise men stand clear of him. . . .

Vol. II, No. 38 Thursday, May 31, 1705

MR. REVIEW DEFENDS MR. DEFOE

I CONFESS the unpleasantest part of this work from the beginning of it has been the interruptions frequently given the reader and myself by the apologies and defenses I have been obliged to make, by the various attacks and assaults of the ill-wishers to this undertaking. And 'tis with such irksome and unwilling necessity I do it, that I every time think it shall be the last.

The enemies to peace are not a few, and he that preaches a doctrine men care not to follow, when they cannot object against the subject they will against the man. He's no scholar, says one. That may be true. He was apprentice to an hosier, says another. That's false, and adds to the number of the intolerable liberties Dr. B[rowne] and Mr. Observator give themselves—he having never been a hosier, or an apprentice. But he has been a trader. That's true. And therefore must know no Latin. Excellent logic this, like Dr. B[rowne]'s moon-blind consistency in his book called *The Moon Calf*,[1] where, pretending to banter the author of the *Consolidator*, in the first paragraph he tells us "that there has been no communication between this world and that in the moon for many ages." And in the next tells us "of an account come from this world by the very last post, *Oportet mendacem esse memoriam*" (*Moon Calf*, page 1).

Asserting of falsehoods provokes me not; personal reflection is none of my business in this paper, nor none of theirs. Those gentlemen that reproach my learning to applaud their own shall have it proved I have more learning than either of them—because I have more manners. I have often advanced it as my opinion that when an enemy begins to rave he is certainly beaten, and must be allowed to quote a poet on this head—though on the other side.

> That disputants, when reasons fail,
> Have one sure shift, and that's to rail.[2]

Asserting of falsehoods, I say, provokes me not; a refuge of lies will in the end expose the authors and not the adversary; and my concern at raillery and forgery is not in the least the cause of my defending myself in this paper. I have no concern to tell Dr. B[rowne] I can read English, or to tell Mr. Tutchin I understand Latin: *non ita Latinus sum ut Latine loqui.* I easily acknowledge myself blockhead enough to have lost the fluency of expression in the Latin, and so far trade has been a prejudice to me; and yet I think I owe this justice to my ancient father, yet living, and in whose behalf I freely testify that if I am a blockhead it was nobody's fault but my own, he having spared nothing in my education that might qualify me to match the accurate Dr. B[rowne] or the learned *Observator*.

If therefore I say anything on my own behalf here, gentlemen, which is not worth your while to read, pardon the digression. All my friends judge for me that I ought to say so much at least as may

[1] *The Moon-Calf, or Accurate Reflections on the "Consolidator," Giving an Account of Some Remarkable Transactions in the Lunar World* (1705), a commentary on Defoe's *Consolidator* (1705), a journey-to-the-moon political allegory concerning England. It was written by Dr. Joseph Browne (d. 1721), who among other things continued the *Examiner* after Swift.

[2] Probably a corruption of the first two lines of the epilogue to Dryden's *All for Love*, which reads, "Poets, like disputants, when reasons fail, Have one sure refuge left—and that's to rail."

convince posterity that the writer of these papers had some reason to know what he said, and for their sakes who in reading these sheets are stumbled at the character of the man, and for their sakes who may see these calumnies when the author is on the other side of time and can say nothing for himself. How should this fellow know these things? And on what ground can he have the face to assert what he does? this is the language of the enemies to this paper. He was bred a mechanic, had no education, and the *Observator*, an author of his own party, upbraids him as an illiterate fellow. Why really, gentlemen, this is very hard; but I'll be very short with these gentlemen.

As to my insufficiency for the vast undertaking of these papers, no man knows it so well as myself; and many a gap in the real capacity I am fain to supply with industrious search of books and precedents, and other men's more polite knowledge is a great assistance to my imperfection. And if any gentleman of equal zeal for truth and of superior genius will attempt this work, such is my sincere desire to have it well done, I'll freely resign it to him—nay, even to Mr. Observator himself, if he will say he can carry it on with temper, integrity, and effect. And by this I will demonstrate that the profits of this paper, none of which I have yet seen, have not been the occasion of its writing, as some have basely insinuated to the world.

As to Mr. Tutchin, I never gave him the least affront; I have even, after base usage from him, in vain invited him to peace—in answer to which he returns unmannerly insults, lies, calumnies, and reproach. To these I answer him doubly.

As to my little learning and his great capacity, I fairly challenged him in a letter I sent him yesterday and which I now renew: that I'll take any Latin author he shall name, and with it one French and one Italian, and I'll translate them into English and after that re-translate them crosswise: the English into French, the French into Italian, and the Italian into Latin. And this I challenge him to perform with him, who does it soonest and best for 20£ each book; and by this he shall have an opportunity to show the world how much Defoe the hosier is inferior in learning to Mr. Tutchin the gentleman.

As to his ill language, his professed resolution to expose me, his abusive treatment of me with his tongue, for he dare not do it with his hands—I'll finish all my replies of this sort with telling him a story;

and if this won't do, I'll tell him another. Two dogs lived near one another, a black and a brown. Black, that was more addicted to bark than to bite, would always run baying and barking after Brown whenever he went by. Brown took no notice of him a long time, but being once more than usually teased and provoked, he gravely turned about, smells at Black, and, finding him of a currish, cowardly breed and not worth his notice, very soberly and unconcerned he holds up one leg, pisses upon him, and so goes on about his business. And so do I. . . .

Vol. II, No. 54 Saturday, July 7, 1705

DEFOE CARRIES A STICK

I HAVE SPENT some time—and some people, I find, think too much —on the subject of peace; I have been moving and inviting all parties to put their helping hands to this necessary work, and principally to choose such gentlemen to represent them in the approaching Parliament as are blessed with those healing principles which seem particularly and absolutely necessary at this extraordinary juncture, AND I HOPE THEY HAVE DONE IT. If in the negative part of my discourse on this head it has come in my way to tell who they should *not* choose, by way of direction to the affirmative, who they *should*, and if it has been impossible to do this without running full butt against the gentlemen of the 134,[1] they must excuse me and blame their putting themselves just in the way of our peace, that we could not pursue it without driving over them. But I am unhappily embarrassed now with a whole party, and assaulted with all manner of malice for endeavouring to show the beauty of that heavenly temper these men want, and which in particular they hate.

[1] Those members of the House of Commons who in August, 1704, voted to tack a bill against occasional conformity onto a money bill. They are frequently referred to in first-decade political writings. Defoe ironically calls them "men of peace," and in his *Consolidator* (1705), the "great bird" (Parliament) has 134 "ill feathers."

It would really be too much satire upon the gentlemen of the other side if I should only publish their own letters to me upon the subject; some that are merely diverting I may give the world a sight of, but some that are villainous and base I conceal for the sake of that peace I would fain move them to by my example. 'Twould even reflect upon the nation in general if I should give the particulars of about twenty to thirty letters, most of which threaten my life, and the world might think England coming into the mode of Italy.[2] Indeed, we have seen too much of this method lately, and justice seems to wait but a few weeks to make a sad example from a set of assassinators, the murderers of the Scotchman of Queenborough.[3] To all the gentlemen who are so exceeding angry at me for inviting them to peace as to threaten my throat, and the like, I make this serious request, let them step to Maidstone gaol and there discourse a little with their brother murderers; and if their condition pleases them, let them follow their steps if they can.

Indeed, gentlemen, the mean despicable author of this paper is not worth your attempting his correction at the price: gaols, fetters, and gibbets are odd melancholy things. For a gentleman to dangle out of the world in a strang [string],[4] has something so ugly, so awkward, and so disagreeable in it, that you cannot think of it without some regret; and then the reflection will be very harsh that this was for killing a poor mortified author, one that the government had killed before. It can never be worth your while, gentlemen, and therefore he hopes you will content yourselves with telling him so, and let him alone to time and age, which is hastening upon us all and will certainly at last do the work to your hand. . . .

I move about the world unguarded and unarmed, a little stick not strong enough to correct a dog supplies the place of Mr. O[bservato]r's great oaken towel,[5] a sword sometimes perhaps for decency, but it is all harmless to a mere nothing; can do no hurt anywhere but just

[2] Defoe here reflects the idea of the period that assassination and poisoning were rife in Italy. In *The True-Born Englishman* (1701) he points out the principal vice of each nation; in Italy it is lust.

[3] I cannot identify either the murderers or the Scotchman.

[4] "String" was a jocular expression for the hangman's rope (*Oxford English Dictionary*).

[5] The *Oxford English Dictionary* gives the meaning as stick or cudgel.

at the tip of it, called the point—and what's that in the hand of a feeble author? Let him alone, gentlemen, and have patience, you'll all come to be of his mind ere long; and then if you had killed him you would have been sorry for it. The days are at hand, I doubt, when you will all own he that persuaded you to peace was in the right of it; and that having despised peace at home, God Almighty in mercy to you will deny you peace abroad. I can much easier jest with the impotent rage of the enemies to the public peace threatening to kill me, than I can with the serious and sad apprehensions I receive from a protracted war, from broken measures, backward preparations, uncertain confederates, and the like.

And yet this bullying method is not the only treatment the author of this has to complain of, but now he has had a storm of a more scandalous assassination, studying to ruin and embroil him, crowds of sham actions, arrests, sleeping debates in trade of seventeen years' standing revived; debts put in suit after contracts and agreements under hand and seal; and, which is worse, writs taken out for debts without the knowledge of the creditor, and some after the creditor has been paid; diligent solicitations of persons not inclined to sue, pressing them to give him trouble; others offering to buy assignments of debts that they might be sued; for others to turn setters and informers to betray him into the hands of trouble; collateral bonds sued, where the securities have been resigned and accepted.

It would take up too much of the reader's time to trouble the world with the barbarous treatment shown a man just stripped naked by the government; 'tis like suing a man just ransomed from Algiers; and, could I descend to particulars, would be too moving to read. That this is all for the party, that this is a pique at the subject as well as the author—speak conscience and tell us: Why were none of these things done before? Under all these designed mischiefs a diligent report has been raised that this unhappy author was carried to Newgate, and some have been so kind to go thither to visit him. Ill tongues may do much; but I cannot but tell a certain gentleman who has offered 100£ to have it so that it will hardly be in his power to effect it. Pardon me, gentlemen, to enquire into the impotence of this malice—a gaol would not check this paper. Perhaps if you could bring it to pass it might furnish me with leisure to perform it better. To those whose designs are different, they may see who they gratify; and I appeal to all the world: What in this paper has merited this persecution? Were all the prosecutions legal, debts just, and circumstances requiring, yet really, gentlemen, when you reflect in what hands he has been in, 'tis something barbarous; common compassion leads men to bear with men whose houses have been burned or who by public disaster are disabled; if his house has not been burned, it has been plundered.

Will you have no compassion! Well, gentlemen, this must all they expect who presume to venture in plainness and without flattery to tell men their crimes. Neither will all this restrain his pen from writing the truth depending upon it, that the author of that truth will one time or other own at least the work, if not the unworthy author. Suits at law, gaol, murder, assassination, and all that malice can contrive are, therefore, without their influence on me; I avoid the first and contemn the last. The law, I trust, will protect me from the first; and I freely run the venture of the last, and so proceed to the next method now taking with me—and this is banter, raillery, and reflection. And what good does all this scribbling do? says one, You had as good let it alone. And whereas you pretend much of the public service being the end, and you would not write but for the public service, since there is no public service in it, pray show your sincerity by laying it down.

The difficulty here lies in what we shall understand by the public service, and doing good. I understand persuading us all to be at peace with one another to be a public service, and doing good. These gentlemen perhaps understand it another way; I am sorry for them. Without doubt they that believe intestine discords, civil dissension, strife, and oppression the needful help to this nation's happiness differ from me, and I from them; and I doubt shall always do so. If I am mistaken in the subject, I ought to be convinced that peace and union is not for the public good; that 'tis better for us to be pulling one another to pieces, tearing and destroying one another, and the like.

Now these gentlemen will undertake to prove [that] laws for persecution of dissenters, feuds and breaches in the legislature, invading privileges, heats, animosities, and violence of parties are particularly for the public service, and help to the public good. If they will make it out that delaying supplies and retarding preparations, wounding public credit, and weakening our hands would be particularly encouraging to our confederates abroad, and support better the Protestant cause; if they can prove that quarrels, heats, feuds, and dangerous experiments will help us to beat the French; that being divided at home we shall be the better prepared to defend ourselves against invasion from abroad; if they can demonstrate that to be all to pieces in our civil interest is the best method to deprive the parties abroad of all hopes that their cause will one day or other be revived among us; that 'tis the shortest way to close all their expectations; that while we are jangling and clashing, writing and fighting in parties at home, it will effectually foreclose the French in their designs of universal monarchy, and sink their expectation of reducing us by force; if these things can be made out, I confess I shall be in the dark and will immediately acknowledge I am in a strange mistake, that all my notions of things are wrong, that I have received false ideas of the public affairs; for indeed I did not know that when our Lord said, "A kingdom divided against itself cannot stand" that the kingdoms of England, Scotland, and Ireland were excepted out of the general rule, with a *cuius contrarium verum est.*

Now as I am and always shall be ready to receive and freely accept the informations of men more knowing than myself, I am in daily expectation of something very considerable upon this subject, which will make out these enigmas, unriddle all this mystery, and prove that Her Majesty was mistaken in her speech for peace and union; that we are all wrong in our construction of the text above; and so by consequence, that I am the Lord knows what kind of an incendiary, a Jacobite, and a public enemy to the nation—and when this comes I am content to be called so.

Vol. VIII, No. 210 Saturday, July 26, 1712

FOR KNAVES—THE CONTEMPT OF SILENCE

IT IS HARD friends should part so ill-natured as I am obliged to do with both our authors of the *Medleys*,[1] for there are two of them, but they are both aggressors. The first attacked me *à la mode de* Billingsgate, and, being a little surprised with the lies and slander of his paper, I had written him a full answer and had actually sent it to the press; but just in the interval I received the letter which I published in my last *Review* but one, by which I understood, if the author of it says true, that he is but a hireling, a tool of scandal, a fellow hired to write for pay, to rail for money, and not worth my notice. Upon this, as I had long ago learned so much philosophy, when an ass kicks me, not to kick him again, or that when a dog barks at me, I should not bark at him again, I laid by my answer resolving by the contempt of silence to let them who employed him know that I am not to seek how best to answer an impotent slanderer, viz., by saying nothing—for answer and answer not, is Solomon's rule.

Only with this promise, which I cannot avoid, that whereas *he says it can be proved that I have taken money for writing* Reviews (those are his words), I challenge all his employers to prove it and to name the person who paid it; and if they cannot, they need not ask me for a name for them, for they give it themselves, and I hate to be always telling people their own names. Let him do it if he would be thought an honest man, or not have honest men ashamed of him; only let him remember his own words, *for writing* Reviews.

But that which I wonder at most was to find the other *Medley* upon me too, and I am the more surprised at this because the letter I published, as abovesaid, has this account in it, that though the other sham

[1] The *Medley*, edited by Maynwaring and, occasionally, by Oldmixon. Defoe is referring to two *authors*, not two different *papers* called the *Medley*. Swift (see note, page 10) calls it the *Medleys*; this title was also given to a reprinting of the *Medley* of 1711.

Medley author was a hireling and a scoundrel, yet he that wrote the true *Medley* was a gentleman, a man of modesty and a man of letters. From this character, I concluded that it could not be the usual author that wrote the paper of that day, or at least that part of it, but that, the gentleman being indisposed, some help was unhappily called in at that time, or that, there being a notorious falsity necessary to be published, the gentleman declining it himself was prevailed with to let some scoundrel take the drudgery of that part upon him. And this I suggest because I know it is impossible that a gentleman should write anything that is scurrilous and abusive upon another who had never injured him, and not be able at the same time to prove the fact.

The case, in short, is that this mercenary which I speak of got it printed in the *Medley*, God knows how, without the author's consent I doubt not: *that he knows who dictates to the* Review (*Medley*, No. [40], July 22). Now, God knows, I write it not to boast, for I have as little money to spare and as much need to save it as any man in England, but I know money is tempting to a mercenary, and if it be in his power he will accept it, and therefore I hereby offer whatever shift I make it, nay, though I should plunder a church for it, I will pay him one hundred guineas at demand if he will prove by any fair, just, and but tolerable evidence either who is the person that ever dictated to the author of the *Review* what he should or should not write, or that he knows the informer he depends on and of whom he may be ashamed. I'll give him all the latitude I can, and therefore I'll add more words to it than he put in: I'll give the same money if he can prove that I have been dictated or directed in, or rewarded for, anything I have written in the *Review*, matters of trade excepted.[2] Now as the author of the *Medley* is a gentleman, I appeal to him whether the person that he was prevailed upon to permit to write that paper be not a worse creature than a gentleman ought to foul his paper with the name of, if after he has said *he knows it* as above, he yet is not able to prove it—being offered so fair a reward for it also? Let him get off of it if he can; if it is true, I challenge him to prove it; if it is a lie, why did he print it?

[2] He probably here means to say that he received money in payment for subscriptions and advertisements—that is, as an act of trade. One must not, however, underrate Mr. Review. Surely such passages as those concerning the wine merchants Brooks and Helliar (VIII, 306, 310, 322; IX, 97) read like "paid publicity."

Who can but smile to see to what shifts men run to cry down the man when they cannot cry down the argument? Certainly what this *Review* writes must have some strange force in it, some unusual energy, that they will not allow me to be the author of it myself—but I must have the materials from the greatest heads in the nation. They do me an honour that I do not deserve, and which they do not design for an honour, but will forever be so in spite of them. Methinks it would become these men better to answer what I say than to spend their time in railing at me, especially since they cannot bestow that labour upon any man in Britain that has less concern for it. But why do they not come to the point? Why do they not confute me instead of railing? Why do they not tell me a reason why the crown of Spain was given to Charles III when his father and elder brother was yet alive? Why do they not answer the IXth article of the Treaty of Partition,[3] where all the concessions of the Spanish monarchy were made, with this express limitation: On condition that they should never descend to the person of an emperor or king of the Romans? Why do they not prove to us the wisdom and necessity of that foolish, headlong piece of politics of the Confederates in making him that they had declared king of Spain be afterwards chosen emperor, which is the only thing that has ruined all the honest designs of the war, and made it unreasonable to carry it on any farther? Why do they not tell us what spirit the Austrian monarch discovered in his late letter to the Swiss cantons? And whether it is not telling us plainly that the old blood runs still in the same veins, and that the spirit of persecution is like the great lip,[4] hereditary to the family? Why do they not tell us which way this nation can stand neuter if the Confederates carry on the war without us? Why do they not tell us, if a war ensue with Holland, what will be our case as to the Protestant succession and the Pretender? Why do they not tell us whether the peace had not better be closed with than that we should run the hazard of all the fatal conse-

[3] In 1698, and again in 1700, England, Holland, and France agreed upon a division of the dominions of the childless Charles II of Spain among three claimants, Philip, duke of Anjou; Joseph, electoral prince of Bavaria; and Archduke Charles. Upon the death of Charles II, Louis XIV ignored the second treaty and placed the duke of Anjou, his grandson, on the throne. This act precipitated the War of the Spanish Succession, 1701–1714.

[4] A distinguishing characteristic of the Hapsburgs.

quences to this nation if a war with the Dutch should happen, nay, though the peace were worse than it is?

If these things can be answered, why do they not do it? That would be a better method than throwing dirt at the author, all which with double stench flies back in their faces. Let them answer, if they can; if they cannot, they shall raise all the scandal upon me that they please and tell untruths till they are black in the face, but they shall never be able to silence that truth which pinches them so sorely. What is it to the argument who dictates to the *Review*, and who pays me for writing? I wish for my own sake they did not lie; and I wish for their sakes, that what they said was true. If it were, it would not be with me as it is, and I would look many of them in the face that now insult me. But whoever dictates to me, let them answer it if they can, I am sure the making lies their refuge is a dishonour to the cause they espouse and to the people who espouse them. But two *Medleys* in a nation! And both espousing the Whig's cause, and both assert what they cannot prove! Fie, fie! The cause of the Whigs was ever a cause that despised the assistance of falsity and forgery, till now. The Whigs never rose by lying and forging. Oliver Cromwell when he was captain of a troop of horse was engaged near Ailsbury with a party of the king's cavalry, who he was obliged to fight at great odds, and the officer thinking himself sure of the victory upbraided him in the heat of the action in this manner: "Now, you roundheaded dogs, where's your Lord of Hosts?" Cromwell, as if he took new force from the words, calls out aloud to his men, thus: "Fall on, gentlemen, the day's our own, the enemy blaspheme." And it discouraged the other so that they quickly fled and were most of them cut in pieces. What will the enemies of the Whigs say when they see their advocates act thus? They'll cry out: The day's our own, for the enemy fly to lies for their refuge. And while this is true, while this accursed thing is among you, you will always flee and turn your backs before your enemies. For shame, gentlemen of the Whig party, either oblige your writers to speak truth or else discard and disown them; if not, your posterity will disown you, for the true cause and interest of the Whigs wants no slander, no lying, no charging falsely, no rage, no fury to carry it on.

What think ye of a printed lie in another case, another lie of the week, a lie with a double aspect and both ways false? Viz., in one paper we are told that the French have not entirely surrendered Dunkirk to us, and that the *Gazette*[5] speaks doubtfully of it and uncertain. And the same author in another paper gives us an account of the terrible works the French are making at Gravelin, and that the port is so much better there than at Dunkirk, that they have two foot water more there for their ships; and that it will be made so much better a port than Dunkirk, and that the putting Dunkirk into our hands will be of less value than we pretend to. All which is not only false in fact, but it is ridiculous to imagine the king of France would have bestowed so many millions of money on the fortifications and harbour of Dunkirk, if in Gravelin, which is the next town, there was two foot water more for the ships.

What dreadful days do we live in that even the best of men, and in the best cause, embrace lies, and fly to falsehood and slander to carry on their own measures. I remember a piece of mob poetry which I saw once upon a sign in the country, which, I think, suits well with this day, and with which I shall close.

The nation struggles with her fate,
We fear she will be wise too late;
Few our true interests understand,
And knaves and fools o'errun the land;
Help Lord and stand unto us,
Or knaves and fools will quite undo us.

Vol. VII, No. 113 Thursday, December 14, 1710

THE *Review* SCORNS ITS CRITICS

IT WAS ALWAYS my opinion that whenever the enemy roared loudest, they were pinched hardest; and that when the patient grew sick, the physic wrought well. Whence I have often asked the rehearsers and the reviewers of the *Review*, and the several people that

[5] Apparently the London *Gazette*. As the mouthpiece of the government, its news was considered official. In 1704 its circulation of 6,000 was nearly twice that of its nearest rival, the *Post Man*.

rail at this paper, why, if they think the author so contemptible and so feeble as they say he is, and in which he never contradicted them, they (who tell us always such great things of their own capacities) should be so moved at him and bestir themselves about what he writes in this paper. For my part, I have always thought that the weakest step the *Tatler* ever took, if that complete author may be said to have done anything weak, was to stoop to take the least notice of all the barkings of the little animals that have condoled him, examined him, &c. He should have let envy bark, and fools rail, and according to his own observation of the fable of the sun, he had nothing to do but to shine on. This I have found to be agreeable to the true notion of contempt—silence is the utmost slight nature can dictate to a man, and the most insupportable for a vain man to bear. Solomon directed it long since—"Answer not a fool in his folly"—from whence I wonder much to hear an author, who first calls the *Observator* and the *Review* stupid and illiterate, should then quit his talking to men of sense and talk to these *idiots*. For a stupid fellow is an idiot. Now what the *Observator* may do, who takes the other end of Solomon's rule—to answer the fool in his folly—I have nothing to say to; but as I have all along practised with *Moderators, Examiners*, and many other such scurrilous, angry sons of emptiness, so I shall still—*answer and say nothing*.

A certain grave lady of my acquaintance having taken something very ill, though not with much cause, from a gentleman, and meeting him at a place where she had an opportunity, fell foul on him in a very furious manner—not without great breach of decency. And letting her passion fly at random, she charged him with several things of which he was perfectly innocent and could with ease have vindicated himself. As often as he could get interval enough for so much speaking, he put in this grave question, "Have you done, madam?" No, she said, she had not done, she would tell him his own. And on she goes again with it till she began to blow, and then, "Have you done, madam?" says the gentleman. After several of these questions at last he brought her to a period, having exhausted her rage, and she answers, "Yes, I have done; what can you say for yourself?" The gentleman makes her a low bow and says "Good b'w'y to ye, madam," and so turned away and left her. The lady took it for such an unsufferable affront that to this day, which is above twenty years, she has not quite been reconciled, though the rest of the quarrel has long been forgotten.

Now, to shew the railers at this paper a method how to contemn a fool, I treat them as this gentleman did the lady, and as they, had they believed me stupid or an idiot when they called me so, ought to have treated me, viz., entirely turn my back upon them and say not one word. Besides, I appeal to all the world whether I should not really prove myself an idiot to talk to one that calls me so—and whether talking to a man that barks, or a dog that barks, is not the same thing? I remember to have read that in our unhappy quarrels between king and Parliament the harsh expressions which were frequently found in their respective declarations were objected as obstructions to all treaty for accommodation. The king had styled the Parliament rebels, had refused to call them the Parliament of England, and they would not treat till these things were revoked again. The Parliament had charged the king with the massacre of Ireland, with being a tyrant, bloody, &c., and His Majesty demanded reparation for that. Now, when a man calls another fool, stupid, idiot, illiterate, &c. and then pretends to enter debate with him—'tis absurd. I am not upon equal terms with him; when I have called him idiot, and fool, and illiterate, then I am upon the square with him, and, it not having been my good fortune to be bred at Billingsgate, I can never come up to this man, and so it is to no purpose for me to begin. Besides, among all the authors of whom the streets abound, with my humble service to Mr. Examiner,[1] I recommend it to him to answer this civil question: If, sir, you have so much learning, how came you to have so little manners? I know nothing can render a gentleman so contemptible in the world as to lose his breeding: to descend to scurrility is certainly the greatest evidence of a man's having no breeding, or having quite forgot that he had any; nor does the difference of persons discharge the obligation of good manners. A footman may talk saucily to a gentleman, and he deserves the cane for it; but if a gentleman is angry at a footman, he will talk still to him as a gentleman, and be angry like a gentleman.

Now the author of the *Examiner*, though he haughtily tells the

[1] Swift, then editor of the *Examiner*, is here meant. So far as we know, Defoe never knew Swift personally, and their relationship was expressed only through the columns of the *Examiner* and the *Review*. See John F. Ross, *Swift and Defoe* (Berkeley, Calif., 1941), for a full discussion.

world (No. 16) he has kept a footman, does not pretend to tell the *Review* that he, the *Review*, has been a footman, and yet treats him as a man of behaviour would not treat a footman. And is this a man fit for the *Review* to engage with? Will any man box with a chimney sweeper, or scold with a fishwife, any more than he will jostle a nightman [2] in his habit? The consequence is very plain. I am not only an enemy to duelling, as it is a sin against God, and therefore never speak of it,[3] but I desire to declare my own penitence upon that subject. But I think staking life upon the occasion of an affront is the most unequal thing in the world; I'll explain myself by telling a story which came within the verge of my own knowledge (and my story shall be very short; I never tell a long one). A gentleman of a courage that had been tried upon many occasions found a man in the very act, and in bed with his wife.[4] The person in bed starts up and says, "Sir, you have surprised me; I hope you'll give me leave to rise and take my sword." "Your boots, you may say, sir, if you please," says the injured gentleman, "and go about your business; I have nothing to say to you. My business is not with you, but with the whore my wife. But as to your sword, sir, I have taken care of that; I shall not fight you upon this head unless you will oblige me in one thing." "What is that, sir?" says the man. "Let me lie with your wife," replies the other, "and then if you have any desire to fight me, I'll be at your service." The case, I confess, seems intolerably hard: that when a man's wife proves a whore and he has the most unsufferable affront in nature, that then he must stake his life upon even terms with the adulterer.

My case is not altogether unlike this gentleman's, in the matter of the *Review*. The *Examiner* falls upon the *Review* with the terms "idiot," "illiterate," and "absurd"; first, let him put the *Review* upon even terms with him for his Billingsgate, and then he may be answered more upon the square. There is a known story of the mastiff and the little spaniel [5] which I could also refer him to, as most proper

[2] A nightman was "a man employed during the night to empty cesspools, etc." (*Oxford English Dictionary*).

[3] Might more accurately read, "speak no more of it," for in Volume I (1704–5) he wrote more upon the subject than any of his contemporaries. See "Duelling" in my *Index to Defoe's Review* (New York, 1948).

[4] Parallels an incident told in Defoe's *Colonel Jacque* (1722).

[5] See above, p. 16. He tells the same story a year later in the last days of 1711 by way of an "Advertisement for the Observator" (VIII, 484).

for such an author; but I leave it and him—when he is tired he will have done; when he has done he will be tired. Happy is the *Review* in pinching this party and making them rave at this rate; it is an immortal testimony of the victory of truth. Given its enemies—why do Tories hate the *Review?* Why do High Flyers damn the author? Why do papists hate Protestants? Turks Christians, &c.? The reason is the same: error always hated truth, thieves the light, and fallacy demonstration. And so much for *Examiners*.

But now because the railing party of this nation shall not want subject for them, most *Moderator*-like, to rave at and with exceeding good manners to examine, I humbly recommend to them a few things which have been the subject of some of my thoughts in this paper and which I suppose they are angry at. And if they would spend their thoughts upon them profitably, they might do the world good service.

1. Has the Queen an hereditary right [6] to the crown of England independent of parliamentary limitation, or has she not?

2. Is there any specific difference between the doctrine of resistance of tyrants and the vigorous withstanding arbitrary power, mentioned in the London clergy's address, and promised in the name of the clergy, by whatever means, without exception of persons, it should meditate a return?

3. Is the national credit to be removed without making the people easy, and allaying the insulting rabbles and tumults of the high flying party?

4. Can taking the Abjuration and the oaths to the Queen consist with drinking a health to the Pretender? [7]

5. Can the vicious lives of the present clergy in England, which is at present grown up to a flagrant, monstrous degree, and the general neglect of discipline in the superior clergy, who ought to examine and censure it, consist with the honour and safety of the Church of England? Are the heretical, deistical, atheistical, obscene, profane books,[8] of

[6] According to the principle set up and acted upon in the Revolution of 1688, bestowal of the crown was subject to Parliament.

[7] A gesture of protest indulged in by Jacobites, High Churchmen (known as "High Flyers"), and other disaffected groups who clung to the idea that the deposed James II, and later his son, the "Old Pretender," were the only true and rightful kings of England.

[8] Just what their titles were is not to be satisfactorily determined. Earlier in the same volume, however, Defoe writes of blasphemous books which "are all written by

which such a just complaint is made, written by the Dissenters or by the Church of England men? And did ever the Convocation [9] think fit to meddle with them?

When the people who pretend to examine writers have examined and answered these things, and either confuted them or proved the *Review* has done wrong in them, then I'll not only subject myself to censure, but to leave off and write this paper no more; but till this, let them expect no answer to a railing accusation but that of the text, "The Lord rebuke thee, thou lying spirit."

Vol. IV, No. 87 Tuesday, September 2, 1707

WHERE'S THE PROOF? [1]

I HAVE for a long time patiently borne with the scurrilous prints and scandalous reproaches of the street concerning my being in Scotland.[2] Today I am sent thither by one party, tomorrow by another; this time by one particular person, that by a body of people; one one way, one another. And I have long waited to see if out of innumerable guesses they would at last make the discovery of the true, and to me melancholy, reason, of setting myself in a remote corner of the world, which if they had done, I should, no question, have been insulted enough upon that head. But since their guesses have too much party malice in them to be right—though there are five or six persons in London who cannot only give them a true account of my removal,

High-Church authors of our own party; almost every one of their authors are Jacobites, Non-Jurors, or profess'd High Flyers." (VII, 81.)

[9] A deliberative assembly of divines of the Church of England. It had an upper and a lower house.

[1] From "Miscellanea," an occasional section of the Review devoted to answering readers' letters or to lighter subject matter. See above, p. 7, n. 5.

[2] During 1706–7 Defoe apparently was in Scotland for about sixteen months. In Volume IV, Preface (written in March, 1708), he quotes a reader as stating that Defoe had been "in Scotland this Twelve-Month."

but recall me from this banishment if they had humanity in them a degree less than an African lion—I therefore cannot but take up a little room in these papers about my own case; not that I shall enter at all into those particulars, which perhaps might be thought too mean, to move the compassion of the reader; I seek it not. There are two sorts of people out of the reach of the world—those that are above it, and those that are below it; and they may be equally happy, for aught I know. Of the last sort I reckon myself one, and declare that as I am below their envy, so I seek not their pity. I am, I bless God, secured in my retreat from their fury, and am fully revenged of the world by contemning all the contempt it can throw upon me.

But I come to the censures of the world. "An under-spur leather," says one angry and raging creature. "Sent down into Scotland to make the Union." "Sent down to write for the Union," "Will not the voyage of the Union bear to send the *Review* into Scotland?" &c., and the like. Angry man! Not purely that I am employed, as he calls it, but that he is not.

But beyond this, behold two new ones. One who is pleased to bestow threatening language gives me his compliment as follows.

REVIEW. Your canting and pleading for the Union loses all its virtue in the just reproaches you lie under of being a hired mercenary sent down to Scotland by the court, and directed there to write for your pay. And like a mere piece of clock-work, strike as the hand that points to you, and as the weight of reward is screwed up—you have been told this by a noble lord long ago, and by several of your wretched brethren, the scribblers of the town. Expect not, therefore, any regard to what you say, for 'tis all lies, forgeries, and counterfeit. Your design is to enflame and ruin the church of God and the nation; and therefore, impudent scribbler, hold thy tongue, or expect not long to have a tongue to blaspheme thy superiours.

Excellent stuff this is indeed! And sufficiently answers itself. But this is not all; I have, with all this, Mr. Rehearsal on my back also. And he has got me a new commission from the Presbyterians. I hope in a few days I may have it down by the post with directions where to go or send for my salary; for it cannot but be very welcome at this distance, I assure him on several accounts. Speaking of a book called *The Short View,*[3] lately published by me, &c., a book I doubt not to de-

[3] *A Short View of the Present State of the Protestant Religion in Britain as It Is Now*

fend against him and all the world, he says, "It is wrote by a remarkable agent of the Presbyterians in England, who has long been employed by them, as their public vindicator here, which he still continues. And he was sent down by them the last winter into Scotland to manage their concern as to the Union there, where he stayed a long time and performs the part of their vindicator to their brethren in Scotland." (*Rehearsal*, No. 220.)

How now shall I do to reconcile these three gentlemen? One says I am sent by particular persons; another, by the Court—who he means by that is not determined; and the third, by the Presbyterians. I wish it had been first true, I was sent *by anybody;* for the work is so just, so good, and so honourable, I would neither have been ashamed of the message nor the sender. But I think the same answer would be very fit to give to these carping, querulous gentlemen as honest Samuel Colvil,[4] the famous Scottish Hudibras, gave when he was complaining of the abuses of those that railed on him about his poetry. "They say," says he, "that I am a bad poet; but I answer in few words. That's true, and yet they are liars, because they aver it in malice, not knowing whether it be true or false." (Preface to *The Whiggs Supplicat* [*ion*], p. 6.) Now, gentlemen, though it were true that I were sent by this or that man, body of men, Court, Presbyterians, or anybody, yet you may find your characters in Sam. Colvil, for none of you know whether it be true or false, and that I am positive in.

But since you have been so very free with me about my being sent, let me tell you and all the world something in which I am persuaded you will be on my side. If I have been sent hither, as you say, I have been most barbarously treated. The Scripture says, no man goes a warfare on his own expense, and I profess solemnly I have not yet had one penny of my wages, nor the least consideration for my time spent in this service. Nor had I had the good fortune to have my brains knocked out in the High Flying mobs here when the name of an Englishman implied one that was for the Union, and that man dangerous to that party—for Union was ever fatal to them. I say, had this

---

Profest in the Episcopal Church in England, and the Dissenters in Both (Edinburgh, 1707).

[4] As author of *The Whiggs Supplication* (1681), which satirized the Presbyterians and imitated Samuel Butler's *Hudibras,* he was often called "the Scottish Hudibras." This term was also applied to the poem itself.

happened, I see no prospect of having been canonized as a martyr for the cause, or having red letters bestowed on my memory in the Presbyterian calendar; but the utmost I could have expected had been what I have met with before in a like case: What business had he with it? What had he to do there? Who sent him? and the like. And is not this hard now, gentlemen Presbyterians, that I should have the testimony of your enemies that I have been serviceable to your cause, and none from yourselves? Pray consider of it, and either discharge yourselves honourably to your poor missionary here in the North, or let these fellows know they are a gang of liars, and you know nothing of the matter.

If the *Observator* will pardon me quoting myself, as he calls it, I will venture to repeat a few lines which had their date in a certain mansion house near the Old Bailey on the like occasion when I suffered like calumnies about the Dissenters paying fines, charges, &c. for me.

> Thus like old Strephon's virtuous miss
>   Who foolishly too coy
> Died with the scandal of a whore
>   And never knew the joy;
> So I by Whigs abandon'd, bear
>   The satire's unjust lash,
> Die with the scandal of their help
>   But never saw their cash.[5]

Indeed, it is very hard, and I hope the Presbyterians will consider of it, that I should have been sent down by them, either to manage their affairs so long ago, and long before employed by them as their public vindicator in England, and have not yet received one farthing salary. I think they have done me a great deal of wrong, and 'tis but small encouragement to anybody to enter into their service again.

But now after all, to leave jesting with this story. I would desire of Mr. Rehearsal, in order to preserve the common decency of good language with him, and to argue like gentlemen, a thing which by former capitulation he has promised: I would desire him to prove things as he goes along, and that I may take him in order, for I doubt not to give a full answer to all his objections upon the book called *The Short View;* I say, to take things as he goes on, and to give a

[5] From his poem, *An Elegy on the Author of the True-Born Englishman* (1704).

reason why what follows should be believed. I fairly challenge him to prove one tittle of what he positively affirms, and begins with, viz., that I have been employed in England, or sent into Scotland by the Presbyterians. If he cannot do this, all the fabric of his florid story falls to the ground, as built on a foundation that is false and suppositious. His reputation also as an author must sink in the eyes of all good men. Nay, even his cause must suffer by it as wanting a refuge of [probity?] to help it out. And to let him know that to help him in this case, and in charity to him, I'll be content with but a very slight proof. Let him but tell the world one Presbyterian, or pretended Presbyterian, in Britain from whom I received the least encouragement to come hither, or the least reward for coming, or from whom, either in his own name or in the name of any other Presbyterian I had the least direction to come northward, or with whom I have so much as corresponded since I came from England. In short, let him take his own words in any positive sense, which by the fairest construction in the world they will bear, as to my being employed in England, or sent hither by the Presbyterians, or Dissenters in general, and make but the least testimony that he spake from good ground—and I'll give up the cause. If not, let the world judge to what purpose I should enter a debate with a man who will venture on such ungentleman, unchristian, and dishonourable a thing as to charge a man positively with no proof of the fact.

Vol. III, Preface [February, 1706/7]

His Proper Employment

It has been the misfortune of this paper, among all the other rubs it has had in its way, that the volumes have been a little too much depending upon one another. Such has been the course of the subject, the length of the circumstance then on foot, or the absence of the author, that the story and the book have not brought their periods to jump exactly. Thus it was in the last volume, which broke off in the middle of the great undertaking which the author at the utmost hazard went through, in pressing this nation to peace and warning them against a sort of people then known by the names of tackers and Tories.

And thus it is now, when pursuing the same general good of his native country the author has embarked in the great affair of the Union [1] of Britain. I must confess I have sometimes thought it very hard that having voluntarily, without the least direction, assistance, or encouragement (in spite of all that has been suggested) taken upon me the most necessary work of removing national prejudices against the two most capital blessings of the world, peace and union, I should have the disaster to have the nations receive the doctrine and damn the teacher; that even those that have owned the truth of what has been said, and even the seasonableness of saying it, have nevertheless flown in the face of the instrument, endeavouring to break the poor earthen vessel by which the rich treasure, viz., the knowledge of their own happiness, has been conveyed. Indeed, I cannot but complain; and should I descend to particulars, it would hardly appear credible that in a Christian, a Protestant, and a reformed nation any man could receive such treatment as I have done—from even those very people whose consciences and judgments have stooped to the venerable truth, owned it has been useful, serviceable, and seasonable.

It would make this preface a history to relate the reproaches, the insults, the contempt with which these papers have been treated in discourse, writing, and print even by those that say they are embarked in the same cause and pretend to write for the same public good. The charge made against me of partiality, of bribery, of pensions and payments—a thing the circumstances, family, and fortunes of a man devoted to his country's peace clears me of. If paid, gentlemen, for writing; if hired, if employed, why still harrassed with merciless and malicious men; why pursued to all extremities by law for old accounts which you clear other men of every day; why oppressed, distressed, and driven from his family, and from all his prospects of delivering

[1] The political union of Scotland and England, accomplished in 1707. The *Review* gives much space to telling the advantages of such an arrangement.

them or himself? Is this the fate of men employed and hired? Is this the figure the agents of courts and princes make? Certainly, had I been hired or employed, those people that own the service would by this time have set their servant from the little and implacable malice of litigious prosecutions, murdering warrants, and men whose mouths are to be stopped by trifles. Let this suffice then to clear me of all the little and scandalous charge of being hired and employed.

I come next to examine what testimonies I have of this work being my proper employ; for some of our good friends whose censure runs before their charity attack me with this. "Ay, 'tis true, these things are so; but what has he to do to meddle with it? What has he to do to examine the conduct of Parliament men, or exhort the people to this or that?" Wise gentlemen in troth—pray go on with it. "Sirs, aye, 'tis true, he did happen to see a house just on fire; but what had he to do to make a noise, wake all the neighbourhood, fright their children, and like a busy fellow cry 'Fire!' in the night. It was none of his neighbourhood; he had ne'er a house there; what business had he to meddle?" Or put it another way. "Ay, indeed he did happen to see a parcel of rogues breaking up a gentleman's house in the night, but what business had he to go and raise the country upon them, cry 'Thieves and murder!' and I know not what, and so bring a parcel of poor fellows to the gallows? What business had he with it; it was none of his house?"

Truly, gentlemen, this is just the case. I saw a parcel of people caballing together to ruin property, corrupt the laws, invade the government, debauch the people, and, in short, enslave and embroil the nation. And I cried "Fire!" or rather, I cried "Water!" for the fire was begun already. I see all the nation running into confusions and directly flying in the face of one another, and cried out "Peace!" I called upon all sorts of people that had any senses to collect them together and judge for themselves what they were going to do; and excited them to lay hold of the madmen and take from them the wicked weapon, the knife with which they were going to destroy their mother, rip up the bowels of their country, and at last effectually ruin themselves. And what had I to do with this? Why, yes, gentlemen, I had the same right as every man that has a footing in his country, or that has a posterity to possess liberty and claim right must have, viz., as far as possible to preserve the laws, liberty, and government of that country to which he belongs; and he that charges me with meddling in what does not concern me, meddles himself with what, 'tis plain, he does not understand.

Well, through all the maltreatment of both friends and enemies, I have hitherto, undiscouraged by the worst circumstances, unrewarded and unsupported, pursued the first design of pressing all people that have any regard to the interest of religion, the honour of their country, and the good of posterity, to come to a temper about party strife; to shorten their disputes, encourage calmness, and revive the old Christian principle of love to one another. I shall not boast here of my success. Let the rage and implacable hatred against me, conceived by the enemies of this healing principle; let the confessions of those who reap the benefit and own the service, though they abandon and despise the instrument—let these be my witnesses, and these shall testify for me that I have not been an unprofitable servant to anybody but myself; and of that I am entirely regardless in this case.

From the same zeal with which I first pursued this blessed subject of peace, I found myself embarked in the farther extent of it—I mean the Union. If I thought myself obliged, in duty to the public interest, to use my utmost endeavour to quiet the minds of enraged parties, I found myself under a stronger necessity to embark in the same design between too much enraged nations. As to the principle from which I have acted, I shall leave to the issues of time to determine whether it has been sincere or no. Hypocrites only make use of masks and false lights to conceal present reserved designs. Truth and sincerity only dare appeal to time and consequences. I covet no better testimony of the well laid design of these sheets than that evidence, time, and farther light into truth, shall discover.

I saw the union of the two kingdoms begun; I saw the principle on which both sides seemed to act look with a different face from what was ever made use of before. All the former treaties looked like politic shams, mere amusements and frauds to draw in and deceive the people, while commissioners met little qualified and less inclined to the general good of the whole. But now I thought I foresaw the success of the treaty in the temper, sincerity, and inclinations of the treaters on both sides. They came together furnished for the work, convinced fully of the advantages on both sides of it and blessed with sincere intentions to bring it to pass. When I saw this, I thought it my duty to do my part without doors. And I know no part I could act in my sphere so natural, so useful, and so proper to the work as to attempt to remove the national prejudices which both people, by the casualty of time, and the errors, industry, and malice of parties, had too eagerly taken up and were too tenacious of, one against another. To this purpose I wrote two essays against national prejudices in England, while the treaty was in agitation there, and four more in Scotland, while it was debating in Scotland by the Parliament there—the contents of all which are repeated in this paper. Nor did I think my time or labour ill-bestowed to take a long, a tedious and hazardous journey thither, or to expose myself to a thousand insults, scoffs, rabbles and tumults—to all manner of despiteful and injurious treatment, if possible, to bring the people there to their senses, and free them from the unreasonable prejudices they had entertained against the prosperity of their country.

And having seen the treaty happily ratified there with some few amendments which I hope are not considerable, I thought this a proper period to close this volume, which had already run beyond its usual bounds, and the next volume will begin at the Parliament of England entering upon the treaty where, I hope, it shall meet with better treatment than it has met with in Scotland, and a better reception with the people. If it shall be my lot to live to see this treaty finished, I think to venture one essay at the general and reciprocal duties of the two nations one to another, in which I shall endeavour to move England to engage Scotland, with all the acts of kindness and all the advantages which can be desired in reason, in order to plant and cultivate the new relation of the two kingdoms; and on the other hand to move Scotland to entertain no jealousies, nor be anxious about any thing without great reason and good ground, as the only way to bring about the general peace of both kingdoms, and settle the doubtful minds of the people on both sides. This I hope I shall pursue with an equality of arguments on both sides, without partiality or affection to one more than another; and in that, shew that the original of my concerning myself in this matter was merely to be serviceable, if possible, to both kingdoms and to the united body in general. I doubt not, however, but I shall give offence in this too; for there is a people in the world who are not to be pleased with anything. But I shall content myself in pursuing what is the true end of the Union—the flourishing of peace and the equalities on every hand in matters of advantage, liberty, religion, and trade.

I am very sensible all coalitions without this will render the Union still imperfect and ineffectual. The Union will never have its full perfection of extent, nor will either nation reap the benefit of it till it becomes a union of affection and a union of interest. This is my business, and let the enemies of God and the nation's peace be as angry as they please; this is what I shall pursue to the utmost. This volume ends with it, the next will begin with it; and those that cry out 'tis too long, and 'tis nothing but what has been heard before, must bear with the prolixity of the author till they please to shorten the occasion. Whenever they please to lay aside their spirit of division, anger, malice, wrath, strife, &c., when they leave off raising unnecessary heats about scruples and trifles, merely to divide, not to inform; when national prejudices on either side cease, and I can see the least prospect of a calm among the men of cavil and continual objection, I shall be the first that shall cease calling upon them to peace. But till then, the tautology is in the crime, not in the reprover, and I shall not fail to alarm them on all occasions.

Vol. VI, Preface [March, 1710]

ASSASSINS DEFIED

I AM COME now to the conclusion of the sixth volume of this work, though like a teeming woman I have thought every volume should be the last. Where it will end now, and when, God only knows, and time only will discover; as for me, I know nothing of it. This particular paper, though written at the end of the work, carries the title of the preface more because it is placed by the bookseller [1] at the frontispiece than that it is anything of an introduction to the volume, for it is really written at the close of the whole, and its subject very particular.

We have had a most distracting turbulent time for the last two months of this year, occasioned by the prosecution and defence of a High Flying clergyman who has undertaken in the teeth of the very Parliament, as well as of the nation, to justify and defend the exploded ridiculous doctrine of non-resistance. This defence has been carried on with all possible heat, fury, and violence among the party; and a strong conjunction of Papist, Jacobite, and High Church madmen has appeared in it, which has made them seem very formidable to the world. Rabbles, tumults, plundering houses, demolishing meeting houses, insulting gentlemen in the streets, and honest men in their dwellings, has been the necessary appendices of this affair. And after all I must own, though the man has been condemned, his principles censured, and his sermon burnt, yet it has not been without most fatal consequences over the whole nation, as it has revived the heats, feuds, and animosities which were among us, and which by the blessed example and exhortation of Her Majesty began to be laid asleep in the nation.

I have been endeavouring to shew you the mischief of these tumults, the bloody design of the persons that have raised them, and how they have differed from all that went before them. I have given you intances of their most villainous designs; such as rifling the Bank, demolishing all the meeting houses, and murdering the ministers, all which they openly professed to be their design. God deliver this nation from the pernicious effects of the present fermentation which we are now generally in on all sides. I have, however, faithfully discharged what I thought myself obliged to as a debt to peace, and in duty to the present constitution, to speak plainly in these cases whatever risk I run, and at whatever hazard these truths are to be told. I have not been afraid to bear my testimony, as some call it, to the liberties of Britain against the reviving mischiefs of tyranny, and have in the midst of all your mobs and rabbles openly declared non-resistance

[1] The early eighteenth-century bookseller often combined the functions of today's publisher and a bookseller.

to be damned by Parliament, and English (now British) [2] liberty to be built upon the foundation of the claim of right and of the Revolution; of which the Protestant Succession, which sets by the more immediate heirs,[3] is the great exemplification. The great King William was the re-edifier of the building; the collective body of the people were the great and happy original; and the Union is the topstone.

I am none of those that boast of their advèntures, and love to tell long stories of the dangers they run. I am not always to be frighted with threatening letters and shams of assassination; I ever thought those people that talk so much of killing folks never do it. Though I am none of those you call fighting fellows, yet I am none of those that are afraid to see themselves die, and I may, I hope, without being taxed with vanity, profess not to practice non-resistance. I have by me about fifteen letters from gentlemen of more anger than honour, who have faithfully promised me to come and kill me by such and such a day; nay, and some have descended to tell me the very manner, yet not one of them has been so good as his word. Once I had the misfortune to come into a room where five gentlemen had been killing me a quarter of an hour, in their way—and yet to the reproach of their villainous design, as well as their courage, durst not all together own it to a poor naked single man that gave them opportunity enough, and whom they had too much in their power. In short, I here give my testimony from my own experience, and I note it for the instruction of the five assassins above, that their cause is villainous, and that makes the party cowardly. A man that has any honour in him is really put to more difficulty how to speak than how to act. In the case of murders and assassination, he is straitened between the extremes of shewing too much courage, or too much fear.

Should I tell the world the repeated cautions given me by friends not to appear, not to walk the streets, not to show myself—letters sent me to bid me remember Sir Edmund-Bury Godfrey,[4] John Tut-

[2] Upon the political union of Scotland and England in 1707, for which Defoe had worked so hard, the proper term for the citizens of both countries was no longer merely English or Scots, but *British.*

[3] In 1701 Parliament passed the Act of Settlement which stated, among other things, that the crown of England could descend only to a Protestant.

[4] Sir Edmund-Bury (or Edmund Berry) Godfrey (1621–78), justice of the peace for Westminster, before whom Titus Oates first brought his story of the Popish Plot

chin,[5] and the like, I must talk myself up for a madman that dares go abroad. Should I let you know how I have been three times beset and waylaid for the mischief designed, but that still I live, you would wonder what I mean. For my part, I firmly believe the villains that insulted honest Sutherland's [6] house, robbed and frighted his wife, and with naked swords bullied the poor woman, threatening that they would murder her husband whenever they met him, knew well enough he was not at home and never will meet him when he is. Wherefore, my brief resolution is this. While I live they may be assured I shall never desist doing my duty in exposing the doctrines that oppose God and the Revolution,[7] such as passive submission to tyrants and non-resistance in cases of oppression. If the gentlemen, being at a loss for arguments, are resolved to better their cause by violence and blood, I leave the issue to God's Providence, and must do as well with them as I can. As to defense, I have had some thoughts to stay at home in the night, and by day to wear a piece of armour on my back—the first, because I am persuaded these murderers will not do their work by daylight; and the second, because I firmly believe they will never attempt it so fairly to my face as to give occasion of armour anywhere else.

I confess there may be some reasons for me to apprehend this wicked party, and therefore as I thank God I am without a disturbing fear, so I am not perfectly secure or without caution. The reasons are such as these: that truly assassination and murder is something more suitable to the High Flying cause, and has been more in use among their

---

in September, 1678. A month later Sir Edmund's body was found in a ditch, run through with his own sword. On poorly substantiated evidence the Court found that he had been murdered by Catholic priests.

[5] John Tutchin (1661?–1707). Author of the *Observator* (1702–7), died September 23, 1707, in the Queen's Bench prison at the Mint. According to Defoe (Vol. V, No. 46), he died of a beating at the hands of hired bullies. Author of *The Foreigners: A Poem* (1700), which Defoe called "a vile abhorred pamphlet in very ill verse," he inspired Defoe to write his own most famous poem, *The True-Born Englishman* (1701).

[6] Probably here refers to one of the dissenters whose house was among the many which mobs raided during the Sacheverell trial in March, 1710. See below, p. 199, n. 1, on Sacheverell.

[7] The Glorious Revolution of 1688, whereby William of Orange was made king of England, and James II deposed. In England it gave the death blow to the doctrine of the divine right of kings, wherein subjects were to submit passively even to a wicked sovereign.

party, than in other cases and with other people. 'Tis the cause of tyranny, and tyranny always leads to blood; oppression goes hand in hand with violence, and he that would invade my liberty will invade my life as he has opportunity. And had their rabble got a little more head, we might have come again into the laudable practice of cutting of throats and cold blood murders. And by the same rule, their downfall being so apparent, this desperate cure may be thought needful to their desperate cause. But I cannot see why they should be so exasperated at the poor *Review,* a sorry despised author, to use the words of one of their party, who nobody gives heed to.

Well, gentlemen, then let your anger be pointed at some more significant animal that is more capable to wound you, and do not own this author to be so considerable as to engage your resentment, lest you prove the unanswerable force of what he says by the concern you are at to suppress him. What will the world say to this way of dealing? You should first answer the argument—that's the best way of murdering the author; to kill him first is to own you could not answer him. If your doctrine of non-resistance will subsist, if it will uphold itself, you have advantage enough; writing against it will be of no force, even the House of Commons must fall before it, for truth will prevail. But if not, if this author and all that open their mouths against it were to be sacrificed by your impious hands, truth would never want champions to defend it against this absurd error. And killing the *Review* would be like cutting off the monster's head when a hundred rise up in the room of it. Upon these accounts I go on perfectly easy. As to the present threats I daily meet with from this cowardly and abominable party—if I am attacked by multitude, I must fall, as Abner fell before wicked men. If I am fairly and honourably attacked, I hope I shall fairly resist; for I shall never practise the notion I condemn; and every honest man ought to go prepared for a villain. This, though it is irksome to me to say, and no man that fights loves to talk of it, yet I thought it proper for me to let you all see that I have my share of this High Church mob. And that whatever may happen to me the world may known whence it comes.

I might, and ought indeed to speak a word or two to three gentlemen, besides those mentioned before, who have been pleased personally to threaten my life—with abundance of preambles and justification of themselves about it. What I shall say to them is—I shall demonstrate my being perfectly unconcerned at the matter by refusing the advice given me, even by their own friends, of binding them to the peace. It seems a little unnatural to me, and what I shall never practice, to go to law with a man for beating me, much less for threatening me. And least of all, when the persons are such harmless creatures as these. Wherefore, all the answer I shall give them is this, with the utmost contempt of their folly,

The cur that barks is not the cur that bites.

These things regard particular men, and I know the persons will understand me when they read it. I assure you it is in courtesy to them that I bury their folly by concealing their names.

Upon the whole, as I am going on in what I esteem my duty, and for the public good, I firmly believe it will not please God to deliver me up to this bloody and ungodly party. And therefore I go on freely in what is before me and shall still go on to detect and expose a vicious clergy, and a bigoted race of the people, in order to reclaim and reform them, or to open the eyes of the good people of Britain, that they may not be imposed upon by them; and whether in this work I meet with punishment or praise, safety or hazard, life or death, TE DEUM LAUDAMUS.

Your humble servant,

D. F.

Vol. VIII, No. 137 Thursday, February 7, 1712

PRINCIPLES, PRINCIPLES, PRINCIPLES

AS I BEGIN to draw nearer the close of this volume, so, as things now appear before us, the time draws on when the liberty of speaking this way will be taken from us.[1] And truly I am one

[1] A reference to the tax of July, 1712, on periodicals and pamphlets (see above, p. 10, n. 1).

of those that rejoice now at the period being to be put to a work which, however now treated by those it has served, yet, and that by the confession of themselves, and of their enemies also, has served them, and shall stand as a monument of the gratitude of the age to their true-born English posterity. I must confess that when they talked of a licenser for the press I offered reasons against it as an invasion of liberty; but I have sometimes thought less of that injury than formerly, when I find our people in every coffee house taking the liberty of every author that writes away from him by censure, raillery, reproach, and the like; that an author if he does not please them, or speaks his thoughts freely, is treated as if he was a servant in their pay, and subjected to their correction; that whoever did not oblige them and say as they said, was dishonest to them, and a breach of the author's duty.

Thus plentifully has a part of the world treated me of late because, forsooth, I have not pleased them in speaking my thoughts freely about the peace. I might ask them, Who of you have I wronged? In whose pay was I listed? Whose wages have I taken and not done their work, that you treat me thus masterly? One particular witty fellow be-rogues and abuses me in a letter signed J. Williamson; but after a friendly advertisement to him to let me know how to direct an answer to him, it seems he is ashamed to own his language. Well, he tells me once I served them and writ well for them, &c. But now! &c. Billingsgate enough. Well, Mr. Williamson, if I served you once, for I must allow you to be a very good judge—what was it for? If for wages, did ye pay me? If for affection and principle, your gratitude is mighty remarkable. And so much to good Mr. Williamson: answer a fool in his folly, &c. Now you are gone from your temper, your principles, your probity, and your party, and I cannot speak for you. What must I do—speak for you against judgment, and conscience, and principle? God knows, I cannot for my life. . . . And while ye rail at me for speaking this truth, pray, what is your authority, and who are ye, gentlemen, that I may not speak my mind as freely as you? If I could have obliged you without belying my own knowledge and experience, I would have done it. But as I have not, for fear or favour, said one word for you, so I can solemnly protest I have spoken neither for gain, or the hopes of it; neither to oblige or serve any one party or person in the world. On the other hand, I never did, nor ever shall, refrain speaking what my own conscience dictates to me to be truth and seasonable, for fear of the face of any man, or body of men, in my life. He that fears the oppression of power can be no servant of truth, nor has any of your fawning scribblers dared to speak the truths that I have done, or to suffer for them either, as I have done. But he that fears reproach and clamour is a slave to his pride, and abject below a criminal. For my part, being fully satisfied that I speak not only from principle but for the public service, I rejoice in the contempt I see put upon me by clamorous and noisy men who are so far from grieving me that they never rob me of a smile, nor ever moved me to any return but to pity the possession of prejudice which they are now under, and which God, in his due time, I hope will deliver them from.

On the other hand, neither can I flatter or refrain speaking with freedom in the cause of truth when men of power take steps to prove them not infallible; my endeavour is to prevent the oppressions which the fury of our parties threatens every side with. When men of honour and figure are pushing their party interests with such an ill-principled rage that they can sell or give up their faithful friends who had for them acted to every extreme of a disinterested affection; who had rejected for them all separate treaties, and all accommodations—when these things are carried on, I have never regarded my own safety or interest to keep me silent. If I have had any interest or favour with men in power, while those I have endeavoured to serve by it have reviled me with acting for the ministry—I speak now of the times as well of the last ministry as of this—I have always improved that interest with faithful remonstrances and representations, as far as duty and decency would permit, to serve and save the interest and persons who have at the same time abused me, and I do so still. And I do it from this principle, that it is the cause, and not the persons, I desire to serve; and he that sees in secret will reward me, if he approves the service. As for the men, I know them too well to expect or desire it from them, nay, I am content they shall stone me, and throw dirt at me while I am doing this for them. My witness is within myself, and yet I am not without witnesses of the fact neither. . . .

Vol. VIII, Preface [July (?), 1712]

MR. REVIEW TREADS THE MILKY WAY

I HAVE now finished the eighth volume of this work, and as this particular part has been the subject of as much clamour and noise as any of the former, though on a different account, and from different people, I cannot close it without giving some account both of it and myself. From the beginning of this undertaking, which I have now carried on almost ten years, I have always, according to the best of my judgment, calculated it for the support and defense of TRUTH and LIBERTY. I was not so weak when I began as not to expect enemies, and that by speaking plain, both to persons and things, I should exasperate many against both the work and the author, and in that expectation I have not been deceived.

I confess I did not expect that if the same truth summoned me to reprove, or differ from the conduct of the people I was serving, they would treat me as they do for it. I own, I thought an uninterrupted fidelity and steady adhering to an honest principle for near forty years would have been some plea in my behalf; and if not that, suffering the shipwreck of my fortunes, which were at that time recovering, and by the bounty of his late Majesty [1] in a fair way of being restored, suffering all the indignities, penalties, and punishments an enraged party could inflict upon me, and about three thousand pound loss [2]—I say, I thought this might have lodged a little in the breasts of my friends and might have allowed them at least to examine, before they condemned me, whether they did me wrong or no. I thought that while I had given such proof that I could neither be bribed from the truth, or threatened, or terrified from my principles, it might at least be a ground for impartial honest men to examine before they cen-

[1] William III, who died in March, 1702.

[2] In 1703, when jailed for *The Shortest Way with the Dissenters* (see above, p. 9, n. 3), Defoe had a manufactory for tiles at Tilbury. During his absence the business failed, and he lost his investment. Elsewhere (see p. 56) he gives the figure as 3,500 pounds.

sured me whether it was true or no that I had been now guilty of both.

But I have found all this in vain; and as if forfeiting my reason as well as my estate were a debt from me to the party I espoused, I am now hunted with a full cry, Acteon like, by my own friends (I won't call them hounds) *in spite* of protested innocence, *in spite* of want of evidence; against the genuine sense of what I write, against fair arguing, against all modesty and sense; condemned by common clamour as writing for money, writing for particular persons, writing by great men's direction, being dictated to, and the like—every tittle of which I have the testimony of my own conscience is abominably false, and the accusers must have the accusation of their own consciences that they do not know it to be true. I cannot say it has not given me a great deal of disturbance; for an ungrateful treatment of a people that I had run all manner of risk for, and thought I could have died for, cannot but touch a less sensible temper than I think mine to be; but I thank God that operation is over, and I endeavour to make other uses of it than perhaps the people themselves think I do.

First, *I look in,* and upon the narrowest search I can make of my own thoughts, desires, and designs, I find a clear untainted principle, and consequently an entire calm of conscience, founded upon the satisfying sense that I neither am touched with bribes, guided or influenced by fear, favour, hope, dependence, or reward of, upon, or from any person or party under Heaven; and that I have written and do write nothing but what is my native, free, undirected opinion and judgment and what was so many years ago as, I think, I made unanswerably appear by the very last *Review* of this volume, where I quoted the very same thing which I write now and which was printed in the fifth volume of this work, No. 155 in the year 1709.[3]

Next, *I look up,* and not examining into His ways, the sovereignty of whose Providence I adore, I submit with an entire resignation to whatever happens to me as being by the immediate direction of that goodness and for such wise and glorious ends, as however I may not yet see through, will, at last, issue in good even to me; fully depending that I shall yet be delivered from the power of slander and reproach, and the sincerity of my conduct be yet cleared up to the world; and if not, *Te Deum laudamus.*

[3] No such reference is made in No. 155 for 1709.

In the third place, *I look back* on the people who treat me thus, who, notwithstanding, under the power of their prejudices, they fly upon me with a fury that I think unchristian and unjust; yet, as I doubt not, the day will still come when they will be again undeceived in me. I am far from studying their injury or doing myself justice at their expense, which I could do with great advantage. It is impossible for the Dissenters in this nation to provoke me to be an enemy to their interest; should they fire my house, sacrifice my family, and assassinate my life, I would ever requite them with defending their cause, and standing to the last against all those that should endeavour to weaken or reproach it. But this is, as I think it, a just and righteous cause, founded upon the great principle of truth and liberty, which I am well assured I shall never abandon, and not that I am insensible of being ill treated by them, or that I make any court to their persons. When any party of men have not a clear view of their own case, or a right knowledge of their own interest, he that will serve them, and knows the way to do it, must be certain not to please them, and must be able to see them revile and reproach him, and use him in the worst manner imaginable, and not be moved either to return them ill or refrain doing them good; and this is the true meaning of that command which I thank God I cheerfully obey, viz., to pray for them that despitefully use me.

I have not so ill an opinion of myself as not to think I merit better usage from the Dissenters; and I have not so ill an opinion of the Dissenters as not to think they will, some time or other, know their friends from their enemies better than they do now: nor have I so far forgot my friends [4] as not to own a great many of them do already. I remember the time when the same people treated me in the same manner upon the book called *The Shortest Way*, &c., and nothing but suffering for them [5] would ever open their eyes; he that cleared up my integrity then can do it again by the same method, and I leave it to him. *Ad te quacunque vocas* is my rule; my study and practice is patience and resignation, and in this I triumph over all the indignity, reproach, slander, and raillery in the world. In this I enjoy in the midst of a million of enemies a perfect peace and tranquillity, and when they miscon-

[4] See below, p. 63, for more specific remarks about his friends.

[5] Another reference to his imprisonment and financial losses resulting from his unlucky pamphlet, *The Shortest Way with the Dissenters*.

struct my words, pervert the best meaning, turn everything which I say their own way, it gives me no other contemplation than this: How vain is the opinion of men, either when they judge well or ill!

This makes me go on steadily, and regard no clamour. When I write *against* a war with the Dutch they rail and exclaim at me and say I write *for* a war with the Dutch. When I write against erecting an Austrian tyrant [6] in the room of a French, they tell me I write for the French. When I write for putting an end to the war, they tell me I write for a French peace, and the like. I have made such protestations of my receiving no reward or directions whatever in or for this work, as none but those who are used to prevaricate themselves can, upon any foundation that is consistent with Christianity, suspect; and the circumstances I labour under in the world are a corroborating evidence of the truth of it; yet without ground, without evidence, without any testimony but general notion they will have it otherwise. Two of their authors have the impudence to assert it, but not one step have they taken to prove it, nor can they do it, though both openly challenged to do it and a hundred guineas offered upon the proof of it; thus they give the lie and the rascal to themselves without my help who quietly let them go on their own way.

My measures are, to the best of my judgment, steady. What I approve I defend; what I dislike I censure without any respect of persons, only endeavouring to give my reasons and to make it appear that I approve and dislike upon good and sufficient grounds; which being first well assured of, the time is yet to come that I ever refrained to speak my mind for fear of the face of man. If what I have said were false, my enemies would certainly choose to *answer* rather than to *rail;* but as I have unanswerable truth on my side they choose to *rail* rather than to *answer*. . . .

I am a Stoic in whatever may be the event of things; I'll do and say what I think is a debt to justice and truth to do and say, without the least regard to clamour and reproach; and as I am utterly unconcerned at human opinion, the people that throw away their breath so freely in

[6] The balance of power was a cornerstone in William III's philosophy, in England's politics, and in Defoe's political writing. The Grand Alliance at the turn of the century was designed to thwart France's chances of adding Spain to her orbit. The disposal of that prize to the Austrian monarch shifted the danger, and Defoe called out upon it.

censuring me may consider of some better improvement to make of their passions than to waste them on a man that is both above and below the reach of them. I know too much of the world to expect good in it; and I have learnt to value it too little to be concerned at the evil; I have gone through a life of wonders, and am the subject of a vast variety of Providences; I have been fed more by miracle than Elijah when the ravens were his purveyors. I have some time ago summed up the scenes of my life in this distich.

> No man has tasted differing fortunes more,
> And thirteen times I have been rich and poor.[7]

In the school of affliction I have learnt more philosophy than at the academy, and more divinity than from the pulpit. In prison I have learnt to know that liberty does not consist in open doors and the free egress and regress of locomotion. I have seen the rough side of the world as well as the smooth, and have in less than half a year tasted the difference between the closet of a king and the dungeon of Newgate.

I have suffered deeply for cleaving to principle; of which integrity I have lived to say, none but those I suffered for ever reproached me with it. The immediate causes of my suffering have been by being betrayed by those I have trusted, and scorning to betray those that trusted me. To the honour of English gratitude I have this remarkable truth to leave behind me, that I was never so basely betrayed as by those whose families I had preserved from starving, nor so basely treated as by those I starved my own family to preserve. The same chequerwork of fortunes attends me still; the people I have served, and love to serve, cut my throat every day because I will not cut the throat of those that have served and assisted me. Ingratitude has always been my aversion, and perhaps for that reason it is my exercise. And now I live under universal contempt, which contempt I have learnt to contemn, and have an uninterrupted joy in my soul, not at my being contemned but that no crime can be laid to my charge to make that contempt my due.

Fame, a lying jade, would talk me up for I know not what of courage; and they call me a fighting fellow. I despise the flattery. I profess to know nothing of it farther than [that] truth makes any man bold; and I acknowledge that give me but a bad cause and I am the greatest

[7] Apparently by Defoe, but I have not been able to find it among his published verse.

coward in the world. Truth inspires nature, and as in defense of truth no honest man can be a coward, so no man of sense can be bold when he is in the wrong. He that is honest must be brave, and it is my opinion that a coward cannot be an honest man. In defense of truth, I *think* (pardon me that I dare go no further, for who knows himself?) I say, I think I could dare to die, but a child may beat me if I am in the wrong. Guilt gives trembling to the hands, blushes to the face, and fills the heart with amazement and terror. I question whether there is much, if any difference between bravery and cowardice but what is founded in the principle they are engaged for; and I no more believe any man is born a coward than that he is born a knave. Truth makes a man of courage, and guilt makes that man of courage a coward.

Early disasters and frequent turns of my affairs, as above, have left me encumbered with an insupportable weight of debt; and the remarkable compassion of some creditors, after continued offers of stripping myself naked by entire surrenders upon oath, have never given me more trouble than they were able, or less than they knew how—by which means most of the debts I have discharged have cost me forty shillings in the pound to pay, and the creditor half as much to recover. I have a large family, a wife and six children, who never want what they should enjoy, or spend what they ought to save. Under all these circumstances, and many more too long to write, my only happiness is this: I have always been kept cheerful, easy, and quiet; enjoying a perfect calm of mind, clearness of thought, and satisfaction not to be broken in upon by whatever may happen to me. If any man ask me how I arrived to it? I answer him in short—by a constant, serious application to the great, solemn, and weighty work of resignation to the will of Heaven; by which let no man think I presume; I have endeavoured, and am in a great measure able to say feelingly and effectually, the following lines which I recommend to the world, not only as the fruit of my own experience, but for the practice of all such as know how to value it and think they need it.

Happy, because confirm'd above,[8]
And t'Heaven's dispose resign'd;
I by His rule direct my steps,
And on Him stay my mind.

[8] This poem, "Of Resignation," appeared earlier in the Edinburgh edition of the

Upon His various Providence
With satisfaction rest,
I unexalted can enjoy,
And suffer undepress'd!

Boldly I steer through storms of life,
And shipwreck of estate;
Without inheritance I'm rich,
And without honours great.

When the world trembles, I'm unmov'd,
When cloudy, I'm serene:
When darkness covers all without,
I'm always bright within.

In labour I enjoy my rest,
In weighty sorrows, ease:
When pride and parties rage with strife,
I'm all in calms and peace.

In scarcity, I fear no want;
In plenty, guard my mind:
In prison I'm at liberty,
In liberty confin'd.

With steady foot, and even pace,
I tread the Milky Way;
I've youth without its levity,
And age without decay.

I scorn the terrors of the world,
And equally her charms;
If those affright, or these allure,
I shake her from my arms.

Often I've been by power oppress'd,
And with deep sorrows tried;
By the same power I've been caress'd,
And I have both defied.

. . . . . .

Review, No. 128, January 28, 1710. Curiously, this version differs principally in using "I" instead of "he."

The HONEST PART I fain would act,
As Heaven shall means restore;
Till then I nurse the principle,
And Heaven expects no more.

. . . . . .

My full dependence is above,
I own and eye His power;
I know I must account to Him,
And wait with joy the hour.

In vain we talk of happiness,
In any state below;
There is no calm on earth, but what
Must from this fountain flow.

Resign'd to Heaven, we may with joy
To any state submit;
And in the worst of miseries,
Have happiness complete.

D. F.

Vol. VIII, No. 123 Saturday, January 5, 1712

DEFOE DEFENDS HIS REPUTATION[1]

I HAD TAKEN no more notice of what the author of the *Observator* had said as what by way of dispute I think merits no reply, if he had not now taken a new course with me, a course which all honest and unbiassed men must abhor, at least if they have any sense either of conscience or justice in the world—and a course which savours rather of a murderer than of a disputant; and in this, the necessity will excuse me.

I thought we might have differed in argument without personal

[1] This bore the heading, "Advertisement for the Observator," and appeared at the end of the issue.

malice. I bless God I entertain none against the worst enemy I have; I have not offered to say one word to him or of him, but what relates to him *as an author*, and to what he has printed in the world; but he, on the contrary, unlike a Christian, as well as a gentleman, has transferred his rage from the *Observator* and *Review*, to Ridpath and Defoe, and for want of better arguments reproaches me with the misfortunes of private circumstances; things altogether foreign to the matter in hand, of twenty-two years' standing, and which he can on no honourable pretense mention but merely *renovare dolorem*, to insult his neighbour. While to make good the deficiency of his reasoning he frequently called me bankrupt, I held my tongue, supposing he took that for a good proof that I was wrong in all I said; for how should a bankrupt have any sense? Or how should he argue that could not pay his debts? But finding this would not move me, he comes closer to me, and publishes in *Observator* No. ——— [2] that nobody will trust me with a shilling. This indeed, though it were true, as I thank God it is a premeditated untruth, weighs not one grain in the scale of his argument, yet forces me to speak a word or two more than I designed.

If I had not at this time in the lawful pursuit of my business (by which, and not by writing, as he does, I get my bread) [to] support a large family, and honestly set apart the overplus to clear the encumbrances he reproaches me with, all which this malicious person has thus endeavoured to blast and overthrow; *if*, I say, I had not in the course of this business, even at this time, the TRUST of several thousand pounds in my hands of other men's goods and effects; *if* I had not, since the misfortune he reproaches me with, been TRUSTED both with public and private money to above the value of one hundred thousand pounds; and *if* I was not every day even oppressed with the TRUSTS of both goods and money by friends whom I act for, much more than I desire —all which business and TRUSTS he has thus done his utmost to ruin and prevent, I should have said nothing. But as this is my case, justice to myself, my family, and such as are daily trusting me as above, obliges me to take notice of it in the following manner.

1. I offer to refer him to several persons of his own knowledge and acquaintance who, having trusted me in business, 500£ and 1000£ at

[2] Volume X, No. 103. Defoe frequently refers to other periodicals in this fashion, but he does not always supply the issue number.

a time, will give the lie to what he has published, and will own those trusts faithfully and honourably discharged; I think this will detect him of malice and falsehood.

2. Had what he says been true, he, a professed Dissenter, ought not to have mentioned it, since thereby he only calls to mind how I suffered 3,500£ loss [3] for a cause that he owns, and a party which he ought to have more respect for than to force me to upbraid them with unkindness, and to tell how easily I could have prevented that loss with advantage if I would have betrayed honest men, even some who have since forgot the obligation, less than which loss would have made him a bankrupt, I doubt, both in cash and in principle.

3. That as he shows himself a man of wicked and malicious principle who without any just provocation can thus attempt to ruin and overthrow a man and his family, who struggles with a known and unwearied diligence to recover his misfortunes, and do justice to all the world; so I cheerfully depend upon it that God will not suffer so malicious a purpose to have its desired effects; and therefore I publish to all those I am dealing with, as follows: that all those people who have now credited me, and whose effects I have in my hands, and who may be influenced by this villainous attempt upon me to be uneasy, on a post letter to me they shall have immediately restored and delivered to them, or their assigns, all their goods, money, and effects, to a farthing.

Vol. I [IX], No. 85 Saturday, April 18, 1713

DEFOE SPENDS THE WEEKEND IN JAIL

THIS IS NOT an age to complain of injustice, but to expect it. Though it is true that I never thought the fury of men could have run so high as I find it, yet since it is so, I shall rather leave it to expose itself than return upon them with what it deserves;

[3] A reference to Defoe's imprisonment for his pamphlet, *The Shortest Way with the Dissenters,* during which his business suffered. See above, p. 47, n. 2.

especially as it is personal, and pointed at me in particular. But because so much malice has appeared, with so little cause for it, and does still appear in the treatment I have just now received from a set of men—Whigs I will not call them—as has scarce been paralleled in any age, I cannot but give you a little brief history of fact, that impartial men may see a little by it to what height our feuds have brought us, and how mankind would be used if these gentlemen had power suitable to their will.

It was above twelve days that two particular persons, who call themselves gentlemen, and whose names may be heard of in due time, began a sham treaty with Mr. Janeway, the printer, to re-print such and such books for them; and then to form this disguise, what lies, what forged stories, what false pretences they made use of! Such as Whigs in former days used to abhor! Of which, all I shall say now, is, God forgive them; for they were shifts nothing of gentlemen could make, nothing of Christians can justify, they were so scandalously untrue in fact. For no good that may follow can justify before God, or man, the committing so much evil to bring it to pass.

When by these frauds and shams they had discovered effectually that he printed the books, which was all they wanted, it seems, they terrify him with telling him it was high treason—another horrid falsity—and frighted the man not only into a confession who he had the copy of, but made him the foolish implement to betray his author, as they call me, into their hands; and causes him to send his servants and workmen with the lord chief justice's tipstaff to my house, to be the officious fools to take me up. Two of his men they terrified so by threats as to oblige them to swear that the copy of the books were my handwriting; though as I said in my last, neither of them either had one bit of copy from me, or ever saw me write a word in their lives. Upon these perjuries they obtained a warrant for me from my lord chief justice.

Having got the warrant, Mr. Janeway's boy comes with the tipstaff to my house, on Friday night. The boy was immediately let in, and spake to me; and the officer who stood at the door when he came out might have followed him, if he had thought fit; nor was he refused at all, till afterward, making a sham story of a false name and refusing to tell any business, he rendered himself suspected of other designs. But it was apparent afterward the design was to bespeak constables and people to make a cavalcade the next day, and do the thing with as much malice and clamour, and as much to alarm and expose me as possible. The next morning, about eleven o'clock, two of Mr. Janeway's people, the same who have sworn so lustily to my hand, came to the door. As soon as the first of them rung the bell at the door, they were immediately let in, and without the least difficulty performed what they came about.

I am particular in this because the author of the *Flying Post* [1] has shown his teeth in this case in so villainous a manner as all honest men must abhor; for in his paper of Thursday, April 16, abandoning humanity, and as much as possible adding to the trouble he thought me in, he says, I having strengthened my house, they were obliged to provide constables, &c. I am sorry to give Mr. Ridpath the lie, it is what is against my very nature and custom; but in so palpable a piece of malice I cannot be just to answer him by any other method; and therefore, asking my readers pardon for fouling their mouths with it in the reading, I say, If thou, Mr. George Ridpath, art the author of the *Flying Post,* thou hast published a LIE; and I shall at any time say it over again to his face if he desires it: Not the least strengthening the house, not the least refusing entrance, not the least occasion to have made a mobbing business of it, was really in the case, for the truth of which I appeal to the officer himself. But the design was plain, viz., to execute the warrant and carry on the whole afterward with as much insult, rage, and noise, and as little humanity as they could—the tipstaff himself being ashamed of them.

To illustrate this piece of malice, let the reason of the case be considered: if I had had the least knowledge of the thing, why was I not gone from home, which had been better than ten fortifyings of my house? And if I had no knowledge of it, how could I strengthen the house against them? Whereas the truth is, all that know my house know there is not a lock, bolt, or bar in it more than when I came first

[1] George Ridpath (d. 1720) was a Scotsman and a Whig journalist, sometimes called "head of the Presbyterian party in Scotland," and an opponent of the Union. Committed to Newgate prison September, 1712, for being the author of three libels in the *Observator,* he was released on bail which he skipped in the following February. He went first to Scotland and then to Holland. After the ascension of George I he returned to England and was given a position by the government. See Vol. I [IX], No. 92 (below, pp. 61 ff.) for Defoe's account.

to it, except a stair-head door to keep down thieves. Such a lie, and so ridiculous, one would think no man of sense could be guilty of. But how a man of conscience, a professor of religion, a member of a dissenting church, can satisfy himself to do thus, and reconcile it to his morality, God and himself only knows. I pray God forgive it him, the injury to me is a trifle.

Well, their warrant being executed, I came readily with them. The officer, who presently saw himself imposed upon, and that there was not the least occasion of violence, admitted me very frankly, being very much indisposed, to ride on horseback, while they came all after on foot, sometimes a quarter of mile behind. Nothing had been easier than for me to have rid away from them all, if I had thought fit, but I had not guilt enough to make me think of an escape.

The next project was that all this was of a Saturday, that they might triumph over me and keep me in their custody two nights in suspense without any release. On the Monday I tendered bail. The scandalous endeavours a set of men made use of, to fright and deter friends that were willing to bail me, will deserve a particular narration, and shall not want it. The unjust endeavours used to represent my bail to my lord chief justice as insufficient, though ready to justify themselves upon oath; the malicious prosecutors pretending to take upon themselves to enquire after and give scandalous characters of my bail, and how my lord in justice delivered me at last, having undoubted testimony of the sufficiency of my bail without giving them the trouble of swearing—these all I reserve for a time when it will be more proper to speak of it. These all are such testimonies of a malice, inconsistent with gentlemen, with Christians, and with a just cause, that I think I need say no more to them.

But when posterity shall read this paper, will they not be apt to ask immediately, What dreadful crime had this man committed that he should be used thus, ho? And what people were they who prosecuted him? For the first, the answer is short; he has wrote two books against the Pretender,[2] one exposing the ridiculous reasons given against the

[2] Pamphlets, rather: *Reasons Against the Succession of the House of Hannover* (1713) and, *And What if the Pretender Should Come?* (1713). Intended ironically, it is hard to believe anything but the malice of enemies could see in these two items expressions prejudicial to the government. Dismissed on these charges, Defoe was jailed for publishing remarks which tended to bring the Court into disrepute.

succession of the House of Hanover, and the other exposing the foolish, senseless advantages which some allege shall accrue to us by admitting the Pretender. This is all the crime, every jot of it, every tittle of it. And which is still more monstrous, the people who have done this call themselves Whigs. But let me not profane the name of a Whig with such scandalous people's characters. I do confess at first I could not think Mr. Ridpath had been one of the conspirators in this senseless piece of malice; but I think he plainly now allows himself to confederate with them. Nor is it possible to assign, hellish malice excepted, any reason why I am singled out to vent this party rage upon —a man that has never been concerned with them, that knows not the faces of one of them, nor ever conversed with them. But as their malice is profound, so is the reason of it.

It has fallen out unluckily for me, it seems, that the three conspirators [3] in this piece of inhumanity upon me are all under a prosecution of public justice for writing real libels against the Queen; and this I suppose made them blush at the thoughts of going with their accusation to the offices of secretaries of state, where their own crimes were well known. And this puts me in mind of a story. A boy who was often, by his truantry and ill tricks, subjected to needful correction, had this unhappy piece of malice rooted in his very nature; that as soon as he was gotten off from a scourging, the first little boy that he met with, less than himself, he would fall upon him and beat him unmercifully; and when anybody asked his reason, his answer was, "My father has paid me severely, and why should not he be beat as well as I?" It happened once he fell inconsiderately upon a boy who, though less in bulk than himself, was equally strong, and truly the boy turned again upon him and worsted him, and indeed beat him very handsomely; and so he was corrected by his father for being a rogue, and by his playfellow for being a fool. Let application make the ass.

[3] William Benson, Whig pamphleteer; Tom Burnet, son of Bishop Burnet; and George Ridpath, editor of the *Flying Post.*

Vol. I [IX], No. 92 Thursday, May 7, 1713

MR. REVIEW MEASURES HIS COURAGE

IT WAS EVER against my principle to fall upon any men, though my worst enemies, while they were under the misfortunes and pressures of public disasters. The hand of Justice is always heavy enough, and the leaden wings of legal resentment, however slow on other accounts, come always swift enough for those who are to bear it. Men in trouble need none to prompt their misfortunes, and I know too much of the afflictions of that kind to desire in the least to add to anyone's burden. And yet the debt of acknowledgment I owe to the wonders of Providences, which have signally appeared in my particular case of late, will oblige me to make mention of the late author of the *Flying Post*, Mr. Ridpath, at a time when otherwise I would, however I have been treated by him, forbear it. But I should be an atheist if I did not see, and no Christian if I did not adore, the infinite and inexpressible goodness of Providence in my own case, and the just retaliation of those injurious things I have suffered from this person and his party, upon his own head, and upon their cause, by the immediate direction of Heaven, which yet I shall do with as few personal reflections as possible.

To see a person who, when I lately fell into public trouble, basely expose[d] in print the names of such friends as had been bail for me—I say, to see him first expose my bail, and then run away from his own! To see a person who in print gave an account with all possible exaggerations of my late disaster in falling into the displeasure of a court of justice, himself not dare to appear before the same court of justice, but fly his country for fear of that punishment which his own conscience gave him reason to expect! To see a person who had frequently reproached me with suffering the indignity of the pillory, though in a cause he pretended to espouse, run away from his friends, and his cause too, for fear of the pillory! To see a person who was not ashamed of his cause enough to restrain him from inimitable indecencies against the government and ministry, yet so much dishonour that cause as not to dare to suffer for it in justification of the integrity of his principles and the justice of his party! To see a person who had reproached me with my private misfortunes in print, when he could no otherwise answer me, fall into those very misfortunes for want of courage to suffer for his friends! To see a party espouse a man in the greatest insolences he could possibly commit against his Sovereign, and to see him desert them and not dare to stand to what he was not ashamed to do! To see a person, after having forged and asserted in print innumerable lies and groundless suggestions—not upon me only, but upon many other innocent persons—fly from justice, and not dare to show his face to justify what he had written! To see a person who has made loud professions of justice and uprightness, and loaded me with infinite calumnies and aspersions, fly from justice, desert his bail, abandon his cause, and run his country!

Glorious is the justice of Heaven on the insolence of those who triumph over the disasters of their fellow creatures.

I have heard many things said in defense of the case, and of Mr. Ridpath's going away: such as complaints of injurious treatment, judging by innuendo, insufficiency of evidence, and the like, which all amount to no more than this, viz., that though the facts were true, yet that being fenced, as he thought, against legal proofs, they would have escaped by the letter of the law. But the true foundation of an innocent person's defense ought to be laid in the real evidence of truth, viz., that the fact is not so, and not a deficiency of proof to fix it upon the man. As to condemning by innuendo, if that be so, and supposing all he can say of it to be true, which, however, I do not grant; yet let the same justice of God be again magnified, that he who has a thousand times reproached not me alone but many others with meaning and designing so and so, which meaning and design was never in the hearts of the persons charged, should himself be condemned, as he says, by innuendo; in which case I recommend to him and to his supporters that awful text, Isaiah 33:1: "Woe to thee that spoiledst, and thou wast not spoiled; and dealedst treacherously, and they dealst not treacherously with thee; when thou shalt cease to spoil, thou shalt be spoiled, and when thou shalt make an end to deal treacherously, they shall deal treacherously with thee." He that does injury shall suffer injury.

I remember a time when in much a juster cause (I am sure), though in behalf of the same people, my case was not the same only, but much worse than Mr. Ridpath's now is.[1] For I had not only the whole weight of an incensed government upon me, but two other weights which he knows nothing of, viz., (1) The resentment of some in power because I would not answer other base ends; and (2) The resentment of the then ignorant blinded Dissenters and Whigs who were enraged at me, as if I had written *The Shortest Way* directly for their destruction, and whose eyes were never opened till I convinced them of my integrity by suffering for them and ruining my family for them.

In this case, I was under bail, and at liberty. The danger was as terrifying as possible, insomuch that when I went to an honest and good man for advice, all he would say was in the words of the disciple to our blessed Lord, "Master, save thyself." My friend[s], for some few friends I had then too, and who were engaged deeply enough as bail for me, were so apprehensive for me and for my family that they earnestly pressed me to go away, and offered to give it me under their hands that they had given me their free consent. But the honour and justice of the cause I was embarked in, the character of the good people I was embarked for, the reputation of my own integrity, and the reproach of running from my bail—these out-voted fear, and out-voted the compassion of my friends, and obliged me to resolve to bear the utmost indignities rather than quit the cause I had undertaken. And do not say this is merit, for I think every honest man who is embarked in an honest cause ought always to do so and never dishonour his cause so as to shun suffering for it. And I can now without boasting say to the good people who then acknowledged I served them and suffered for them, Ye had a man once who could have died for you, had you kept fast to the honour and integrity of your own principles, adhered to justice, and acted with moderation, and would die still for the ancient principles and temper of the Whigs or Dissenters upon those terms. But when the best men quit the substance and run into desperate extremes, those men must be quitted and the blessed medium of truth and moderation be adhered to by every upright man.

[1] He here refers to his pamphlet, *The Shortest Way with the Dissenters* (1703), the irony of which was lost upon the government. He developed the arguments of the High Church preacher Sacheverell to their logically illogical ends—that the Dissenters, a third of the nation, be purged and rooted out. He was arrested and imprisoned on the grounds that his doctrine endangered the peace. See above, pp. 9, 47.

And now behold, to what end does all the violence of your enslaving instruments tend? Will they stand the test for you? Will they suffer for the cause they rail for? Is their passive courage equal to their clamouring fury? No, no! They fly from the fiery trial, disgrace the cause they appear for, dare not look the laws in the face, for there can be no courage in suffering, without innocence of design in acting. Nothing but truth can make men bold; nothing but suffering for truth can make us look upon the world with contempt, or to Heaven with confidence. Guilt is the shame of punishment, as sin is the sting of death.

If a man is not sure his cause is right, his pursuit of it just, his design honest, his principle clear, no wonder he flies; but if truth be his foundation, if his country's good be his clear disinterested view, gaols, pillories, gibbets, and death have nothing in them to terrify him. I bless God I can say this was my case, and therefore when danger threatened, friends exhorted, and bail consented, Nehemiah's words followed me: "Shall such a man as I flee?" I considered it would reproach the cause I suffered in; that many thousands would hear I was run from my bail, to a few that would know my bail gave me their consent; that it would be remembered to posterity that I had left my bail, when it would be forgotten that they gave me leave; that it would reproach my principle, my friends, my children, and my party; and upon these considerations I resolved to hazard all rather than fly, and suffered the utmost accordingly. But the success I have had in faithfully serving and steadily suffering for the good people whom I sacrificed my family for, and their usage of me now, is, I confess, a good *memento mori* to Mr. Ridpath, and one of these things may be justly concluded. Either he has not thought the cause, or the people, worth suffering for. The last I'll join with him in, but the first all honest men must condemn him for; for if it was not a good cause, why did he embark in it? If it is a good cause, why is he afraid to suffer for it?

I forbear to say any more, because I would not add to his misfortunes.

MEMORANDUM

I am obliged here for the satisfaction of some honest but prepossessed people in the country to mention one thing more relating to myself. It has been very maliciously reported, written in news-letters, and even printed in the north of Britain, that the trouble I have been lately in was for being the author of that insolent and unmannerly libel called *The Ambassadresses Speech, &c.*[2] To which my answer is in short this, viz., that it not only is false, but not rational; and that it is not possible that I can be either such a villain to Her Majesty, or such a fool to myself.

Vol. I [IX], No. 104 Saturday, June 6, 1713

THE *Review* REVIEWED

I AM NOW bringing this long work to a close; and this is the last, or very near the last paper I shall trouble you with.[1] It has been my misfortune that several of my writings, however otherwise designed, have given offense to the legal authority I live under, and whose power it is many ways my duty, and was always my inclination, to submit to. And though I have the satisfaction of having never designedly spoken or written anything that should displease, yet as well to testify the deference I pay to the laws and to give others an example of a dutiful subjection to them, I willingly impose a silence upon myself for the future, as a just though voluntary penance for involuntary offending. I gave one testimony of my disowning a temper of insolence to superiors [2] in my late submission to the court of

[2] This is typical Defoe: one may read this statement several times and still not *positively* know what Defoe meant. He has two subjects: the cause of the trouble, and the authorship of *The Ambassadresses' Speech.* I leave it to a more percipient reader than I to assert confidently that Defoe is denying (1) that his trouble resulted from the pamphlet, or (2) that he was the author of the pamphlet, or (3) both. It is not included in his bibliography.

[1] Two issues were to follow. At the end of the last, No. 106 (Thursday, June 11, 1713), Defoe writes, "Exit *Review.*"

[2] In the *Reviews* of April 28 and May 5, 1713, Defoe made a formal apology to Lord Chief Justice Parker for having written disrespectfully of his lordship on April 16 and 18. His remarks had lodged him in jail April 22, and he was released on May 2. Final pardon was issued on November 20. See note on pages 100 ff., below.

justice, which I had unwarily affronted; and I had the satisfaction of seeing that submission accepted in a manner that will encourage all well-meaning men to fly TO justice, not FROM it, when they fall into mistakes. I think it always my duty to acknowledge what I cannot defend, and to own myself in the wrong when I am convinced of it. If the resolution I have taken to write no more be likewise acceptable, I hope no man will envy me the silence and retreat I am now going to enjoy, or grudge that this penance should atone for the errors committed in too much speaking.

And now being [resolved] to take leave of the world as to writing, according to that Christian temper we ought to show at leaving the world itself, I freely and heartily ask every man pardon whom I have in the least offended or disobliged in anything I have written; and I as heartily and freely forgive all those printed injurious things which I have received from others, which indeed are not a few; and if this asking pardon is not sufficient in any case, though I hope it may [be], I am ready to make any other submissions to them which can reasonably be required. Pursuing to extremities a man willing to acknowledge and sin no more, and if he has sinned already has done it by inadvertency, is not the custom or usage of the English temper, especially where the offense is not capital and where the usual adverbs of an accusation, viz., the "seditiously" and "maliciously," are not very apparent; and from this general felicity of this nation I promise myself some favour.

But I shall say no more to the public part of my case. The state of my conduct as to particular persons and parties requires that I should say something at parting, in which I shall study to give as little offense as I can. I have struggled long with the buffoonery of the age, and have opposed with my utmost skill, cool argument, and calm reasoning to party rage, personal prejudice, and universal clamour. I have the satisfaction of an honest appeal to Him who knows better than all of us what the ends of His Providence are, in suffering us to be thus fatally divided. That I have acted nothing by party, personal influence, or pecuniary reward, nor against the principles I always professed—this appeal will be heard, though the noise here is so great that no appeal to man, to reason, or to conscience will reach your ears; I speak now to our party divisions.

If God has any part among you, any people that He will own in Britain, and has any designs of mercy and goodness to them, He will give you all another spirit. I shall be a quiet spectator of those wretched abominable divisions that I can do no good in attempting to cure, and I shall be a silent mourner over the miseries of my country, which I expect this rage that now governs our parties will bring us to. I know and am fully assured that the spirit that now guides us, as well one as the other side, is not the spirit that ye shall have when Heaven resolves upon your deliverance; and from thence I conclude that some dreadful consequences of your divisions must first appear. Whether your judgments shall come immediately from Heaven, or you shall be made to execute the sovereign decree of Providence, one upon another, I do not pretend to determine, though I must own I fear the latter.

I acknowledge I cannot find that either recent as in memory or remote as in history, I ever saw, heard, or read the story of any nation, or of this nation, when such heats, such feuds, such rage of men among themselves ever went off without blood. How it should do so now, I know not. Your eyes are upon men and means, without the least deference to the first cause of things; you are erecting party against party, one idol to pull down another, potsherd against potsherd; and if you meet with disappointment, you rage against instruments, as if He that made them all, and can dash them to pieces at His pleasure, had no hand in it; or as if there was some evil in the city, and He had not done it.[3]

When I have seen even those who I have thought good men, and still hope they are so, run this length, I have not been able to follow, believing I ought not to be distracted because my friends were so. Though this was enough to stigmatize me for a deserter, yet I could not rest there, but have had the boldness to reprove them and the weakness to hope that they might be convinced, not remembering that state lunacies and party madness, like that of melancholy, are never cured. When I saw the world of God turned into bullying and burlesque, and the pulpit sound to party war; when I saw those hands which used to be spread forth in prayers to God and blessings to men lifted up in virulent imprecations, cursing and bitterness against this

[3] A paraphrase of Amos 3:6.

or that particular person, as if on one hand the Sovereign Agency had been committed to that person to act by, and on the other the sacred prerogative of vengeance had been taken out of God's hand, and man was to repay for himself; when I saw the Dissenters embrace a set of men that avowedly sold and betrayed them, and who indeed never did anything else but sell and betray them; nay, when I saw them willing to be sold and betrayed so they might but pull down one man, as if God could not pull him down for them if their cause was right, or they could pull him down without God if it was wrong; when I saw the contention creep into societies, into church communion, into relative affection, and into all sorts of duty, destroying religion, charity, justice, honour, nay, even natural affection, I could not but speak; indeed, who could, or who can refrain?

Difficile est satyram non scribere, nam quis iniquae
Tam patiens urbis, tam ferreus ut teneat se?
Juv. *Sat.* I.

But I considered not that the rage is too great; I have been like a man that runs in between two duellers to part them, and who to prevent the losing their lives, loses his own; the furious gladiators run both their swords into him that would part them, and he falls a sacrifice to his own zeal. On one side I am reproached with writing for gain, payments, and pensions. Alas! I have seen no gain but enemies, and these I have increased without number. Whatever endeavours I have used to persuade you to peace on both sides, I have enjoyed none myself, but am loaded with scandals, lies, reproaches, and menaces of various kinds, in your common discourse, in your libels and prints, even from them that know me not. But since I can convince nobody by words, I shall satisfy them now by letting them see my gain is so small I can lay down the employment; and as I shall not only be out of the business but out of the nation,[4] as soon as public engagements will give me leave, I hope slander shall not follow me so many hundred miles as my designs at present propose to lead me.

I once thought to have retired from state affairs, and yet to have kept this paper up for the sake of the few friends I have left who from the beginning have been benefactors to the work, and without

[4] So far as we know, he did not leave the country.

whom I could not have supported the expense of it; and in doing this I thought to have confined my future discourse to matters of TRADE, thinking this a safe retreat, and that both sides might have been quietly talked to on this head, as what had no concern in the national feuds we were embarked in. But alas! trade too is now become a bone of contention; and unless I will say as you say, viz., that our trade is ruined by the peace—which I cannot do, and that only because I know it to be false (a poor and unfortunate reason)—I shall displease you there too. Nay, in but giving my reasons about the French trade, I have been so treated in your coffeehouse politics as is intolerable; where behind my back I meet with such foul, abusive, monstrous language, instead of argument, as no man of sense ought to give and no temper can well bear; and this from such a crew who, I may without any boasting say, dare neither answer me with their tongues or their hands.

Again, should I set up to cry down the great things some say of the peace, more by half [even] than the government who made it designed it for, or will promise for it, I should provoke the other side; and who knows where the disasters of a man crushed between two weights shall end? And would I go about to clear up your general errors about the commerce, as now settled in a middle, an equitable, and impartial way, what then? Should I hope for success? Alas! who has temper enough to bear it? However, as this I thought was needful, I was going about it and had made a beginning in three papers relating to the trade with France, when on a sudden I found my province invaded, and that work taken out of my hands by an unexpected paper without an author, and called the *Mercator*.[5] This work, I soon discovered, if not done by the government's direction, is so far encouraged as to have the helps of original papers, documents and authorities to speak from—things which without doors an author cannot expect, and which I never pretended to. If then this paper goes on with such authority, my parade is over; and as there will, on the other hand, be no need of me, so there will be no room to say anything, when an account vouched by such authorities shall come out three times a week.

Thus I am become an invalid even in that thing which I thought my

[5] Devoted to the subject of economics, the *Mercator* appeared twice a week from May 26, 1713, to July 20, 1714. Defoe himself was the editor.

peculiar, and I am very well satisfied if I may but be quiet and enjoy my share of the public peace. If not, I resolve to leave you; and if I trouble you no farther with my talk, it is but just ye trouble me no more another way. However, before I lay down this work, I shall give a summary [6] of what matters in trade I had designed to speak of, and of my opinion in public matters as I think they stand now in our view; that if ever I should write again (as I believe I shall not), I may know where to begin, and you may know where I left off.

[6] In neither of the two subsequent issues of the *Review* does he carry out this promise.

The Press: License and Liberty

OF TRUTH, AND FREEDOM OF THE PRESS

I ALWAYS THOUGHT it was the right of Englishmen to have liberty to speak freely in things relating to their general interest, only with this just restraint, viz., that they spoke TRUTH, but I never thought that liberty extended to a general latitude of forging what stories they thought fit, and speaking by their own authority whatever they pleased, without respect to matters of fact. The justice of our nation is eminent for correcting the manners of the age, and though there may be a deficiency in our law, that a man cannot be punished for lying, yet he may certainly be punished for *printing* lies. Spreading false news is punishable by several statutes, and those particular laws well known; nor is this any breach of the liberty of the subject, for doubtless liberty of speech, which is a British privilege, extends no farther than to speak truth; otherwise we pretend to reckon the liberty of lying to be a privilege of an Englishman.

I speak this with a melancholy retrospect to the sin of the day, in which raising and publishing mere fictions, mere forgeries of our own, and spreading them about for news, to please or serve the parties we are concerned for, is grown so general a practice that indeed it is become the jest of the town, and 'tis the common greeting now in a morning—Well, neighbour, what news? Truly, says t'other, I am but just come, I don't know, pray, what is the lie of the week? Or what is the lie *courant* [1] for the day? What a wretched posture are we come to that [we] receive lies, knowing or believing them to be so, and please ourselves with them, to confront one another, and make good the scandal we deal in!

It would be too dirty a piece of work to rake in the general laystall of parties and expose the wretched particulars; how do our newswriters carry on the wicked war, and throw lies at one another every post, just as our boys throw dirt at one another in the street. To come off of this we have a new invention, for what cannot our projectors for Hell do in that case? Viz., to dress up a formal story and call it "a letter

[1] A pun upon the *Daily Courant* (1702–1735), which Defoe criticized frequently for its inaccuracy. Founded in 1702, it was the first daily paper to be printed in England.

from Holland"; the concern whether it be true or no is then no more upon us, it is a story left on the reputation of somebody abroad. This way we have every post a packet of such forged stuff, as well of one side as the other, that it is intolerable. I clear none of the parties of it; the crime is general. And what's the lie of the week now? Alas, this very week has been so fruitful of lies that it is hard to determine; but I think the lie of the greatest magnitude, the master lie that came over this post at the head of the swarm, may be allowed to be that of the Duke of Ormond's army [2] burning a church and burning 270 of the poor people, inhabitants of the village, alive in it, not suffering them to come out. Is this story likely to be true? Do Englishmen use to do thus? Is the Duke of Ormond of such a bloody, barbarous disposition? This I could not omit taking notice of. And what a day do we live in that such a piece of news will go down with us! We had another coined in the same mint a while ago, viz., that a certain gentleman told the deputies of the States in a conference that if the States did not comply with Her Majesty's measures, and agree to a cessation within forty-eight hours, the British troops would all join the French army. Another, that Prince Eugene [3] had ordered all the governors of the towns in Flanders not to admit any Englishmen into the towns. The first is contradicted by matter of fact, and the last is contradicted by this post by an account printed in the *Post-Man*, the only impartial paper we have left—the English officers having in their march been received at Lille, Tournai, &c., with all possible civility, and an excuse made by Baron Hompesch, governor of Douai, and by Prince Eugene himself, for the incivility of some refusal at Douai.

I refer the general author of scandal on the other side to farther

[2] James Butler, second Duke of Ormonde (1665–1745). He displaced Marlborough as general of the British troops. In July, 1712, he had the unpleasant duty of carrying out the terms of the secret treaty between France and England by marching the British troops off the field of battle in full view of their allies. That his troops committed such atrocities as Defoe mentions can only be left to conjecture.

[3] Prince Eugene of Savoy (1663–1736). Denied a commission in the army of Louis XIV, Eugene served gallantly under the Austrian emperors Leopold I and Charles VI, and inflicted several defeats upon the French. An ally of Marlborough, he has been called one of the great captains of history. His campaigns were marked by audacity, courage, and perseverance regardless of the cost to his men or himself. He was wounded thirteen times. Under him the Austrian army attained a fame never equaled before or later.

remarks, but take notice of these first, because they are the manufacture of a party that do not use to deal in that commodity, and whose cause, did they rightly adhere to it, stands not in need of any such weak support. A refuge of lies has always been the mark of another side, and I would fain have it be the peculiar of those people who have so long had the title to it. I do not love invading of properties, and as the other party can plead the oldest title to the practice of lying in print, I would e'en have had them held it, nay, though they made a monopoly of it, but it seems envy will not permit them that privilege.

I have somtime wondered at the folly of those people who are satisfied in lying if a printed lie will but hold *one day*, and though it be detected the next, they think it worth while to go through with it. But now I am convinced of the usefulness to them of this way of lying, though it be but for a few hours. How often has a formal lie come hot out of the oven into Exchange Alley, served the interest of the contrivers to the tune of 2 or 3 per cent in the price of stocks between nine o'clock and two? And though it has been cold again before night, nay, though it has been traced in those few hours, how have the managers made it answer all the ends of truth to them? Sold their stocks off at a good price, and stand and laugh at you into the bargain? Nay, make the advantage of the very detecting their own forgery, and make a second gain, by buying in cheap what before they sold out 2 or 3 per cent dearer.

In politics it is the same. A lie, like General Grovestein [4] in his late expedition into Champagne, if it gets but one day's march, it spreads so swiftly, and runs so far, truth can never overtake it, and this is the way that this kind of bare-faced lying becomes useful. How bloody and barbarous! What a dreadful thing was it, says an hundred poor well-meaning people, to burn the poor creatures that were fled into the church for the safety of their lives, and not let them come out when the church was on fire! Why, says another, did you not hear that it was a mere lie, and that our men had no hand in any such thing? —No, indeed I never heard a word of that, I thought it had been true.

[4] Frederik Sirtema van Grovestins (1668–1750), major general in the army of the States General. On June 10, 1712, he set out with 1,800 hussars and dragoons and traversed 403 leagues in eleven days, and a total of 800 leagues in forty-eight days, pillaging and burning his way through the heart of Champagne.

Thus the mischief of a lie spreads; so poison searches into every pore, and finds its way through all the meanders of the blood, and though an antidote well applied may follow it so effectually as to preserve the life, and drive it out of the vital parts, yet its secret paths cannot always be traced where it works and breaks out. Thus, often, if the man escapes, he loses his hair, his nails, his teeth, and sometimes his senses. Thus a lie spread but this hour, though it be detected the next, and openly contradicted, yet the diffusion cannot be stopped, and the infection spreads whither the cure can never reach. Slander and reproach is just the same kind of thing, and a lie once published upon the most innocent man in the world, all his innocence shall never prevail, but he will for ages after have some of the reproach left, and perhaps shall have it break out like a fresh wound when all his defense, ay, and defenders too, lie buried too deep in time to have them rise again for his deliverance. Fifty year hence the Duke of Ormond shall be branded with cruelty in burning alive 270 poor innocent people in a church, when it shall be in no man's power to say whether it were true or no.

How many well-meaning people to this day positively charge the memory of King William with innocent blood, as they call it, and with cruelty in the affair of the Glencoe-men,[5] when the just vindication of his conduct in that case is forgot, or has not been seen by them! Ages to come will have cause to reproach the men of this generation with leaving such magazines of scandal and forgery, and so far separated from the true accounts of the same fact, that they will not be able to know from our testimony when they speak truth or report lies. In the decay of trade, occasioned by the war, lying is taken up as a new manufacture for the employment of the poor; and as we were very good at improving before, we are in a fair way now to be esteemed as good at inventing. In a few years more there is no doubt but this

[5] In 1691 the Scottish clans were exhorted to submit to William and Mary by December 31. All but the Macdonalds of Glencoe, about three hundred fifty persons, complied. On January 16 King William signed an order "to extirpate that sect of thieves." In the middle of February soldiers fell upon the people and massacred thirty-eight. The rest escaped to the hills, many to perish in the bitter cold. Ironically, Dalrymple, secretary of Scotland, had not notified William that on January 6 the Macdonalds had taken the oath. This event, the full truth of which was never widely known, plagued William continually throughout his reign.

new manufacture may arrive to greater perfection and may be fit for exportation; meantime, if Her Majesty pleases but to encorporate the present remarkable people who are set up for proficients in this new undertaking, some of the authors of the present age whose works stand every day upon record in their favour ought to put in for nominations as governors and directors of the Lying Company, for the first year. As to precedency among them, whether Protestant or pagan, *Flying Posts, Lying Posts, Medleys, Examiners, Plain Dealers,*[6] or what else shall stand foremost, be it to them as they merit; I leave that to justice.

Vol. VIII, No. 2 Thursday, March 29, 1711

A PROPOSED TAX EXAMINED

HE THAT will speak at all must speak quickly; and he that has but a little while to speak ought to speak to the purpose. This I observe not from the proposal in a printed paper only, but from a letter I have sent me, insulting me with what the *Examiner* gives a hint of, viz., laying a tax upon public prints and pamphlets. I am no projector of ways and means; if I were, I should say something to what paper and print may or may not be able to raise, and perhaps might venture to tell you that a handsome fund might be raised by that means, without being any discouragement to letters, or prejudice to trade; but when these people speak of a tax upon public papers, anyone may know their meaning, and that the project they would have go on is not raising a fund, but suppressing the thing. And I must say a word to them upon that supposition.

[6] Besides calling Scotsman George Ridpath, editor of the *Flying Post,* a "son of scandal," Defoe taunted him with being a foreigner and "not an Englishman." This from the author of that defense of all foreigners in England, *The True-Born Englishman!* The *Medley,* edited by Arthur Maynwaring, and the *Examiner,* edited by Swift, were frequent targets in Defoe's war upon party-journalism and irresponsible journalism.

1. It will be forever a brand upon any cause that attempts to suppress printing, and will leave it upon record, to the infamy of the party that espouses it, that it could not bear the energy and force of truth bearing witnesses against it.

2. It will be a fair acknowledging that they cannot answer the arguments by reason and fair disputing; that demonstration is against them, that words cannot defend them, and they dare not bring their logics to the test with their enemies.

3. It is a tacit owning that having blinded the poor hoodwinked people by clamour and noise, they are afraid these poor people should have their eyes open again by reason, argument, and matter of fact.

4. It is fairly acknowledging that their practices, whether in politics or morals, will not bear the light; and that 'tis their interest to prevent the secret histories of their persons or party being made public.

The method of suppressing fair reasoning by power seems to have three things in it that I doubt not, if ever it comes to be debated in Parliament, will weigh down all the reasons that can be given for such a thing.

1. It has something of arbitrary cruelty in it, and a little resembles a late barbarous practice of the same party in Scotland who, when they had the power in their hands, and exercised it with fury and blood, caused the drums to beat when the poor victims they were sacrificing came to die, that the testimony of their innocence, and the dying honour they gave to God, His church, and cause in the world, might not be heard or known by the abused spectators—an act something beyond the cruelty of death itself.

2. It has something in it which seems inconsistent with what, we thank God, this nation has always been chary of, viz., the liberty of the subject—which I must acknowledge I think is evidently infringed in it. And here I cannot but make two observations of my own upon it, which if I am mistaken, any man is welcome to confute me, and let the impartial on both sides be the judges, for I am speaking of no side in this matter.

1. A design to suppress printing on either side can be nothing but a design to suppress *truth;* since if falsity, scandal, slander, or anything that merits reprehension is published, the laws are already strong against them; and if in anything they are defective, the Parliament is

sitting to add such new provisions as may seem necessary. But to lay a universal load upon everything, or, in English, to silence mankind, is a plot against truth, against the friends of virtue, learning, and religion, as might be made appear on many occasions.

2. To make such a thing general, without distinction of the subject, prevents all the attempts against vice, profaneness, and immorality; all the helps to instruction, education, and religion, and all the useful essays in learning, improvement, morality, commerce, religion, or other useful things which in small manuals have oftentimes had good effect upon the world, and may still. And therefore, no doubt, whenever such a thing comes to be debated, there will some exceptions be admitted in cases not concerning government, parties, or politics, or else Britain will do a thing no nation in the world dare do before, except where both God and man have been defied and insulted.

3. The attempt will not answer the design; for though it may suppress useful things, as above, and rob the world of the advantages from the labours of honest men—yet party rage will break through, lampoons, pasquinades, and inveterate satires will swarm more than before and be diligently handed about by parties all over the kingdom, whose darts will be keener, and poison stronger than anything printed; and perhaps the more so as they shall be received with more gust by the people on either side. And I appeal to any man that remembers the days of King Charles II, when the license tyranny reigned over the press, whether that age did not abound in lampoons and satires that wounded, and at last went far in ruining the parties they were pointed at, more than has ever been practiced since the liberty of the press. And he that does not know it must be very ignorant of those times and has heard very little of Andrew Marvel, Sir John Denham, Rochester, Buckhurst, and several others, whose wit made the court odious to the people, beyond what had been possible if the press had been open.

I may add one thing with respect to public news which will be the consequence of suppressing public prints, which was formerly found most pernicious, and will be much more so now; and that is the filling the world with written news-letters,[1] in which men take always an un-

[1] Handwritten and sent direct to subscribers only, these would not be touched by the proposed tax.

bounded liberty, as they neither direct them to, or subscribe them by, any name. This leaves them free to write what they please; leaves them obnoxious to no law—even a House of Commons cannot deal with them, for they can make no man the author, and no man the publisher. And if this does not first or last amount to a greater evil than the public prints whose authors are known, and who are answerable for what they write, and may by a few clauses be made more liable, then I have no foresight of things, and I leave this testimony of it to be proved by the consequence.

These things I offer to the thoughts of those people only who flatter themselves with the happiness of silencing their opposers by the advantage of the law, let them be of what side they will. Laws may be made to refrain circumstances, to silence such or such subjects; they may prohibit printing anything relating to government and parties, to politics and national affairs; and I'll show my satisfaction in it by being the first to lay down, as I have often offered, and to show that I am not speaking self or private interest. But to lay a prohibition in general, without exception, is to suggest they have something to do they dare not let the people hear of; it is to padlock the mouths of the free people of Britain; it is to deprive men of their fair and just defense or vindication; and, which I think may merit a consideration by itself, it is to invade the properties, the livelihoods, and the employments of families and trades innumerable whose dependence and whose estates lie in several parts of the printing trade not at all concerned with the state or the government, and who in common justice must be made exceptions in such a general design.

Among these are to be reckoned patents and properties in copies of smaller books such as almanacs, catechises, psalms, little manuals of many sorts, religious and moral, the copyright to which are estates to many families, and to preserve which right from piracy and invasion, a very just and necessary law was made last Parliament, the advantage of which is happily found in many cases since. Besides these are to be considered the proceedings in law in our united neighbours in Scotland, the briefs and states of every cause in which proceedings are done in print, and must be so, and a tax cannot be laid on them but it would infringe the Articles of the Union. Innumerable other cases will clash with the design of these gentlemen in a general loading the lesser publication of things in print. And when they come to push their project in their own way, they will find it.

Meantime, that some restraint should be put to scandal, ribaldry, and reproach, to insulting governments, vilifying ministers of state, invading men's reputation, and the like, by obliging every man to *set his name* to what he writes, making the proceedings in personal injury summary and decisive; giving double costs of suit, and such other amends to the person[?] injured as may be thought fit; preventing allusive descriptions; printing initial letters of names,[2] and oblique pointing at persons in matters scandalous, &c.—some law against these would have every wise man's assent; every honest man would be desirous of having such a law made, the sooner the better. All the rest savours of guilt, party interest, encroachment upon liberty, arbitrary imposition upon the people, besides invasion of property, ruin of families, and unhinging men in their lawful employments—with this addition, that they will leave the mischief proposed to be remedied in a worse condition than they find it.

Vol. VIII, No. 172 Tuesday, April 29, 1712

OF TAXING THE PRESS

IN MY LAST I inquired a little into the present affair before the Parliament, viz., of stopping the press.[1] As to putting an end to the strife of the street, and the railing at one another from the press, no man will ever find me offering to say one word against it; I have

[2] Defoe himself indulged frequently in this practice. It probably represented a kind of defense against physical and legal retribution rather than a device for titillating reader curiosity.

[1] Near the end of Queen Anne's reign, newspapers, broadsides, and pamphlets were of such a violent party nature that the Tory government was determined to put a stop to it. Defoe here objects to a proposal which would double the cost of much printed matter. The tax as finally adopted, and in effect until the mid-nineteenth century, applied to pamphlets and newspapers at the rate of a penny per half sheet. As was intended and predicted, it effectually silenced most of the newspapers. See above, p. 10 and note,

wondered some years that no steps have been taken to do it before. But that to prevent a flux of scandal and quarrelling of parties, a universal stop should be put to all manner of small press-work, by laying a duty on all sorts of little books, which by the nature of the thing is an effectual prohibition—this is what, if rightly represented to the Parliament, I cannot think but they will consider very seriously of, before they pass it. And this makes me take the liberty to speak to it in this manner; if it had been to suppress *Reviews*, *Observators*, *Examiners*, *Medleys*, scolding pamphlets, and the like—nay, if all papers had been forbid to speak of, or relate the public affairs—I should have been the first to join in with the thought and prove that I write not to preserve or promote strife, but peace, among us. But the suppressing pamphlets is a thing which extends itself so far, and affects so many other things useful and advantageous, both to public and private persons, to learning, to religion, to education, to trade, to justice, and in short, to the whole nation, that I cannot but humbly represent it to our superiors to think at least of making just exceptions in proper cases, as to their own wisdom and judgment shall seem meet. As to newspapers and party tracts, papers of faction and public strife, I give them up at once, as not concerned in the case. But in behalf of trade, some concern may be allowed to affect us.

As I said in my last, trade, during this tedious war, has no need of more discouragements; and to take from the poorest people the meanest shift they can honestly make to live, especially at such a time as this, is by all means to be avoided. To burden trade may be necessary, but to suppress it cannot be so. I humbly refer it to common judgment where I err, if I say that the tax upon paper and print, as now in view, will entirely suppress many little articles of trade very useful and profitable to the nation, unless the House pleases to hear of some just exceptions. What though they are mean and trifling branches, yet they are a part of trade. They have a proportion in the employment and subsistence of our poor; and if three thousand poor families are thereby divested of their employment by it, as speaking with submission I believe will be the least, those three thousand families must push into some other employ, for starve they cannot, and thereby lessen the labour which employed three thousand other families before, and those again must look farther, and so on, till the injury loses itself in the multitude but affects the whole, as when you toss a flat tile into a pond of water you shall see the motion which begins in the center extend itself every way, and the little undulations push on and into one another, till they extend to the extremes of the whole surface.

It is not to the purpose to say the thing is small. Small as it is, great numbers of the poor are fed by it, who, if you dispossess of their way of getting their bread, you must maintain them some other way. When I say *you,* I mean you the general body of traders in the nation. For example, the paper manufacture in Britain is a small but improving thing, and employs many families. We reckon above two hundred paper mills in England; most of the paper they make is used in printing small tracts, pamphlets, &c. They are not arrived to an improvement able to supply for greater pieces. A tax upon their goods had been nothing, nay, though it had been 50 per cent it must have been born with—the consumer must have paid it. But suppressing the pamphlets which consume it is first laying a tax upon the manufacture, and then taking away the market that should vend it. This is bringing forth a child and then killing the mother, or taking away the breast that should give it suck. To tax the goods might hurt and discourage the trade, but to stop the consumption is to destroy it; the one may wound, but the other kills outright. And I believe I am within compass if I suggest that at least fifty of those paper mills, erected and carried on at great expense, must be laid by, and the poor employed at them must seek other ways to get their bread.

Come we next to the printing houses. We have now about twenty-five presses employed in the several parts of Britain, besides London and Edinburgh, which are all wholly employed in printing small tracts, little odd pieces, and get their livings very well by it, and are very useful to the countries in several respects as to trade, as at Exeter, Bristol, Norwich, Canterbury, Chester, Nottingham, Stamford, York, Newcastle, Glasgow, Aberdeen, and many others, not reckoning our universities. Perhaps not one of those ever wrought a bound book, but prayer books, psalm books, catechisms, sermons, story books, song books, and a thousand such trifles. Not one of these can bear the tax now proposed, nor can one of these printing houses stand, besides several in London. Immediately all the poor people are divested of the means they had to live. I have little to say of the poor wretches that cry these things, and carry them all over England—I am no great friend to the manufacture of ballad singing—but let these be what they will, they cannot starve, and their number is unaccountably great.

The sum of all is this, that, as above, if three thousand families of poor are immediately put out of their employment by this projected tax, I doubt not but the Parliament will think of some method to prevent it. This, I affirm, may be done without difficulty, without destroying the tax or lessening the sum to be raised by it. Nay, it may be done, and the sum to be raised shall be the greater, for as it is, I cannot see it is calculated to raise money so much as to suppress the thing. To tax any trade so as that it cannot subsist under the payment is not a means to raise the money, but to destroy the trade. Two ways this tax may be made effectual, the check intended to be put to the insolence and licentiousness of the press be made to answer, and yet the trade not be destroyed, the paper manufacture not lost, or the poor turned out of their employment: first, by moderating and proportioning the sum charged on each article so as that it may be paid, and the thing paying be left to subsist; secondly, by limitations and exceptions such as shall be thought needful to suppress such as ought to be suppressed, and preserve such as ought to be preserved. There is no doubt but under a moderate tax the trade may subsist; an immoderate tax stifles and destroys it. High duties, more than the goods will bear, were always esteemed the best method of prohibition. If a moderate tax be laid, the money will be paid. If the manufacture taxed sinks under the weight, it raises nothing; in the grave of a manufacture no payment can be expected; and therefore when I prove that the working part cannot subsist, I need go no farther to prove that it will raise no money.

As to exceptions and limitations, they are manifestly just and very easy. I shall never suppose that an English Parliament will deprive the poor of the few helps they have—for God knows they are few enough—to instruction, to Christian knowledge, to education of their children, or of the advantage of reading because they have not money to buy large books; this would be to damn the age to ignorance for want of money. It is true there is a great deal of ribaldry, fiction, lies, fables, and foolish stuff sold about the nation; but there are abundance of useful, nay, necessary books, proper for the use of the poor, to propagate Christian knowledge and teach the children of the meaner people, proper for the use of families, and intended by the authors for the use of the poor, and these as well by Church of England divines as others. These are accommodated not only to the capacities but to the purses of the poor, made short and cheap, that religion might be no oppression, and are often given by well-disposed Christians as gifts of charity to the poor; such as prayer books and books of devotion; such as Gauden on the Sacrament, Rawlet's *Christian Monitor*, Countess of Morton's *Devotions*, *The Winchester Manual*, *The Week's Preparation*, Lake on the Sacrament, *A Posie of Prayers*, and a vast number of the like, all which must now pay 2*d*. a sheet tax, and be raised to the poor from 2*d*., 4*d*., and 6*d*., to 6*d*., a shilling, 18*d*., two shillings, and so on, above the price and pockets of the poor, who for want of money must now be without these things which in all ages have been allowed to be very useful. And they who know, or have seen anything of the darkness and ignorance of the poor people in the countries in this enlightened nation, will acknowledge they have little need to make the small helps they have to gain Christian knowledge harder to come by. In behalf, therefore, of the poor, I cannot but earnestly recommend to the Parliament such exceptions for the propagation of Christian knowledge, the fear of God, and the instruction of the children of the poor, as they shall, in due consideration of such a case, think fit.

God forbid I should seem in this to favour parties or sides. The excellent books left among us by several Church of England divines are chief in my plea; he that labours to instruct the poor is of God's party, let him be who he will. Drexelius was a Jesuit, yet his *Considerations on Eternity* is an excellent piece, and has been as useful to and valued by Protestants as any book on that subject in the world. It is the work, not the author, I am distinguishing. Family instruction is a work so generally neglected by all sorts, and the consequences of it appear so plain in the profligate youth of this nation, even of all opinions and parties, the like of which no age could ever be charged with, that it would be a lamentable act of Parliament, and what I hope we shall never see passed, that would farther discourage it among us. There are many just exceptions more which might claim the consideration of the Parliament in the passing this tax, viz., small tracts relating to science, literature, and improvement, which being confined to large books, learning must needs receive great discouragement by it; cases and papers of reasons, in affairs depending in Parliament, which are not sold but given away, and the like; all which limitations may very well consist with a complete suppressing a faction, strife, atheism, heresy, lewd and vicious books, and the like, to suppress all which would be the honour of the Parliament, and the advantage of the nation.

In behalf of religion, of learning, and of the bread of the poor, I have written this paper; if it may influence our superiors to consider these three articles, I shall rejoice; if not, I have done my duty, and let the issue be what it will.

Te Deum laudamus.

Vol. VIII, No. 180 Saturday, May 17, 1712

THE NATURE OF SATIRE

Happy the man, who when his station's high,
  Calmly contemns the envy of mankind;
Without resentment can their rage defy,
In peace his own prosperity enjoy,
  And guides his lofty steps with a well-govern'd mind.

Happy the man, who when his station's low,
  Keeps up a cheerful heart, and steady hand;
Without disgust can to disaster bow,
Find every sorrow sweet, or make it so,
  And keep his rising passions at a full command. . . .[1]

WE HAVE in the town two animals, men I cannot call them, for I choose to speak in the first person of the papers, rather than of the authors, viz., the *Examiner* and the *Medley*. These two, like hornets about the traveller, assault the noble per-

[1] From an untitled poem by Defoe in the Preface to Volume VIII of the *Review*.

sons above,[2] in all the most unsufferable, and indeed criminal, ways that ever I have seen practiced; as if the patience of the persons were only to be made conspicuous to the world by their bearing the grossest abuses, and they were to stand trial of this ordeal to give the world a testimony of their passive valour. And all this seems only to be the consequence of the authors' writing against one another as if the eminent character of the great men they affront were only to be sacrificed to the scolding of two pamphleteers. Far be it from me to enter the lists with either of these combatants, as to their quarrel with one another, or the arguments they have to use; but my observation lies equally against them both.

One ungenerously falls upon a person of the highest rank in the nation, and whose eminent character the world, and even his enemies, acknowledge. He treats him by way of libel with all the indignity, calumny, and reproach that words can express, or a too keen fancy invent, without respect to the dignity of his person, the merit of his actions, the character he has born in the nation's esteem, or the trusts he has been in under our sovereign; and all this at a time when by the vicissitudes of human affairs he is fallen under the displeasure of his prince, and under those things the world calls misfortunes, and thereby divested of that power which perhaps he might be said to have [had] before to do himself justice, which no doubt adds to the baseness of it.

The other flies higher, and he, as if he designed it as a return to his opposer, attacks the prime minister of state, and therein the Queen herself; flies in the face of him whom Her Majesty has honoured with the greatest trust in the nation. Not the character he bears, not the dignity of his office, not the favour of the Queen, are of any weight against the fury of the man, the foulness of his language, or the grossness of the insult. To say it is upon the Queen herself, to say it is unsufferable by the government, to say it is a reproach to the very nation, that even the highest characters, ministers of state, and men vested with supreme authority are not spared in the openest and most scurrilous invectives—all this is to say nothing. Nay, to say on either hand that the reproaches cast are satires without a sting, scandals with-

[2] The Tory *Examiner* was bitterly attacking Marlborough, charged with profiting on the sale of bread to his troops. The Whig *Medley* was assailing Harley, Earl of Oxford, who was lord high treasurer.

out truth, sarcasms without any edge, and malice without wit, is still to say nothing; but the two cavilling writers fall upon two of the greatest men in the nation by way of battle against one another.

What if the two persons are opposites to one another in their politics? What if their interests clash, and are incompatible; they differ after another manner, they do not make war in this way of battle, and throw dirt after this fashion. Now let us examine what's the exercise this gives to the two great persons I speak of? I make no doubt it must be seen with regret by the first, that it is very provoking, and that he thinks himself very ill used; but what does he say? Why, it is but a dog, let him bark; I may find a time to scourge him hereafter by the whip of the law. It is his time now, like Shimei's, to curse; let him alone. And in this contempt of such treatment the true greatness of a man of honour appears.

The case differs, indeed, in circumstances in the other, but is the same in kind. Here's a man of the first dignity in the kingdom, vested with full power to do himself justice, wearing the trophies of him whom the Queen delights to honour, able with his hand or his frown to crush the little monsters that bark at him, and make them resign that life (as a paper) by which they are made capable of offering him these insults; and yet the author lives, raves on, and goes on to abuse him. What does the injured yet powerful man do in the case? The example is eminent; he is so far from using his power that, contemning entirely the venom of the reproach, he sits above the reach of the malice. It is below him so much as to resent; he restrains all the dictates of the passions, and rather pities the lunacy of the wretch than punishes his insolence. Nay, he shows so much of his being untouched with his rudeness that he scorns to suppress his paper, but gives him full liberty to say what he pleases.

This is the present case with these two. I have nothing to do with party debates here, but sure no man can defend this practice, nor, if it goes on, will any man in the nation be free from it. The foulness of it is so gross that nothing that calls himself a man can say anything for it. If it were clean satire, the wit, the good humour, and a hundred things might atone for it, but mere calling names, mere railing, calling fool, beggar, knave—that is, in English, *rogue*, and *rascal*—this was never suffered in any age. I remember the case of Mr. Dryden, the author of *Absalom and Achitophel:* Mr. Dryden had described the Duke of Buckingham with a great deal of wit, but in one line had given him ill names, as *fiddler* and *buffoon.* The Duke was a lover of wit, and had as much himself as most men of the age, but resolved to take some advantage of the author's weakness in that part; to which purpose His Grace finds him at a coffee house, and charging him with want of decency, as no true part of satire, caned him very smartly. "There, sir," said the duke, "is for your ill manners; and here, sir," says he, "is for your wit," and threw him a purse with thirty guineas at the same time. Now I would recommend to all those gentlemen who take upon them to write satires on great man that they would take care to merit the guineas without the cane; but really when they descend to be grossly abusive, and rail without wit or manners, they merit the correction without any pretence to the reward.

It is not at all to me how the noble persons touched at in this case are stated as to parties; if the world will allow me at any time to be speaking without respect of persons or parties, I do so now. They are both in condition to do themselves right, but it is the general practice that I condemn; nor, I think, can I be charged with anything like it, though I may have had my share in satire too. My opinion of satire is that first of all the character should be just, which in these cases cannot be pretended; secondly, that the thing satirized *be a crime;* thirdly, that the language, though keen, be decent—in every one of which these authors are faulty. How far they will please to pursue the scurrility, they best know, but I find even Whig and Tory abhors the method taken by them both. The truth is, the issue generally is only mischief to themselves; and when they have thrown all their filth about, they will give over, as two dogs barking and foaming at one another a long time, at last when they are out of breath they leave off. It was a good saying of the Macedonian king to one of his soldiers, who was always cursing and railing at the Romans: "I hired thee," said the king, "to fight with the Romans, not to rail at them."

Vol. VII, No. 114 Saturday, December 16, 1710

IDIOT *Review* AND SCURRILOUS *Examiner*

THE AUTHORS that have drawn up in order of battle against this paper I fancy are of a kind with the creatures the blessed apostle engaged with at Ephesus. For 'tis certain they were not lions or dragons, but strange things in human shape, such as *Examiners, Moderators, Rehearsers,* and the like. And how was he treated by the men of that generation? *Babbler, sorcerer, deceiver,* and the like, was the best they could say to him—but not a word of answer to his argument. Confounded with the force of his reasoning, they fell to raillery, just as the like kind do now; frequently raised the mob upon him, as at Jerusalem, at Ephesus, at Athens, and at other places. When from the stairs of the castle in Jerusalem the apostle spoke to the enraged multitude they stamped, fumed, shouted, and threw dust into the air for madness. Not able to contradict by reasoning the force of his words, they bound themselves by an oath to murder him. When he came among the wise, learned Athenians, they bantered and ridiculed him, called him idiot, and illiterate, and their EXAMINERS fell upon him with this, "We will hear what this babbler says."

I am not comparing the *Review* to the apostle, they cannot take me there; but the rabbles of both times may be compared without offense, for there the parallel will exactly hold. The poor author of this has been treated just like that blessed man, and, saving the difference, which I regard with all possible reverence, with the same kind of justice (see the story, Acts 21:27). First, the apostle having brought men into the temple who he had purified, though they knew it not, they fall upon him with the usual violence of a rabble, crying out, "A Whig, a Whig! He has polluted the temple! He has polluted the temple!" And were just a-going to murder him when the Roman governor rescued him (v. 32). All this was before they understood anything of the matter, see the text: "Some cried one thing, some another, among the multitude" (v. 33). And he, the governor, "could not know the certainty for the tumult." Paul desired to speak to the people, and the first question the chief captain, who so far joined with the people, asked him was to reproach him with ignorance, like our *Examiner* to the *Review* (v. 37). "Thou speak to the people, thou idiot! thou illiterate!" (*Examiner*, No. ———). "Canst thou speak Greek?" *Anglice*, are you not an illiterate fellow? And again, "Art not thou that Egyptian, and a leader of murderers?" Well, the innocent pleader confuted that folly, and goes on; and when he had spoken at large, words of truth that flung them to the quick, *how did they examine it?* What [s]aid the *Moderators?* Excellent arguments! Chapter 22:22, 23—"Away with such a fellow from the earth, for it is not fit that he should live." Raging in their fury, they turn quite mad, "cast off their clothes, cried, and threw dust into the air." And when they could not get him into their hands, they swore to murder him (23:14).

Now, gentlemen, lest I may sometime or other, as God shall let loose their hands, for like the devil they are chained, fall into the power of this enraged crew, give me leave to show a little how they have treated the author of this paper, that it may stand upon record against the party, and I'll be very brief. When railing in print, bullying and hectoring would not silence him, letters were sent threatening to murder him. His house was marked to be pulled down by the rabbles, and he was assured by writing and by messengers that he had not long to live; the very printer was threatened to have his house mobbed for printing it. Several attempts were made to prosecute the paper at the Old Bailey, at Guild-Hall, and at Westminster, &c. But when no jury could be found to present it, no crime found in it to present it for, that was let fall. Other measures were taken to embroil him with the government, and to involve him *à la Scan*[*dalous*] *Mag*[*azine*] with great men, but still all was in vain.

When this failed, endeavours were used to rouse sleeping lions, and harass him with dormant creditors—men who, satisfied with the frequent offers he had made of complete surrender of his whole effects to them upon oath, had declined for seventeen years a fruitless cruelty upon a man who had given such evidence of his integrity. However, some mischief of this kind they brought him into, and when he had extricated himself from that, the same perjured villain that insulted Mr. Daniel Burgess,[1] for a sham pretence well known, assaulted him, took 15 guineas of him to get out of his hands again, which extortion he is now under legal persecution for, and may speedily be brought to justice upon that score. Not content with this, the same villain insulted his house on the Sabbath day, without any legal warrant or the least just pretence, in order upon a sham to get him into custody and betray him, whether to murderers or creditors he yet knows not. Other sets of rogues were employed after this to take sham writs out in names not known, and to men that were not officers, pretending to arrest him without any real debt in the least—which pretended officers are now under prosecution also, and one of them has confessed the fact. He has been often beset, often waylaid, and often dogged into dark passages; yet when they have actually met him and found him prepared for his defence, and resolved not to die as a fool dies, their hearts have failed them, for villains are always cowardly, and he still lives and defies them. And all this, 'tis evident, is for writing this paper.

And now, gentlemen, as if this was not enough, Mr. Examiner is falling upon me. And behold his first volley is shot off—much powder, much noise, no bullet, like the French army on the Rhine, which, having made a great bluster and done nothing, was thus bantered.

Comme une bête dans la Rhine,
Qui faisoit mille fracas;
Et qui l'avoit cent mille têtes
Mais n'avoit pas les bras.

Much powder, I say, much noise, much ill language, much call-names, no argument. After *idiot,* which is the first mark of distinction, comes *illiterate.* Much wit in that truly is—how should an idiot but be illiterate? This brings a remark into my thoughts which I have often taken occasion to make on affairs in the world; we have abundance of learned fools in the world, and ignorant wise men—how often have I seen a man boast of his letters, and his load of learning, and be ignorant in the common necessary acquirements that fit a man either

[1] Daniel Burgess (1645–1713) was a Presbyterian minister whose church in Lincoln's Inn Fields was gutted by a Sacheverell mob on March 1, 1710. The government offered a reward of £100 for the arrest of the culprits, and also repaired the building.

for the service of himself or his country. I know a man at this time a minister; he is a critic in the Greek and Hebrew, a complete master of the Latin. Yet it would make a man blush to read a letter from him, sleep to hear him preach, and sick to read his books. He is a master of languages, and buried in letters, but cannot spell his mother tongue, knows nothing of the world, and has never looked abroad. Such learning, I confess, I despise, and covet to be illiterate rather than thus a scholar. Again, I know another that is an orator in the Latin, a walking index of books, has all the libraries in Europe in his head, from the Vatican at Rome to the learned collection of Dr. Salmon at Fleet Ditch; [2] but at the same time he is a cynic in behaviour, a fury in temper, unpolite in conversation, abusive and scurrilous in language, and ungovernable in passion. Is this to be learned? Then may I be still illiterate!

I have been in my time pretty well master of five languages, and have not lost them yet, though I write no bill over my door, or set Latin quotations in the front of the *Review*. But to my irreparable loss I was bred but by halves, for my father, forgetting Juno's Royal Academy,[3] left the language of Billingsgate quite out of my education; hence I am perfectly illiterate in the polite style of the street, and am not fit to converse with the porters and carmen of quality who grace their diction with the beauties of calling names, and curse their neighbour with a *bonne grace*. I have had the honour to fight a rascal, but never could master the eloquence of calling a man so; nor am I yet arrived to the dignity of being laureated at her Majesty's Bear Garden. I have also, illiterate as I am, made a little progress in science. I read Euclid's *Elements*, and yet never found the mathematical description of a scurrilous gentleman. I have read logic, but could never see a syllogism formed upon the notion of it. I went some length in physics, or natural philosophy, and could never find between

[2] The allusion is generally accepted as referring to Swift. Nathaniel Salmon (1675–1742), was a historian and antiquary. Fleet Ditch is now closed over and is used as a sewer under Farringdon Street, and New Bridge Street to the Thames runs across Fleet Street from Holborn to the river.

[3] In *The Pacificator* (1700) and again in *A Hymn to the Pillory* (1703) Defoe identifies Juno's academy as Billingsgate, a riverside area in London frequented by fishwives notorious for their swearing. In Seneca's tragedy *Hercules furens* Juno in her jealousy swears mightily. Burton in *The Anatomy of Melancholy* speaks of Juno as "miscalling, cursing, swearing and mistrusting everyone she sees."

the two great ends of nature, generation and corruption, one species out of which such a creature could be found. I thought myself master of geography, and could have set up for a country almanac maker, as to my skill in astronomy; yet could in neither of the globes find either in what part of the world such a heterogeneous creature lives, or under the influence of what heavenly body he can be produced: from whence I conclude very frankly that either there is no such creature in the world, or that according to Mr. Examiner I am a stupid idiot and a very illiterate fellow.

Vol. IV, No. 46 Tuesday, May 27, 1707

JOURNALIST DYER REBUKED

THE REMARKS made in my last on our news-writers has appeared so needful as obliges me to proceed with Mr. Dyer [1] a little farther. It is very strange that any man who pretends to write public news should offer to make remarks of his own, so personally and publicly injurious, and for which he seems to challenge even the correction of the mob. I shall invite nobody to use him ill, and this remark is far from designing any such thing; but I should forsake all manner of public justice if I did not take notice of two of the most abusive, intolerable, and barbarous clauses that ever I saw offered in public, the persons especially considered, in my life.

I shall no longer lead the reader about in the case; the first clause is in his letter of the 6th of May, in which, speaking of the Duke of Marlborough's journey to Saxony [2] to the King of Sweden, he has this expression: "It's believed His Grace carried with him a powerful

[1] John Dyer was author of a privately circulated handwritten newsletter which Defoe considered particularly irresponsible and libelous. Defoe contemptuously calls Dyer the "famous country trumpet" of the High Church party, and, "that scribbler."

[2] A dramatic meeting of two famous soldiers at Altranstadt in the last days of April, 1707, in which Marlborough proved himself diplomat as well as soldier. Charles XII,

argument which Count Piper[3] could not withstand, the same which has been often made use of by the court of France." This horrid suggestion is big with so many slanders, and so hellishly pointed, that were it not that this wretched author is not capable of much thought, one would think he had laid his malice deep enough to reach all the parts of the present government.

1. Here is the Swedish general and minister bribed by the English general.

2. The English government stooping to the scandalous French custom of bribing the servants of foreign princes to act against their masters.

3. Here is Count Piper accused of betraying his master; for he that takes money to move his master to this or that, though it were to his own interest, betrays him.

4. Here is the Duke of Marlborough accused of bribery in so many words.

I could enlarge very pleasantly on all these, but I shall not endeavour to bring the public resentments upon anyone; I shall only go as far as to me appears necessary in order to clear up the case. . . .

First, 'tis observed that he ushers this account in with "it's believed," a certain signal that he knew what he was doing, that he was publishing a slander and durst not be positive. Though to say "it's believed" is forward enough; for to say "it's believed" in a public paper is to say it is generally believed, which is still a barbarous suggestion. For it really is not so believed by anybody but the public professed enemies of the present government. Secondly, 'tis a certain token that 'tis a bare suggestion, that he has no positive assurance of any such thing, and therefore provides for it by an uncertain way of suggestion. Lastly, this is a most intolerable scandal upon the Duke of Marlborough that no less a messenger could be employed upon so scandalous an errand when the general of the British armies; that the victorious terror of France and prince of the Confederate armies should

who had defeated the Russians at Narva, had conquered Poland, and was at present in possession of Saxony, now threatened Austria. Marlborough, victor at Ramellies and Blenheim, persuaded Charles not to attack Austria but to turn his energies upon Peter the Great, whose forces later routed Charles at Poltava and drove him into exile among the Turks.

[3] Secretary of state to Charles XII of Sweden.

undertake a journey at such a season of the year too, and when he was so much wanted, on a message so base, so little and unworthy either of the sender or of the person sent.

Horrid suggestions! Why this upon the English, and why upon the Duke of Marlborough? The French have indeed by bribes, pensions, and corruption of other courts carried on their intrigues, and made their conquests easy. But why was this? Because in the matter of fighting they always knew themselves inferior, and on all occasions but with advantage, shunned fair fighting. But have the English ever shunned the field, have the Confederate forces ever baulked their enemies or avoided battle? Has the Duke of Marlborough ever declined to push the French upon all occasions, and bravely met them under all disadvantages; nay, have not they attacked the French in their advantageous posts, and in their entrenchments? Has not His Grace beaten them out of their fastnesses and broke in upon all their cautions? Has he not fought them behind their strongest lines, and within their fortified passes? What occasion is there for bribery where a war is made successful by true courage; bribery is generally made use of to supply the defect of bravery, and where the latter is not wanting, the former is seldom useful. . . .

I come now to a second scandal which Mr. Dyer is pleased from his own fruitful invention to put upon the world, and that is upon our honest seamen, especially those brave though unfortunate fellows who have been lately taken in the *Grafton* and *Northumberland* men-of-war.[4] His words are these: "According to the best accounts of this action, the commanders of her Majesty's ships did their duty; but there are fears the crews did not theirs; but this will best appear when upon the return of the officers they shall be called before a council of war to give an account of the loss of her Majesty's ships." I was in Scotland when I met with this letter. "How," says a gentleman at the reading of it, "dares any man in England suggest that of the seamen before he knows anything of the fact?" "Where does that fellow live," said another; "Sure he does not live about Wapping or Redriff."[5]

[4] Two seventy-gun ships-of-the-line, the *Grafton* and the *Hampton Court*, were captured by the French off Beachy Head on May 3, 1707. The *Northumberland*, however, was reported on convoy duty in September of that year.

[5] The riverside district on either side of the Thames in London below the Tower. Redriff is now known as Rotherhithe.

I confess 'tis very barbarous upon the whole body of English seamen in general, but 'tis particularly cruel to the poor fellows that are taken prisoners by the enemy after a brave resistance.

And why, Mr. Dyer, why so unkind to the seamen? Can you tell us a time when if the officers on board an English ship behaved well, the seamen did not do their duty? It has always been observed in England, both by sea and land, the common people, whether seamen or soldiers, never flinch from their duty; and this to me appears a visible case between us and other nations, that abroad if the men will follow, the officers will always lead on, but in England or Britain, if the officers will lead on the men will always follow. This observation, I believe, was always just of them, and strangers will do them this justice; it has never been their character abroad that they will not fight; if anything has been their fault it is that they are too forward, that without examining disadvantages, either of number or situation, either of ships or guns, they would always cry out for fighting. But what countryman is this Mr. Dyer, that he should, and without any proof too but his own opinion, say it is feared the seamen did not do their duty? Indeed, I think there is the least fear of that of anything else, and I dare say if there was any defect of duty, it was not among the seamen.

I shall say no more to this blessed reporter. . . .

Vol. VII, No. 13 Tuesday, April 25, 1710

THE PUBLISHER OF THE *Review* KIDNAPPED

THE *Review* had given you an account of the prisoners taken, and the number of the slain and wounded in the late great High Church battle,[1] of which our former treated at large. But alas poor *Review!* The rage of the party has reached thee among

[1] The trial of Reverend Henry Sacheverell, whose prosecution in 1710 for a violent sermon against the Whigs, Dissenters, and moderate Tories united the Tories and overthrew the Whigs. See note, p. 199.

the rest, and the world is thus deprived of this day's publication. For behold a party of the runaways of the defeated High Church army falling upon Mr. M[atthews], the honest publisher of this, have taken him prisoner of war, and the man being entirely in their custody, and consequently not *sui juris*, you are to expect no more *Reviews* from his hand. Nor can anybody blame him; for when people are frighted, they are not masters of their usual resolution, or indeed of their understanding.

The whole of the case is explained by the above—but farther thus. It has been observed in several *Reviews* past that great endeavours have been used to stifle and suppress this paper; sometimes the author has been threatened and bullied, sometimes the printer; sometimes they carry it to this grand jury to get it presented, sometimes to that; sometimes the government is solicited to discourage and silence it; sometimes the indignation of the party is shown one way, sometimes another; but finding all in vain, and that the author continues to gall them with plain truth, their last poor, and indeed very weak and foolish, shift has been to tamper with the publishers and dispersers of it. This has been practiced upon other papers as well as this; the *Observator* [2] gives you an account of his having been served in the same manner; nay, even the Queen's proclamation could not obtain to be regularly published or cried about streets as usual.

This I endeavoured to rectify a little, by appointing the *Review* to be had at two several houses in town besides the usual place, viz., at Mrs. Pye's at Charing Cross, and at Mr. Nathaniel Cliff's in Cheapside, near Mercers Chapel. But this not being sufficient, and the party continuing to solicit every publisher to suppress it, we have now removed it from the usual place of publication, and put it into hands that will not be biassed, terrified, or anyway prevailed upon to keep it back; and from henceforward, this paper will be published by Mr. Baker, as is printed at the bottom in the usual place. And what has the *Review* done, gentlemen? Either it speaks good or evil, truth or falsehood: if evil, bear witness of that evil, and prove it—the author has asked you no favour. If it speaks truth, wherefore are you angry? It must be that this truth is something that pinches you so hard you cannot bear it. The physic really makes the party sick; I hope it may work kindly and do them good.

[2] A Whig newspaper started by John Tutchin in 1702.

How many endeavours have we had to present and prosecute this paper, and all in vain? Once it was presented, and some teeth shown, but lo, an impeachment rose up that appeared at a distance like the cloud in the Scripture, about the bigness of a man's hand—but soon overspread the High Church horizon and drowned all the designed building. Since that the courts of justice (may I say it with pardon) have been teased with the impertinence of the party—the benches of justices, grand juries, nay, superior powers have been importuned—but justice reigns still, and clamour cannot prevail. God be praised, our judges are not to be led by noise, biassed by parties, or prevailed with by importunities. And thus hitherto the endeavours of the party, though they thought they had the fore horse by the head, have proved abortive, and they have attacked the *Review* in vain.

I am sorry to see the party so angry—not that I fear their rage, or will go one step out of my way for all they can do, having truth and the law on my side; but methinks there is something very melancholy in seeing so many people so furiously bent to embroil and disturb their native country. And not that only, but they are come to that pass that they think even courts of justice are to be affronted and insulted by them. But they found themselves deceived. It can hardly be believed how insolent some of these people were, even in the court when their criminal[3] was in the hands of the law. How did they harden the poor wretch to behave himself with a confidence not at all suitable to his guilt, though indeed very suitable to their cause! How did they boast to the world that the jury would acquit him, even before they knew what would be testified against him! A particular insult upon the jury, as if those gentlemen were to act by party, and not by evidence. As if they would acquit him in spite of proof of fact, and that they were men [who] had no regard to their oath. It was an insult also upon the officers that empanelled the jury, as if they had packed them of knaves to the purpose—and yet without regard to any of these, they endeavoured to spread it all over the town that the man could not be condemned. Nay, they persuaded the poor man so himself—which he discovered by the dreadful surprise he was in when he saw his doom certain, and his sentence near at hand. Thus they have affronted justice, insulted government, and cheated the poor man out of his life.

All the effect this has upon the *Review* is that it has baulked a very

[3] Sacheverell.

merry paper which was written to oblige them, and would have made them laugh, though perhaps on the wrong side of their mouths—which now must be adjourned to our next, when they shall have it with interest.

Vol. I [IX], No. 89 Tuesday, April 28, 1713

MR. REVIEW APOLOGIZES TO THE COURT

IT WAS always my opinion that a wise man ought never to be ashamed to acknowledge himself to be in the wrong, or to beg pardon when he is in a mistake. This I have so often professed to be my judgment, in print, that you cannot reproach me with making it my practice. It is true that we ought to consider well before we speak, and not offend, especially those who we ought not to offer any offense to. But as any man may unwarily offend, for no man is infallible, the retreat an honest man always makes in such a case is, by a just and voluntary acknowledgment, to make *l'amende honorable* to the parties offended, and in the humblest manner possible to ask their pardon.

If I should say that I voluntarily and of set purpose affronted and offended Her Majesty's court of justice [1] and my lords the judges in what I have written, I should add to my offense, should say what is not true, and should load myself with guilt of a kind which I abhor; for I bear the greatest and truest veneration to the office and authority of a judge that I can possibly express. But that I have unwarily and for want of circumspection offended is very true; and I do freely acknowledge the displeasure of my Lord Chief Justice and the court is very just; and this I say most voluntarily, and of my own accord.

[1] He was jailed on the complaint of enemy journalists who ostensibly could not see the irony in two Defoe pamphlets upon the Hanoverian Succession. In two issues of the *Review* Defoe angered Lord Chief Justice Parker by criticizing him, as Defoe's biographer James Sutherland puts it, "with injudicious frankness" while the case was still in the hands of the Court (*Defoe* [Philadelphia and New York, 1938]).

I esteem the execution of the law to be the sum and substance of the people's liberties; and the persons, therefore, to whom that great trust is committed are, in my esteem, so far sacred, and ought not to be any way insulted or offended. Nay, if I were to be brought before the judges in a foreign nation, yet, as the laws of that country were committed to them, and I lived then under the government of that country, I would behave myself with decency and respect to the judges in mere veneration to their office; much more here, where I have not the least objection either against the laws themselves or the uprightness of the persons to whom judgment is committed. For my submission, therefore, to the judges of England, whom I have unwarily offended, let no man reproach me, since it is every man's duty so to do. We see the apostle Paul when he returned too warmly to one whose person he mistook: when he came to know he was the judge, who had a right to resent what he had said, he immediately begged pardon. "I wist not that it was the high priest; for it is written, Thou shalt not revile the ruler (or judge) of thy people."

For these reasons and many other, as soon as I perceived my mistake in the *Reviews* lately written on the subject of my prosecution, I presently waived all the defense I might think to make of my writings (as of their being innocently and unwarily done; or of my meaning the private persons only that had fallen upon me, &c.), for I saw I had wanted due caution in explaining myself and that the uncertainty of my meaning gave my Lord Chief Justice sufficient and just cause to think himself affronted and ill treated. Upon this, as an honest man, I say, ought to do, I immediately by my petition to my Lord Chief Justice acknowledged myself in the wrong, and with all possible and sincere humility asked his lordship's pardon, and in a second petition to the whole court did the like again. And I have here given the world a true copy of both these petitions, as well to give all possible satisfaction to their lordships, as to let everybody see that I am ready to make any submissions where I own myself in a mistake.

How, not justly only, but generously also, I have been used by their lordships upon these submissions, I shall not be backward to let the world know; and if I am at any time guilty of reflections upon either, it must be when my senses forsake me, as well as my principles. If any man insults me upon the meanness of these things, I contemn his insult; for it is beneath no man to submit himself to the just magistracy of his country, especially when he is in the wrong. We see instances of this daily before the two houses of Parliament, where it is esteemed no reproach for any man to humble himself when he has offended; and I fear much for those gentlemen who think it below them to ask pardon, especially of just authority, when they have offended it, whether they would not treat their Maker in the same manner if they could? But I profess myself of another opinion in both cases, and therefore very freely and willingly publish my two petitions aforesaid, as follows.

To the Right Honourable Sir Thomas Parker, Kt., Lord Chief Justice of England.

The humble petition of Daniel de Foe of Newington, in the county of Middlesex, now a prisoner in the Queen's Bench,

Humbly sheweth that your petitioner is extremely afflicted at the offense he has given to your lordship in the two printed papers entitled the *Review;* and for which offense he stands committed, that as your prisoner assures your lordship he did not foresee the just displeasure of your lordship, so he is heartily sorry for it; and, avoiding all excuses or extenuations of the fact, he throws himself upon the goodness and compassion of your lordship in the humblest manner possible, and with the lowest submission asks your lordship's pardon for the same: humbly imploring your lordship that his other unhappy circumstances, such as a large family, his private affairs long in a perplexed posture, and the public prosecutions which he is now under, may move your lordship to forgive his said offense, which otherwise will be his utter ruin and undoing.

Your petitioner therefore most humbly prays your lordship's pardon; and, that he may be discharged from his present confinement, assuring your lordship of his dutiful behaviour to your lordship for the future.

And your petitioner shall ever pray [&c.].

DANIEL DE FOE

To the Right Honourable Sir Thomas Parker, Kt., Lord Chief Justice of England, and to the rest of the judges of Her Majesty's court of Queen's Bench.

The humble petition of Daniel de Foe, prisoner in the Queen's Bench prison,

Humbly sheweth that your petitioner humbly, and without any reserve, acknowledges the justice of your lordships' displeasure at what he had written in those *Reviews* for which he stands committed, and is sincerely sorry for having given your lordships offense therein. And though he did not foresee the same, yet he is very far from excusing or extenuating the fact upon that account; but humbly throws himself upon your lordships' mercy, begging pardon of your lordships for the said offense in the humblest manner possible.

And whereas some words have been printed in another *Review* which are also justly offensive to your lordships, he humbly assures your lordships the same was actually printed and wrought off before your lordships' displeasure at the other papers was known. And he humbly assures your lordships that as he is heartily afflicted at having thus incurred your lordships' displeasure, so he will be careful to avoid the like for the future; and particularly that he will never take the liberty to mention anything in public which relates to your lordships' proceedings in any respect whatsoever.

Wherefore your petitioner humbly prays your lordships that he may be discharged from his present confinement, without which he and his numerous family will be utterly ruined and undone.

And your petitioner shall ever pray, &c.

DANIEL DE FOE

There may be objections by some to the manner of my submissions; for my part, all the objection I make to them myself is that I think they are not full enough in the acknowledging part; and if I could have made them more complete, I ought to have done it, because the lenity shown me by their lordships, when this resentment might have been much heavier upon me, even to my ruin, calls for very large and very open acknowledgments. And therefore, as I have published these petitions by their lordships' command, so if I knew what to add as a voluntary expiation for this offense that would be more to their lordships' satisfaction, I should think myself bound to do it. And I do take the liberty to say that this is not all the acknowledgment I purpose to make of it, but shall let the world see I am sensible both of the offense and of my duty, even when the hands of justice are taken off.

Economics and Trade: Britain's Mystery and Bulwark

Of Divinity in Trade [1]

And what if, being writing of commerce, I should tell you there is a kind of divinity in the original of trade, and if I spend one *Review* to put you in mind that God, in the order of nature, not only made trade necessary to the making the life of man easy, and towards accommodating one part of the world with what they might want for their conveniences from another part, but also qualified, suited, and adapted the vegetative and sensitive world to be subservient to the uses, methods and necessities which we find them now put to by the ingenious artists for the convenience of trade? And it cannot be amiss to remind you how unfitted for trade, and how uncapable to carry it on the world had been, if these things had not been at first ordered by the wise hand that governs the world.

Providence has adapted nature to trade, and made it subservient in all its parts to the several necessary operations of commerce. What a turn would it give to affairs of commerce in the world if Heaven should either withhold the constant influences of natural instincts in the creatures, or alter anything in the first stated law of things? If floaty bodies, by natural levity adapted to swim on the surface of the water, by change of climate or other accidents could assume gravity, there at once would be an end of all navigation, and a ship that swims in one sea would immediately sink to the bottom in another. If the law of gravity, by which every heavy body tends downward, should either cease in general or alter in particular places, upon every storm of wind the waters of the sea would stand in clusters and heaps, vast chasms would appear in the deep, and navigation be of course impracticable; and innumerable instances of like kind would be found in all the other common operations of obedient nature.

How naturally does the water, moved by the mighty winds, flow into every hollow and fill up every vacant part in the sea; the innumerable particles diligently crowd on the heels of one another to supply the place of those forced away, and those that are forced from

[1] Defoe here seems to reflect his reading of Dr. Thomas Burnet's *The Sacred Theory of the Earth* (1681).

their place by an unusual gust immediately return to fill up the first emptiness they find? When the ship, tossed by the fury of the contending element, and mounted on the surface of a rolling body of disordered water, seems to be falling into a vast gulf of destruction, how do the same waves hurry into the hollow place, and catching it in their soft arms, prevent its descent to the solid bottom, where it would be dashed in a thousand pieces, and gently raise it up again by their united force, and having brought it to their surface launch it forward to receive the same kind usage from the next? Thus obedient nature, true to its own laws, preserves the communication of one part of the world with another, and lays the foundation of commerce which would otherwise be altogether impracticable and impossible.

Let us take a short view of the land. The subjection of all the creation to the dominion of man, when his Maker first made him lord of this wide place we call the world, is to me the most signal discovery of a sovereign invisible power that can be found in the whole frame of it. What has made the useful part of the creatures tame, docible, tractable, and submissive, while the less needful part are left wild and at war with us? Should the sovereign Lord of this globe arm the creatures against us, cause them to declare an universal war with mankind, and let them loose to the exercise but of that strength and those weapons which he has given them; nay, should he but remove that fear and awe of man that stands fixed in their nature, how useless would they be to mankind, and with what difficulties should we live; what a turn would it give to trade, what a universal stop to all manner of commerce!

If the horse would not be rid, nor the ox draw, nor the cow be milked; if your sheep were not the tamest, quietest, submissivest creatures in the world, that lay their throats down to your knife and their backs to the shears; if the ox would not go into your very slaughter-house to be killed, instead of having the trade of a butcher, and a few men in every village supplying us with provisions, all business would be set apart, and we should be forced to turn hunters, archers, and gunners for our food. Your country would all be thrown open and turned into common; and enclosing of land would be only to keep cattle out, not to keep them in; property in cattle would cease, the ox would no more know his owner, nor the ass his master crib; the horse would show you his heels, and the cow her horns; the dog would bark at you, not for you, and hunt for himself, not for your table. You must draw your own ploughs, and carry your own burdens; the ladies must go on foot, and the kings and queens be content with the services and labours of their own kind. Commerce would cease, and no more people could dwell in a country than the land itself would maintain.

How blind, then, must those people be that can look round them on the disposition of the creation, how subjected to man's authority and adapted to his use, and not acknowledge the infinite superintendency of invisible Providence! If such depravity rests still on the minds of any creature vested with reason, I can only recommend to him the exercise of his reason upon some such contemplations as these; and whether it will lead him to the gate of that knowledge to which life and happiness is annexed, I will not determine, for that appears to have different channels of conveyance. But certainly it will carry him thus far, that he must immediately conclude that there is not a power supreme only, but supremely wise and supremely good, which governs the world. The force these natural convictions have on the dark reason of unenlightened nations seems to me to be original of that universal inclination to acknowledge a God, where it has not pleased God to give any other discovery of himself.

This is a large field, and too great to enter into here; but the present use I shall make of it, and indeed the reason of my bringing this subject into these papers is this, to let thoughtless people see how Providence concurs in, and seems to have prepared the world for, commerce; assists us in the diligent pursuit of needful improvement, and seems to expect trade should be preserved, encouraged, and extended by all honest and prudent methods, as a stated provision made for the support and maintenance, employment and improvement of his creatures, especially for mutual assistance, comfort, and support of nations and families, where more people are collected than the bare fruits of the earth can maintain.

Without these methods of trade, the due disposition of what the wisdom of God has furnished the world with could not have been made. Metals designed, no doubt, for universal use, but stored up by nature in proper receptacles, could not be dispersed to the several parts which are left without; the wines, oils, silks, fruits, iron, marble, steel, wool, brimstone, and sundry other goods produced in France, Spain, Italy, &c. would not have completed the delightful habitations, accommodations and comfortable living of the inhabitants without the gold and ivory of Africa, the silver of Hungaria and America, the lead and tin of Britain, the copper of Swedeland, the sugar and tobacco of the Islands,[2] the furs of the north, and the spices of the south—none, or very few of which, are found in all those delicious countries of France, Spain, or Italy.

Shall any tell me that God in His infinite providence did not guide nations by invisible directions into trade, and lead them by the hand into the methods, manner, and consequences, to render commerce both easy and useful? The very position of things in the world would confound the opposer of such a plain assertion: the navigation of rivers letting us into the very bowels and center of countries, from whence the growth and produce of those countries, otherwise too remote for any tolerable conveyance, is to be brought away; the natural assistance of long undiscovered guides to navigation, such as the fixed stars, magnet, &c.; the wonderful assistance of human art, doubled by experience, in the mere perfection of the science of navigation; the furnishing all maritime nations with materials for shipping and the like—as they are instanced before to be foundations of commerce, so they are undeniable testimonies both of the infinite foreknowledge of divine wisdom and of the appointments Providence had made for the employing and improving the people that were to come upon this earth.

The increase of this commerce, therefore, receives its rise from the daily discoveries more and more of what lies treasured up in the bowels of the earth, or in the remote parts of uninhabited climates, and unnavigated seas, bays, channels, and retreats of the waters. The search after these things has met with wonderful success, and the finger of Providence has been more than usually visible in the bringing things to light, in these latter ages of trade, which our ancestors knew not of; and doubtless Providence has yet an inexhausted store of undiscovered advantages in trade, both to encourage the industry, and re-

[2] The West Indies, particularly Jamaica, Barbadoes, and the Leeward Islands.

ward the hazards of enquiring posterity; into some of which, perhaps, these sheets may make no unpleasant inquiry.

Vol. VIII, No. 16 Tuesday, May 1, 1711

TRADE, THE BULWARK OF ENGLAND

MY TIME is so little that I can spare upon the subject of trade, and the scene so large, that I own I can but touch at things as I go; yet I cannot but bestow a few lines upon the subject of our credit—a thing I touched more largely when I thought it in some danger, and say the less to it now I think it secure.

I confess I have thought one of the pleasantest things in the world is to see men struggling against themselves grow happy by being defeated of their own desires, rich by having their interest ruined, and safe by having their own measures crossed and disappointed. To see them, like a man in the water that cannot swim, struggling to drown himself, and endeavouring to pull him under water that comes to save him—this, indeed, I take to be the case of our high-hat gentlemen that would fain have thrown the heels of our bank up, and with it have ruined both it and themselves.[1]

Those gentlemen talked loud of credit, but understood it so ill that really a man would rather have pitied them than have laughed at them, because they had a great deal of money at stake to lose. Did ever men that had any money in the stock strive so earnestly to ruin that stock as these? Did ever men that had a cargo in the ship bore a hole in the bottom? What wretched stuff was it, to hear these men talk of credit without trade, and banks without money. And this has been

[1] Upon losing the elections of 1710 to the Tories following the Sacheverell fiasco (see note, p. 199), the Whigs, who largely represented the moneyed interests, thought to overthrow the Tories by depressing the national credit as it was reflected in the young Bank of England. When bank stock dropped from 129 to 95, Defoe warned them that they were cutting their own throats.

all their cry. It is true, land is a fund—unhappy is the *Examiner*,[2] to bestow so much wit on so dull an argument! What makes land a fund? Let any man go back and enquire what was land in the days of Henry I? The ground stood just where it does now; the sweet dews of heaven, the refreshing showers, the warm beams of the sun, all invigorated the earth as much, as constantly, and as seasonably as they do now—but where was the fund? What was the rent? Where the improvement? Alas for the ignorance of our men of learning! Land is a fund! But what had your land been without trade? Go dig your lead mines in Wales, and turn them all into silver, as Sir. H. M.[3] has done into dross, and see how rich you will be; shear your sheep and see what you will do with the wool. Till trade brought you gold and silver, and fetched away your manufactures, found vent for the produce and labour for your people, what was all your wealth? Your natives must have wandered abroad and been hirelings and mauls for Europe, as the Swiss are to this day. Your gentry and nobility might have been kings and princes at home, and the poor people drones and slaves—but where had been your fund? Where your wealth? *It is trade* has made your commons rich, your merchants numerous, your poor able to maintain themselves. *It is trade* has made you great, strong, terrible abroad, and busy at home. *It is trade* has kept your people from wandering like vagabonds on the face of the earth. People consume the produce, trade has filled you with people; the produce raises the rent, and the rent makes the land a fund. Mark the climax—your land might go a-begging but for trade; and for the landed men to rail at trade is like the members mutinying against the belly. 'Tis from trade as the magazine that land receives its value and life. Land is a fund of wealth, that's true; but trade is the fund of land, from your trade springs your land's wealth. Let such men but view the land in other countries. What was the land in Barbadoes good for when the island was unpossessed by us? It was as rich as now, the fund was

[2] The *Examiner* was a Tory periodical begun in 1710 by Bolingbroke and continued by Swift.

[3] Sir Humphrey Mackworth (1657–1727), politician and capitalist, attempted to develop collieries and copper-smelting works in Wales under the corporations known popularly as the Mine Adventurers. In 1710 the House of Commons voted him guilty of fraud in his ventures. Defoe frequently attacked him in the *Review*. Earlier, in a pamphlet, *Peace without Union* (1703), he replied to one of Sir Humphrey's tracts.

there—but that trade gave that fund a value. It was a fund and no fund—a fund of nothing; and take trade from that island now, with all its wealth, and what will it be good for still? Will it feed and employ 60,000 Negroes, &c., in a place of but 25 leagues round?

Stop but trade in England and see what your lands will soon come to! Let no more clothes or stuffs be made, or in general, no more wool spun except for private use; no more ships built, no more correspondence with foreign nations; no exportation or circulation—and let any man but imagine what a state this nation will soon be in! The poor would eat up the rich; the land would not feed the multitude; your rich trading and encroaching neighbours would hire and entertain all your youth, who would fly to them for bread, and being armed by them, would come back and conquer you; your provisions, of course, would fail; that failing, rents of lands must fall. Customs, excises, and taxes would fail of course, all your subsidies must lie upon land, your gentry would sink, a thousand pounds a year in land would not be worth a hundred, and where then is your landed fund?

I blush for the ignorance of those men that would contemn trade to raise land. No, no, gentlemen, if you will have land be a fund, you must encourage trade. Land and trade are like the monster of Glasgow, of which I have often spoken on another occasion—it had one body from the navel downwards, but two bodies from the navel upwards; they had different hands to work, different heads to contrive, and, no doubt, different souls to direct; they received nourishment two different ways, and had two stomachs to digest, but they had but one pair of legs to walk with, one belly to receive and vent, one receptacle; and from hence it followed that they had but one and the same life. The foolish creature would sometimes, just like our landed men and trading men, quarrel with itself; one side would be for going this way, and the other that, an evidence it had two wills. And what was the consequence? Why, the legs were fain to stand still till the heads were agreed, for there being but one pair of feet, and the locomotive faculty receiving its orders from the will—and there being two wills—till they concurred, the legs were perfectly useless. Would to God our people would consider how apt this creature was formed to describe our case. Really, good people, if trade and land, which are the wealth of this nation, are divided and differ, the whole body will soon stand still. And this, like the circulation in the body, will throw the whole into apoplexies, dead palsies, and every mortal disease.

Wretched folly! Land despise trade! and trade set up against land! Can anything be more absurd? Is not trade the nurse of land? And is not land the nourishment of trade? Does not land supply the materials of trade? And does not trade enable the land to supply these materials? Land produces wool, corn, cattle, timber, hemp, metals and minerals; trade produces a market for all these, gives a price to them, brings home silver to circulate that trade, and feeds the people who take off these provisions at a price, and by this, land lives—what would land be without it?

The monster I tell you of was really born at or near Glasgow, and lived many years in that unhappy conjunction, came at last to this miserable end—and is an emblem to our purpose in its end, as it was in its life; one of the bodies died before the other. What was to be done then? What course to be taken to preserve the living part? Indeed, nothing. No. Nature had it not in her power, art could give no help, the living body was tied fast to the dead; it mourned, it grieved, it wept, it struggled, it pined, but it could not be. The mortification conveyed itself on gradually to the living part; it languished and became a carcass by mere natural consequence. Let your landed men that would crush our trade take the hint. Whenever trade dies, land will, of course, feel the beginnings of death. Land will pine, fade, languish, and at last die into its original poverty and its mere native condition.

Trade then, is the life of the land's wealth, and land will be no fund without it; and those people that think to make land a fund, must cherish trade to support the value or rent of land, or they destroy that fund themselves. . . .

Vol. VI, No. 33 Saturday, June 18, 1709

CONSUMER CREDIT THE RUIN OF TRADE[1]

THERE IS but one objection to credit, and that lies in the last consumer. No man ought to take credit, or give it for food or cloths; for as that is the point or end of trade, so a credit there tends not at all to the increase of commerce, but to the decrease of it. The retail of the goods sold is the last act of trade; this we call the consumption and is the end of circulation. To trust here is a kind of stagnation, not a revolution, because there is no rolling on. Trust to him that sells enables him to trust another, and him a third, and so on to the retailer; but trust to the consumer is putting a stop to the motion. The first increases trade, the last straitens it. If a man trusts me with 100£ in trade, I can perhaps return this twice a year, which is 200£. The next man I trust with it returns it twice a year also, and so on perhaps through ten hands. If everyone gets 10 per cent let this but be cast up, the 100£ original credit causes 2,000£ to be returned in the year, and the profits of that in ten hands is 200£ increase to the public stock. . . .

To all these here is a profit, and every profit is an increase of wealth to the general stock. The circulation nourishes every part it passes through, and credit thus supplies the room of stock. I could enlarge on this subject, but experience is our common instructor. Let any man but look round him, what proportion is there between the stock of England and the credit of England in trade; there is no naming them together. Though the stock is great, too, credit carries on trade; its circulation is infinite and not to be expressed.

Again, it is to be observed what lessens and what creates credit. Giving credit as before to the last consumer is the destruction of credit; and ever while you live you shall find it where the circulating credit is least, that dead credit prevails. And this is the ruin of the credit of trade, as I shall take the freedom to say more largely hereafter. To

[1] The first four paragraphs have been omitted.

preserve credit, whether personal or political, one essential is to be taken care of, viz., a punctual, fair performance of contract, and compliance with appointments. This is something equivalent to what you call parole of honour in gentlemen, and is indeed not improperly called the honour of trade. Upon this, credit and trade and everything depends; and indeed, without this there is no carrying trade on. They tell us that when Sir Thomas Gresham built the Exchange of London, he raised it upon pillars which he called his props of honour, intimating that the honour of merchants was to be the support of the Exchange; [2] and hence we have a usage of accepting bills for the honour of the drawer when the merchant on whom a bill is drawn refuses or delays the payment.

And I cannot but take notice here that this credit in trade is very much sunk of late in Britain, and I could demonstrate how the value as well as extent of our trade is lessened in proportion. We complain of the war, and our losses at sea [3] lessening our trade, and I doubt not but it has so; but I must add also, the breaches made upon our trade by the ruin of credit, and that ruin beginning at the breach of honour in traders, have been the greatest blow to our commerce that this nation has felt for many ages. This has helped on our running our money into loans and public funds, and has supplied that stock to the government which would otherwise have been employed in trade; for as I noted before, though the credit of our public funds is a great reputation to the kingdom in general, an honour to the government, and particularly to the ministry who have raised it to such a head, yet I cannot say it is an argument of the increase of trade, but just the contrary. . . .

As credit enables a tradesman to do wonders, to trade without a stock, trust others with what is none of his own, and extend his commerce to a hundred times his foundation; so has credit wrought wonders for the government. Who can blame the King of France for

[2] Sir Thomas Gresham (1519?–1579), merchant and financial agent for Henry VIII and Elizabeth, built at his own expense the Royal Exchange. He contributed to other public objects, including a college in London which later housed the Royal Society.

[3] England, as a member of the Confederacy, had been at war with France since May, 1702, over a successor to the Spanish throne. In the first six years more than eleven hundred ships were lost to the French.

venturing a war with the Confederates, believing they could never have exerted such a force as they have done? If any man of the sublimest knowledge in the world was to have been asked twenty years ago if England could go through a war that should in twenty years cost her 120 millions sterling, besides above 30 millions in losses at sea, would he not have laughed the enquirer to scorn? And yet this have we done, and are pushing to have this war continue still, disdaining to talk of being unable to carry it on. Well might I say, he that manages your treasure is the general of your generals, and the soul of the war. All this is done by credit, and this credit formed among ourselves upon the solid basis of honourable compliance, and vigorous circulation. . . .

Vol. VI, No. 31 Tuesday, June 14, 1709

CREDIT, THE INVISIBLE PHANTOM[1]

THAT substantial non-entity called CREDIT seems to have a distinct essence (if nothing can be said to exist) from all the phenomena in nature. It is in itself the lightest and most volatile body in the world, movable beyond the swiftness of lightning; the greatest alchemists could never fix its mercury, or find out its quality; it is neither a soul or a body; it is neither visible or invisible; it is all consequence, and yet not the effect of a cause; it is being without matter, a substance without form. A perfect free agent acting by wheels and springs absolutely undiscovered, it comes without call, and goes away unsent; if it flies, the whole nation cannot stay it; if it stays away, no importunity can prevail for its return. No law can reach it, acts of Parliament cannot influence it; its motions are natural to itself, and never to be constrained; it is sullen and ill-natured enough in its actings, and perfectly imperceptible in its mov-

[1] The first three paragraphs have been omitted.

ing; it comes to a man, or a body of men, or a nation, insensibly, as dust upon the cloths; it goes imperceptibly as light vanishes into darkness; it comes with surprise, and goes without notice. Where there is no occasion for it, it will stay whether you will or no, and seems to love those who have no use for it; once to want it, is effectually to lose it; like the vermin in a house, it always flies when the house is falling, though with this unhappy difference, that where this flies, the house not only may fall but *must*. Where it stays it has strange qualities: it is the best philosopher's stone in the world, and has the best method for multiplication of metals; it has the effectual power of transmutation, for it can turn paper into money, and money into dross. While it lives with a merchant, he can trade without a stock, draw bills where he has no effects, and pay bills without money; if it forsake him, his trade dies, his money won't circulate, the vitals of his management stagnate, his ships won't sail, his bills won't be accepted, and nothing will go any faster than 'tis driven; while it dwells in a nation, it doubles their strength; they can fit out fleets without money, have money without funds, and funds without deficiencies. What has this invisible phantom done for this nation, and what miserable doings were there here before without her? She cuts all the notches in your tallies, and the obedient nation takes them for money; your exchequer bills have her seal to them, and my L—— H——x [2] sets his hand to them in her name; 'tis by her you raise armies, fit out fleets, clothe your soldiers, establish banks, sell annuities, pay equivalents, and in short by her you found your grand alliances have supported the war, and beat the French. By this invisible *je ne scay quoi*, this non-natural, this emblem of a something, though in itself nothing, all our war and all our trade is supported. The commerce of England is at this time carried on to a hundred million sterl[ing] a year of returns more than there is specie of coin to negotiate; the war is carried on with an hundredth part of the ready money that it would otherwise require. 'Tis all done by the aid and assistance of this machine called *credit*. This is the wheel within the wheel of all our commerce, and all our public transactions. By this you have fought, and by this you conquer.

[2] Charles Montague, Earl of Halifax (1661–1715), a Whig whom William III made Chancellor of the Exchequer. He issued paper money to counteract clipping of coins. Ousted by the Tories in 1703. President of the Royal Society 1695–98. As patron, he assisted Addison, Congreve, Prior, and Newton.

I might concern her in private affairs. And how many families does she keep alive now that must starve without her? How many shops does she keep open that must shut up without her? Pay homage to her image, O ye thousands that walk the Exchange, who trade largely, live high, and sink deep into the pockets of your substantial neighbours and have not one penny of foundation to stand upon. But with the assistance of this charm, flatter your fellow traders to put their stocks into your hands, flatter yourselves to go on, and make your fortunes out of nothing. Pay homage to this idol, I say, and be very tender of her; for if you overload her, she's a coy mistress—she'll slip from you without any warning, and you'll be undone from that moment.

I cannot now enter into her private recesses where she concerns herself with families, persons, and things. Long account might be given of her there; there she blesses and blasts just as she pleases; she tyrannizes over youth, beauty, virtue, estate; she makes honest women whores, and whores honest women. By her the homely get husbands, while all men shall shun the fair; if she forsake the honestest woman in the world, nobody will touch her; if she covers the most scandalous behaviour, it passes for virtue; the spouse deceived by her takes a prostitute, and swears she was a virgin; demonstration will hardly convince against her evidence; and a whole life of virtue won't repair the injury she does, where she falls off. But that by the by. . . .

Vol. V, No. 149 Thursday, March 10, 1709

OF THE LAWS ABOUT INSOLVENT DEBTORS[1]

IN GIVING my list of particulars, I mean of the several classes of miserables in this nation whom we call insolvents, I promised to explain myself as to the last article, viz., those in actual confinement, and subdivide them again. The number of these I call 5,000, who are actually immured and kept close, and many of whom without

[1] This is Defoe's own title.

Parliamentary relief must perish there, having no hope of liberty but by death or an act of Parliament, which act, I confess, I do not see so much hopes of as I once thought I should—I mean as to its extending to the relief of such whose debts are considerable, though their distresses equal, if not exceed, those who are in for smaller sums. I shall therefore divide the supposed number of 5,000 into the following parts; and though it is done but by probable conjecture, yet if I am near the truth, 'tis as exact as the argument I am upon requires.

1. Of these 5,000, I suppose, of meaner tradesmen, poor handicrafts, and labouring people, whose debts are from one hundred pounds downward, about two thousand. These live, most of them, in the common sides, and are there fed by the basket, as 'tis called; or live by begging at the grates of the prisons.[2] And though many of them suffer hardship enough, yet generally speaking, these live better than many in the master-sides of prisons, whose wants are inexpressible.

2. Of more capital tradesmen, gentlemen, and some clergymen, whose characters and education, rather than substance, have prevented going among the other, that cannot beg or feed on the basket, but endure a thousand more miseries and extremities than those that do, whose hardships and sufferings are born with silence and mourning of soul rather than noise and loud complainings—of these I believe there languishes, for I cannot call it living, in the several gaols of this nation, two thousand more. Of these 'tis observable there dies three for one of the first sort, and that more miserably.

3. There are a higher sort yet, and these consist of such tradesmen and gentlemen who, though not able to pay their debt and free themselves, have yet something left to bear them up under prison charges, though it is wasting every day, as well by the chargeable subsisting in prison as by their families abroad; all their affairs suffering a general shipwreck, and the industrious hands locked up from looking after their own affairs. These are wasting and consuming, and being without prospect of deliverance, though for the present they live, yet are hastening apace to the miseries of the first two classes; and these I reckon to be about eight hundred.

[2] Treatment of prisoners varied from prison to prison. At Newgate the common sides (free ward) prisoners were fed one loaf of bread daily, but were obliged to provide their own fire and beds. Friends or visitors could feed them through the grates of the prison door.

4. There are yet remaining two hundred more miserable than the worse of the other; and these are such as seem condemned to perpetual imprisonment, sealed up to darkness and oblivion, men that ought to bid the world good night. *Les enfans perdue*, in a true literal sense, *lost men*, given up to death and murdered by inexorable creditors. Generally these are sacrifices to revenge, private grudge, and every unchristian passion; and such is the severity of the late Act [3] that there seems no possibility of escape for them. Pay they never can, and without pay the law will not release them. These are such as are in upon extents from the Crown, or the new murdering writ, as I call it, or escape warrant, as the law calls it. I believe I am very much within compass when I reckon up these but two hundred, among whom are a great many gentlemen of worth, and of great personal merit, but unhappy to the last degree; and some of these have continued in this condition of the first sort eight, ten, to fifteen years—till they are grown grey in their misfortunes and are quite lost to their families; and of the last, several ever since the first month of the Act, which is now about five years old.

And now, gentlemen, are these men to be pitied or no? Is human nature so capable of cruelty? Can it be imagined that a man who has lain seven, eight, or ten years in prison can pay? Is it not punishment enough to satisfy any man's revenge? Is it possible the rage of a creditor can hold so long, for a mere debt? If the debtor cannot pay, and can give you an account how he became unable, is it fit to keep a fellow creature longer in misery? What signifies acts of Parliament to relieve poor creatures for trifles, whose circumstances are sometimes worse out than in? The misery lies in these people I am speaking of, who are loaded with debt as with a crime unpardonable; that being perfectly unable, are kept up and continued unable, and punished more for debt than others are for robbery. But, say some, they are not unable. What, lie in prison, and yet able to pay! What sort of creatures are they, and how will you convince any man in the world that a man who lies in prison is able to pay? But suppose human nature so far degenerate that a man could choose a prison with knavery rather than liberty and honesty. This might be for some time. But how many years could that baseness of spirit hold? I cannot but think it may be

[3] Probably referring to the regulation adopted in 1707 whereby the commissioners were required to assign all the bankrupt's effects to assignees chosen by the creditors.

ventured upon as a true rule—he that lies in prison for years and ages, as seven, ten, twelve, fifteen years by the obstinacy of a creditor, it may be presumed is not able to pay and obtain his liberty. Seven year is a long apprenticeship to a gaol, and he that serves it certainly wants money to buy his freedom, or else I know not what rule to judge by.

I might now go back to our laws, and it is not difficult to prove that not only other nations do not deal thus with their poor insolvents, but also that it was not the intent and meaning of our most early laws that the person of the debtor should be arrested or attached in *mesne* process. . . . It's clearly evident that the design of the law of England in this respect agrees with the civil law, and that of Scotland, that the person shall not be ordinarily subject to arrest in the first process. But here by a sort of practice contrary to the intent of the law [4] the attorneys or under-sheriffs return a *nihil*, of course, and so take out *capias's* universally in all cases, and subject people's liberty to be a prey to sergeants and bailiffs who commit horrid and intolerable extortions sometimes by fob or sham actions, at other times by excessive high actions for small debts; and often for a debt of ten or twenty shillings it costs a poor man in custody under an arrest thirty or forty shillings. . . .

To what, then, are we corrupted, and how has the practice of the lawyers altered the very meaning of the law; and under this error of practice how many thousands of souls perish in this nation. To reform this the present law will not extend, but it may relieve the miserable sufferers, and indeed there is need enough for it. I shall next show you how remote also it was from the thoughts of our forefathers to let the debtor, after he is a prisoner, perish in prison, and this I shall quote very good authority for.

[4] A short-cut, and perhaps an abuse of power, is here indicated in carrying out the law. Normally there would be an inquiry into what the defendant had before a return was made that he had nothing (the *nihil*). Only after this investigation could he properly be taken into custody.

Vol. III, No. 2 Thursday, January 3, 1706

MR. REVIEW PLUMPS FOR FREE TRADE[1]

GENERALLY SPEAKING, all the innumerables of trade come under these two heads: natural produce, and manufacture. The different climates and soil in the world have by the wisdom and direction of *nature naturing*, which I call GOD, produced such differing species of things, all of them in their kind equally necessary, or at least useful and desirable, as insensibly preserves the dependance of the most remote parts of the world upon one another, and at least makes them useful to each other and contributing to one another's convenience, necessity, or delight. And here I might digress to good purpose in setting out how the most plentiful country receives from the most barren; how every nation has something to fetch from and something to send to one another; every nation something to spare which another country wants, and finds something wanting another country can spare. And this occasions exchanging with those countries to the advantage of both; and that we call TRADE. This necessarily implies convenience for portage, and that we call navigation; and thus general negoce began to be improved by human industry to strange and unaccountable enlargements. This variety also is not only natural, but artificial; and as the climates and soil have produced in every country different growths or species of things, so the differing genius of the people of every country prompts them to different improvements, and to different customs. They eat, wear, and dwell after differing manners; and as all people, tenacious of their own way, seek what qualifies them best to pursue it, they seek to foreign climates to furnish themselves with what they cannot have so much to their purpose, or so suited to their occasions or inclinations at home. And this is again revolved into necessary correspondence; they must send to those countries some equivalent to satisfy the people for what they take from them, and thus we are again brought home to TRADE.

[1] The first three paragraphs have been omitted.

To examine this variety a little may not be unpleasant, nor in its end unprofitable to the reader, because it will tend to open our particular scenes of trade, of which, in course, I shall come to treat more particularly and largely than perhaps is expected. The variety, both of the produce and manufactures of the several countries, are the foundations of trade, and I entitle Providence to it; not only as it is found in nature, but as it is found in customs and consequences of things; for God, in whose infinite foreknowledge all the accidents of time are always present, who is one infinite substantial essential *now* in which is no past or future, must be supposed to foreknow that natural causes considered—*and to natural causes He had in His infinite wisdom by laws of nature submitted all the variety of consequences*—the generations of the world could not subsist in the manner prescribed, without the mutual assistance and concurrence of one another. The bare produce of the earth in many of our neighbouring countries could by no means have maintained the numbers of people which the consequences of trade have brought together. To answer for this, navigable rivers, as well as a navigable sea, has made the communication of remote parts practicable; and floaty bodies are adapted for vessels, that the light bodies may bear the heavy, and goods that will not bear it may be fenced from the inconvenience of weather and preserved fit for use and convenience. The rivers and roads are as the veins and arteries that convey wealth, like the blood, to all the parts of the world; and this wealth is the life of kingdoms and towns, the support of their people, and test of their power.

I wonder sometimes at the ignorance of those people and nations whose gentry pretend to despise families raised by trade. Why should that which is the wealth of the world, the prosperity and health of kingdoms and towns, be accounted dishonourable? If we respect trade, as it is understood by merchandising, it is certainly the most noble, most instructive, and improving of any way of life. The artificers or handicrafts-men are indeed slaves; the gentlemen are the plowmen of the nation, but the merchant is the support and improver of power, learning, and fortunes. A true-bred merchant is a universal scholar, his learning excels the mere scholar in Greek and Latin as much as that does the illiterate person that cannot write or read. He understands languages without books, geography without maps; his journals and trading voyages delineate the world; his foreign exchanges, protests, and procurations speak all tongues. He sits in his counting house and converses with all nations, and keeps up the most exquisite and extensive part of human society in a universal correspondence. He is qualified for all sorts of employment in the state by a general knowledge of things and men; he remits and draws such vast sums that he transacts more value than a large exchequer.

By the number of these, cities rise out of nothing and decay again into villages. If trade abandons a port, if the merchants quit the place, it languishes of course, and dies like man in a consumption, insensibly; if these flock to a town, home trade crowds upon them, seamen increase, people flock in, and the village soon becomes a city. In nations and empires 'tis the same; what infinite crowds of people flock into Holland; cities without number, and towns thick like the houses in other countries, that the whole country seems to be one populous city; people in such multitude that all the land in the country can't find butter and cheese for them, much less maintain them! All these attend upon trade; by trade they possess the world and have greater stocks of goods in each country's growth than the countries from whence they have them can show. Their rivers are thronged with shipping like a wood; their naval stores are inexhaustible; they can build a navy and fit it to sea sooner than any nation in the world; and yet have neither the timber or plank, the ironwork or cordage, the pitch or the tar, the hemp or the rosin, in any part of the country. All this is done by trade; the merchant makes a wet bog become a populous state; enriches beggars, ennobles mechanics, raises not families only, but towns, cities, provinces, and kingdoms.

How then can that be dishonourable that it in its kind is the support of the world, and by and from which nations and kingdoms are made to differ from one another; are made to excel one another and be too strong because too rich for one another? The merchant by his correspondence reconciles that infinite variety which, as I noted, has by the infinite wisdom of Providence been scattered over the face of the world. If England has wool and Spain has oil, Spain sends her oil over to England to enable England to work that wool into cloth, bays, sayes, perpets, and stuffs, and so they may be sent over to Spain for their clothing. Has Spain wine, England has her beer and fine ale, which in those countries where there they have wine is justly esteemed before it. And again, we send for their wines to drink here, our prelates inclining to seek those liquors which we must fetch from abroad. We cloth[e] all the islands and continent of America; and they in return furnish us with sugars and tobaccoes, things by custom becoming as useful to us as our cloths is to them. Trade carries the very soil away and transposes the world in parts, removing mountains and carrying them over the sea into other countries. What a quantity of the terra firma has been carried from Newcastle in coals, whose ashes lie mixed with the soil in most parts of the world; what cavities and chasms in the bowels of the earth have we made for our tin, lead, and iron in the respective counties of Cornwall, Derby, and Sussex! These we carry abroad, and with them we purchase and bring back the woods of Norway, the silks of Italy and Turkey, the wines and brandies of France, the wines, oil, and fruit of Spain, the drugs of Persia, the spices of India, the sugars of America, the toys and gaiety of China and Japan.

An infinite variety might here be run through; every country communicates to its other corresponding country what they want, and these [that] can spare them *vice versa* receive from that country again what of their growth these want; and not a country so barren, so useless, but something is to be found there that can be had nowhere else. All the world could not have thought of such an increasing trade as has been established in our colonies of America; for tobacco and sugar and abundance of useful things, the cochineal, cocoa, bark, and drugs of America; the fish of Newfoundland and New England; the whales from uninhabitable Greenland, and the like; no nation so hot or so cold but it contributes something to another, by which wealth is advanced, people benefited and employed; and this in its true original called TRADE.

In the pursuit of this matter of general trade, the nature of the thing led mankind to a necessity of a general medium of trade; and the original of this is found in this absolute necessity. For example, one country demands more goods from another than it can pay for in goods of its own growth or procuring, or than that country will take in exchange; now trade labouring under this dilemma, necessity drove men to form a medium of trade—something whose value being always intrinsic, would be accepted everywhere, and that always must attend to form the balance and pay the overplus; and this is MONEY. When this money could not be either readily as to time, or sufficiently as to quantity be procured, the honour and character of the persons raised from experience of probity and punctual payment made the men easy; and in confidence of the integrity of the person trading, he will be content with tomorrow which cannot with convenience be had today, and accordingly he stays the day appointed, and then receives it; *and this we call* CREDIT, of both which in our ensuing discourse.

Vol. I [IX], No. 43 Thursday, January 8, 1713

THE TRADE IN BAUBLES AND TRIFLES

THE SUBJECT of trade which I am now entered upon has this one excellency in it, for the benefit of the author, that really it can never be exhausted; and indeed, such are the follies and absurdities of our present notions of trade, that should I go on as I have begun to treat of them first, before I come to discourse solidly of real improvement, I should be in danger to spend my whole life to satirize and divert you, and die before I came to profit and improve you—like the famous reader of divinity at Prague, I think it was, or Vienna, of whom Mr. Fuller writes in his *Holy State*, who being appointed to lecture upon the prophecy of Isaiah, read two and forty year upon the first chapter and never got through it till he died.

I am jesting with you a little upon the mighty improvements we are arrived to in trade, and I gave you some of them in my last—the truth of which I cannot but illustrate by some extraordinary examples I instanced in our coffee, tea, and chocolate, which it is well known are now become capital branches of the nation's commerce. That the fact is true nobody will question when they view the custom-house books and see whole ships entered there laden entirely with coffee, and when they read the cargoes of our East Indiamen with 300,000 pounds of tea imported at a time, and cocoa in its due proportion. [These] will be found so assistant in the duties paid to the government, that I defy any nation in the world showing an equal revenue raised from three such foreign trifles, the importation of which within this three score years did not all together pay ten pounds a year custom.

I am now to examine a little the real advantages these mighty improved trades are to us, how many families and what multitudes of hands they employ—for these are the things which recommend any article of trade, and make a manufacture valuable to a nation. I remember some time ago I gave you a hint about the mighty alteration in the face of trade in this city; I cannot but touch it again on this occasion, because it relates to what I am upon. Let any man who remembers the glorious state of our trade about thirty or forty years past view but the streets of this opulent city and even the Exchange of London—nay, even our courts of ———.[1] It must of necessity put him in mind of Ezra 3:12, where the ancient men who had seen the old temple wept when they saw the weak foundations of the new.

However, to go on as I began and examine our new increase of commerce which we so must boast of: Let me note a little to you with what mighty advantages the chasms, gaps, and breaches of our trade are filled up of late, and let us see it, I say, in the streets. Here, in the room of a trifling banker or goldsmith, we are supplied with a most eminent brandy shop (Cheapside). There in the room of ditto you have a flaming shop for white tea pots and luted earthen mugs (Cornhill), the most excellent offspring of that most valuable manufacture of earthenware. It is impossible that coffee, tea, and chocolate can be so advanced in their consumption without an eminent increase of those trades that attend them; whence we see the most noble shops in the city taken up with the valuable utensils of the tea table. The china warehouses are little marts within themselves (and by the way, are newly become markets of clandestine trade, of which I shall say more very quickly), and the eminent corner houses in the chief streets of London are chosen out by the town tinkers to furnish us with tea kettles and chocolate pots—*vide* Catherine Street and Bedford Buildings. Two thousand pound is reckoned a small stock in copper pots and lacquered kettles, and the very fitting up one of these brazen peo-

[1] The word has been omitted in the original. I believe he intended the word "law."

ple's shops with fine sashes, &c. to set forth his ware costs above 500£ sterling, which is more by half than the best draper or mercer's shop in London requires.

This certainly shows the increase of our trade. Brass locks for our chambers and parlours, brass knockers for our doors, and the like add to the luster of those shops, of which hereafter. And the same sash works, only finer and larger, are now used to range your brass and copper, that the goldsmiths had always to set out their less valuable silver and gold plate. From hence, be pleased to look upon the druggists of the town who are the merchants of these things. Bucklers-Bury and Little Lombard Street were the places which a few years ago held the whole number, a very few excepted, of that difficult nice employment, whose number is now spread over the whole town and with the most capital stocks, whose whole employ is the furnishing us by wholesale and retail with these most valuable of all drugs, coffee, tea, and chocolate—the general furniture of a druggist's shop being now three bales of coffee, twelve boxes of chocolate, six large canisters of tea, and an hundred and fifty empty gilded boxes. In like manner the rest of the town—how gloriously is it supplied! How do pastry cooks and periwig makers, brandy shops and toy shops, succeed linen drapers, mercers, upholsterers, and the like. A hundred pounds a year rent for a house to sell jellies and apple pies; two hundred pounds to fit up a brandy shop, and afterwards not a hundred pound stock to put into it. These I can show many instances of.

Look, gentlemen, upon the particular parts of your town, formerly eminent for the best of tradesmen! View the famous churchyard of St. Paul's where so many aldermen and lord mayors have been raised by the trade of broadcloth and mere woolen manufactures, and on whose trades so many familes of poor always depended, that Sir William Turner used to say his shop alone employed 50,000 poor people! What succeeds him? A most noble, and to be sure, a much more valuable vintner's warehouse, *Anglice,* a tavern, more vulgarly a bawdy-house. And the next draper's shop, a coffee house; what takes up the whole row there? and supplies the place of eighteen or nineteen topping drapers? Who can but observe it! Cane chair makers, gilders of leather, looking-glass shops, and peddlers or toyshops—manifold improvements of trade! and an eminent instance of the growth of our manufactures! Go from hence to Holborn Bridge, a place where once was a flourishing business, and let anyone but count from thence up Snow Hill and through Newgate Street and tell me how many shops of eminent trades are now, most comfortably to the landlords, shut up there, and ready to be let at half their usual rents? It is not many months ago since I reckoned up eight and thirty empty houses in that part particularly. But of this I shall say more when I come to speak of the decay of our wholesale trade, and of the circulation of our manufactures among ourselves.

As to the face of the city of which I am now speaking, I shall conclude it with this one remark: Let any man who thinks our trade improved and increased walk through the principal streets where our trade formerly flourished, such as Cheapside, Cornhill, Leadenhall Street, Newgate Street, Fleet Street, Snow Hill, the Strand, Paul's churchyard, Paternoster Row, Grace Church Street, Cannon Street, Watling Street and such like places. And first let him reckon up all the houses which are now to be let and are actually shut up, and then let him set aside all the pastry cooks, coffee houses, periwig makers, cane chair men, looking-glass shops, tinkers, china or earthenware men, brandy shops, and the like—I mean such as deal in baubles and trifles, and whose trades used to be found only in lanes and alleys, or back streets and by-places, and are fittest for such places; I say, let him look upon all these *as shops shut up*, and *as houses empty* and to be let, as indeed they ought to be esteemed, comparing our trade to what it has been, and what a sad, tattered condition will this improving city look in?

How the town may appear now, I know not, having been out of it some time; but I'll tell you what my own observation about five months ago was, and I doubt it is but little better since, viz., that there were at that time shut up and to be let in the capital streets of London, 317 large capital shops and houses; that, of the trades above-mentioned, and such others as within my remembrance it would have been thought very odd to have seen in the high streets of the town, there were 1,322, so that we might reckon at that time 1,639 houses and shops empty and to be let, above 67 of which were between Ludgate and Temple Bar, among which I reckoned neither alehouse nor tavern that had ever been alehouse or tavern before.

These are the evidences to be drawn from the nature of things to prove the improvement and increase of our commerce. I shall inquire a little into the causes and remedies of these things in their order. I assure you, however the war may have helped forward these things, it is not the best peace in the world will remedy them, without some other measures to be taken also.

Vol. IV, No. 106 Thursday, October 16, 1707

MONEY, MONEY, MONEY[1]

O MONEY, MONEY! What an influence hast thou on all the affairs of the quarrelling, huffing part of this world, as well as upon the most plodding part of it! Without thee Parliaments may meet, and councils sit, and kings contrive, but it will all be to no purpose; their councils and conclusions can never be put in execution! Thou raisest armies, fightest battles, fittest out fleets, takest towns, kingdoms, and carriest on the great affairs of the war. All power, all policy is supported by thee; even vice and virtue act by thy assistance. By thee all the great things in the world are done; thou makest heroes, and crown'st the actions of the mighty. By thee, in one sense, kings reign, armies conquer, princes grow great, and nations flourish.

Mighty neuter! Thou great Jack-a-both-sides of the world, how has thou brought all things into bondage to thy tyranny? How art thou the mighty word of this war, the great wheel in the vast machine of politic motion, the vehicle of Providence, the great medium of conveyance in which all the physic of the secret dispensation in human affairs is administered, and by the quantity of which it operates to blessing or cursing? Well art thou called the god of this world; for in thy presence and absence consists all the heaven or hell of human affairs. For thee what will not mankind do; what hazards will they run, what vil-

[1] The first seven paragraphs have been omitted.

lainies perform? For thee kings tyrannize, subjects are oppressed, nations ruined, fathers murdered, children abandoned, friends betrayed. Thou art the charm that unlocks the cabinet, unscrews nature; for thee the traitor fawns, the parasite flatters, the profligate swears, and the hypocrite prays; for thee the virgin prostitutes, the honourable degenerates, the wise man turns fool, the honest man a knave, the friend turns traitor, the brother turns a stranger, Christians turn heathens, and mankind devils.

Thou art the test of beauty, the judge of ornament, the guide of the fancy, the index of temper, and the pole star of the affections. Thou makest homely things fair, old things young, crooked things straight; thou hast the great remedy of love, thou can'st give the blind an eye, the lame a leg, the froward a temper, and the scandalous a character. Thou makest knaves honest, whores chaste, and bullies justices of the peace. Thou creepest into all our towns, cities, corporations, courthouses, ay, and churches, too. Thou makest the difference there between the great and the small, the high and the low, and to thy charge it is justly laid why sots lead, blockheads preach, knaves govern, and elected fools make aldermen and mayors.

In the armies thou workest wonders too. There thou makest the coward fight, and the brave run away. Thou givest victory, and leadest triumphs; all the caps and feathers stand upon thy head, and thou hast the passing of all commissions. Thou makest mareschals of France, governors of provinces, and lieutenant-generals; thou makest bullies admirals, sodomites captains of men-of-war, cowards commodores, and brutes leaders of men. For thee the poor soldier strives to have his brains beat out; the officers court thee through all the paths of death and horror; for thee the generals shift hands, serve anybody, nobody, and everybody. Thou makest Christians fight for the Turks; thou hirest servants to the devil, nay, to the very Czar of Muscovy.

For thee the kings of the earth raise war, and the potsherds dash against one another. Thou art ambition, for pride is really nothing but covetousness. 'Tis for thee the mighty sell their rest, their peace, and their souls in quest of crowns and conquests. They talk sometimes of other trifles, such as liberty, religion, and I know not what; but 'tis all for thee. I never knew but two exceptions in our histories, viz.,

Gustavus Adolphus, and King William.[2] Thou art the mighty center of human action, the great rudder the world steers by, the vast hinge the globe turns on. O money, money, who can form the [thy] character!

And yet, thou necessary evil, thou hast some panegyric due to thee also, and they that rail most at thee seek thy favour. Thou assistest the injured to shake off their chains, the invaded to defend themselves, and the oppressed to regain their liberty; and thou art equally necessary to one as to the other. In thy [the] excesses and the excursions of men about thee consists all this scandal. Thou encouragest virtue, rewardest honesty; and art the reward given to man for his labour under the sun. Without thy help tyrants would never be dethroned, nor ambition restrained, nor any of the capital diseases of the world cured.

And how art thou to be obtained? How must we court thy favour? Truly, just as the rest of the world does: where thou art, we must seek thee; where thou art legally provided, thou shouldest be legally demanded; but where fraudulently, oppressively, or violently amassed, by the same violence thou art to be lawfully seized upon; such are pirates of nature, and ought to be plundered for the public good; and if their power cannot be subdued, you may doubtless use the best means you can to remove out of their possession the prisoner, MONEY.

And this brings me down to the times. Money is now the business: raising money is the affair, ways and means is the word. The answer is ready: where money is legally obtained, it must be legally obtained again. Subjects honestly labouring, honestly possessing, ought to be left quietly, enjoying what they are masters of; and this is the foundation of what we call law, liberty, and property, and the like modern words very much in use. This is the end of parliaments, constitutions, government, and obedience; and this is the true foundation of order in the world, and long may it be our privilege to maintain it. . . .

[2] Gustavus Adolphus (1594–1632) was king of Sweden from 1611 to 1632 and one of Defoe's military heroes. Defoe makes much of him in the *Review* and in his *Memoirs of a Cavalier* (1720). William III was the object of Defoe's lifelong devotion.

Vol. VI, No. 35 Thursday, June 23, 1709

REFUGEES: ENGLAND'S GOOD FORTUNE[1]

I KNOW, when the late act of Parliament for naturalizing foreign Protestants was passing, it was a common objection, and some people thought themselves witty upon the subject in saying, that all the beggars of Europe would come over hither. And now they allege, here is the experiment made, and that in time we shall drain all Germany of their poor. I shall meet with all these objections in my way as I go on without being obliged to form them again, and speak to them in distinct heads.

To examine whether this be a grievance or an advantage, it will be necessary to enquire: (1) How the increase of people is our wealth? (2) Whether an addition of poor people are really advantageous? (3) Whether England really wants people or not?

1. How the increase of people is our wealth? It is an old and often demonstrated argument, and I need say but little to it. Every labouring man is an increase to the public wealth, by how much what he gains by his labour amounts to more than he or his family eats or consumes —for every increase is an article in the credit of the general stock— and for this reason, I say, it is an addition to the public wealth to have the price of labour dear; of which hereafter.

Every labouring man, then, however poor, increases the public wealth. Nor is it enough to say that the public stock is the same; for that what A gains, B pays, and it is still all in the kingdom, both A and B being members and residents of the whole body, for still the circulation is the wealth, and everybody increases the value till the last consumer pays it. And this almost in every article of trade falls upon foreign export; but be it that it were at home, yet the profit is the same thing as it increases the value of the thing, and that increased value is an addition to our wealth. It is an advance upon the general valuation of all things among us, and let it seem to be upon

[1] The first three paragraphs have been omitted.

ourselves alone, yet it is evident, it is upon everything and must at last affect every part of trade. The domestic and the foreign depend upon one another; and let them be what they will, they give new value to every thing advanced above what it was before, and that thing so advanced will purchase any thing in the world at the advanced price I speak of, whether there be an intrinsic value or no.

I think therefore this must be plain, whatever value we can put upon our labour, which we can make our neighbours pay, must be clearly our gain. As it is in the value of labour, so is it to the quantity. If the labour of the industrious is our gain, then the more of these industrious people, the more gain—with this one proviso—that there is labour enough to employ them; and this is an inquiry by itself, in examining which I shall make no question to prove that there is no want of work in England for the inhabitants, but evidently the contrary. The increase of people is then our wealth, by the improvement upon their labour. But they are profitable another way still, and that is, as they make labour; for be they never so poor, they must eat, and be clothed, and live in houses. And this brings in the second query above mentioned.

2. Whether an addition of poor people are really advantageous? Beggary and sloth, I allow, is bringing in a disease upon us—and that is not our case; the question is, whether an addition of people be an advantage to us, though they are all poor. My answer is short, poor and industrious *are* poor, and slothful or begging are *not*.[2] Let the man that labours be never so poor, he is fed—here is a help to the employment of land for the produce of corn and cattle. He is clothed—there is the consumption of the wool, and the increase of labour; so that be the man never so poor, he is something, an increase to the consumption, to the labour, and by consequence to the wealth of the nation.

If we had 100,000 of these poor people here, be it that they wrought their own manufactures, made their own household stuff and clothes—but this is certain, they do not produce the corn they eat, or the wool they work with. This is the produce of the land, and this is clear gain

[2] No satisfactory explanation appears possible, but the Poor Laws did give some relief to the "slothful" and the "impotent" poor, while the "industrious" poor were left to care for themselves. There was a growing concern, which Defoe echoes, with a pernicious unwillingness among laborers to work more than just enough to keep themselves alive.

to the public, because some is consumed that was not consumed before. However poor these people may be, if they are but industrious, they are your gain, and must be so while you have a foot of land uncultivated or a pound of wool unwrought in the whole nation.

The last question is whether England really wants people or not? And this, I think, will be best answered by another question; is there any land in England that is not improved to the best advantage? If you improve land at all, you must have more people to do it with, or else you must prove that the lands in England are capable of no farther employment, which, I believe, nobody will pretend to. It remains to enquire in what our want of people appears, and I hope to make it clear to you all, though methinks any that have viewed the face of England might be able to satisfy themselves without my help. But one says, we want no people in our country; another says, we have a great many people in our country want employment; a Yorkshire man says, all our people run up to you in the south for want of employment; a Colchester man, or a Norwich, or a Canterbury man tells me, we have such a vast number of people with us, that if there be but a little stop upon trade they are ready to eat up one another, and the like.

Let me examine these apart. And first I must lay it down as a fundamental, whether in manufacture or husbandry, if there is any land unemployed, or any trade unattempted—it is either want of people, or want of stocks, that is the occasion of it. I am loth to put in the words *sloth* or *ignorance,* for it is manifest we do not want industry or knowledge in improvement in England, if we have either hands to do it, stock to compass it, or a prospect of advantage by doing it. Now, have we any grievance in our trade at home but what increase of people would redress? Is your produce of corn or cattle too great—though that be an absurd notion in the main—but is not remedied by the increase of people to consume it? Is the quantity of wool in Britain too great—though that is a complaint equally foolish—but it is not for want of an increase of people to wear it?

Upon a rational conjecture I may allow that every single person living at the common rate of plenty in England, especially here in the south, consumes in food two quarters of wheat, four quarters of barley, five quarters of peas or beans green, a bullock, six sheep, two calves, and a hog, and a hundred pound of butter, or cheese, or milk, in a year; besides fowls, fish, fruit, and garden-stuff. Now to examine how much land the proportion of this will employ is pretty difficult to do nicely, but I believe I shall be allowed not to exceed if I say the corn part, according to a middling crop, will take up two acres, the feeding part for the produce of the cow at least an acre, and for the flesh, at least two acres more.[3]

Now lest I should be thought to calculate extravagantly upon our food, as if all England lived as luxuriantly as we do here in the south; or as if the poor lived as plentifully as the rich (though it is manifest our poorer sort—I don't mean the miserable poor, but the working poor —live in a manner that does not lessen the consumption; for if the rich, who live in plenty, eat more flesh, beef, mutton, veal, &c., the poor again eat more milk, butter, and especially cheese; if the rich eat more pies and puddings, the poor eat more bread; if the rich drinks more wine, the poor generally drink more strong beer, and the consumption of the produce is not the less)—but to avoid all possible cavils at my calculation, which perhaps I may yet make more exact in my next, I'll take it at near half the quantity; and casting the consumption of food, and the ranks of people into a medium, I believe whoever knows the manner of our living in England one with another will allow my calculation to be modest, and rather over than under.

Vol. VI, No. 41 Thursday, July 7, 1709

WAGES, PEOPLE, PROSPERITY

I HAVE BEEN talking of the happiness of nations consisting in the increase of people, and have dwelt pretty much upon the real advantages of entertaining numbers of foreigners among us, be they Palatines [1] or others. I find your mouths full of objections, and I

[3] Defoe is here indulging in guesses in that area known then as "political arithmetic" and today more simply as economics. Sir William Petty and Sir Josiah Child were the foremost contemporary "arithmeticians."

[1] Protestant refugees from the war-torn Rhine area of Heidelberg, Mannheim, Worms, and Speir. England offered 10,000 of them refuge, but upon their arrival

could spend a great deal of time in confuting those objections; but I am sorry to say it, the difficulty is in your tempers, not in your reasons. There is a kind of native national aversion rooted among us, though we were all strangers ourselves, though a Syrian ready to perish was our father, though we came hither as refugees, *or worse,* and were nourished and fed, and this country has been a nursing mother to us. Yet we have a principle of aversion to other strangers settling among us, be it that their numbers would more completely cultivate and improve our land, increase our produce, increase our labour, and by consequence our wealth—yet we will not, because we will not. We will not have strangers settle among us, because we will not.

Some tell us it will lower the price of wages and under-rate the labour of the poor. And very learnedly they argue that this will, of course, lower the price of provisions, and that will lower the rent of lands; rent of lands falling sink the value of our general fund, lower the taxes, and by consequence our strength in war, which, it is apparent, now depends upon our wealth of money, not the number or valour of our men—and all these consequences I readily own. But on the contrary, I shall at any time make it appear that this increase of people shall raise the wages, because it shall increase the labour of the poor. I do confess I am not of the opinion of some who, to increase the export of our manufactures, would reduce their value, and consequently the labour of the manufacturer, from the general received maxim that cheapness causes consumption. And I doubt not in the process of this debate to prove that keeping up the goodness that is the true merit of our manufacture, is the true way to increase its consumption. And I must lay down a maxim or two in our manufacture in general, that perhaps everyone will not grant, but which I have a full satisfaction of the truth of—viz., that it is already sold cheaper than any nation in the world can make it. If it be said that the Dutch and the French undersell us in Spain, Italy, Turkey, &c., I answer, it is a vulgar error; all price of goods is dear or cheap in proportion to goodness, and all labour or wages for labour is dear or cheap in proportion to the rate of provisions. The Dutch and French sell a manufacture cheaper than

---

public sentiment ran high against them, principally because they threatened to take jobs away from "true-born Englishmen." After camping on Blackheath they were at last shunted to Ireland and the American colonies, particularly Pennsylvania.

we (and a manufacture that mimics or imitates ours), but neither the Dutch or French can make any part of the woolen manufacture equal in goodness to ours, lower in price than we. But this is by the way; I shall be more at large in this article hereafter.

Meantime, I insist upon this—that numbers of people among us will neither take any labour from our poor, nor sink the price of the labour of our poor—but rather the contrary. To make this clear: Pray, look into any of your neighbouring countries—nay, look into some parts of our own—and tell me if this is not a general maxim all over the world, that where there are the fewest people, there the labour of the poor is cheapest and the wages lowest. I except our European colonies in America only for evident reasons which make the difference, particularly the dependence on Europe, by whose commerce the produce of their country is taken off. But else look round you and you will find that want of numbers of people has always made a want of work for the people, and consequently want of price—for as numbers of people decrease, trade and employment will more decrease.

By the same rule, as your numbers increase, trade and employment must increase. And every number that you add, adds still some labour to be done, more than that number can do. Upon this depends the whole argument, and I think it is easy to make it out. If a million of people were to plant here they would make more labour than they could perform; this overplus of labour then must fall upon those that were here before. And this is the reason that in this very nation, as our people increased, our wages, provisions, and land have risen in value. Look back to the days of Edward III in England, you will find us then a flourishing, victorious nation—yet a fat sheep was sold at 3*s*. 4*d*., a fat ox at 20 to 30*s*., a lamb for 6*d*., and the like. And how was labour? The wages of the poor were to some 1*d*. a day; to many, less; to some few 2*d*., to artificers 3*d*. or 4*d*. per diem, which was great pay. How has this increased but just as your people have increased? With them has come trade, trade brought wealth, people improved land, and increased manufactures; this brought home money, money bettered their way of living, increased work; work increased wages, wages raised provisions, provisions increased the rent of land, and thus you grew rich just as you grew populous—and thus you may go on to be more populous and more rich, if you please.

I grant again, there are ways to plant people so among us as to make them for the present burdensome to us, and destructive to our manufactures. For example, should you take these ten thousand Palatines,[2] be they more or less, and place them at Colchester, or at Exeter, or to come nearer in Spittlefields, and there force them to get their bread by spinning, winding, &c., the common works of the manufactures, the poor people would starve themselves and the poor they came among immediately, because wanting bread, they would be obliged to work for little or nothing. But as there are in all cases ways to turn our blessings into curses, so this does not at all argue but that they may at the same time be so ordered as to be made an advantage to us; and that is what I argue for in placing them upon our unimproved lands. There every ten thousand that shall be planted in England will add to our produce, and increase the labour of the whole body, and consequently enrich us.

But now I am talking of our poor, and indeed we are filled with the clamours of our people about our poor—with the least reason, and the least project of rectification, that ever was seen in any like case in the world. I might say it is our rich poor, not our needy poor, that are the clamorous and uneasy people of this nation, and these want sundry regulations which I cannot speak to now. However, being thus entered upon the subject of our increase of people, and improving our lands, I shall lay down a few heads in which, I suppose, the general management of our people in Britain is defective, and which, if they suffered a due regulation, would open your eyes to the several advantages of commerce, and to the true methods of planting and managing not the people you have only, but all those that shall seek settlements and refuge among you. I shall only lay you down generals at present, and speak to them apart, as occasion presents.

First, the several impositions and encroachments we make upon the industrious poor[3] in the ordinary methods of trade, whether by

[2] See note 1, above.

[3] By "industrious" poor Defoe and his contemporaries meant the poor who worked, as opposed to the "slothful" and "impotent" poor who did not or could not work. Towns and cities as corporations had set up restrictions governing labor, trade, and industry which Defoe and others charged hampered growth and expansion. Thus laborers were in effect denied freedom to follow high wages by the difficulty of convincing the authorities that they would never come on the town as paupers.

corporation-tyranny, as I call it, which confines men to labour in such or such places only—a thing which requires a long series of regulation in Britain; or as by the oppressions of usury, tallymen, pawnbrokers, &c., a sort of people who, as some say, and I am apt to believe, in this very city only, gain 100,000£ yearly out of the labour and industry of the poor by horrid extortions and barbarisms, which I am very loth to rake into—such as extravagant interests, advance-money, &c. upon pawns and pledges—including a little, or rather not a little, Exchange-usury, or Lombard-Street extortion such as discounts on bills, advancing money for customs, &c. We have been told of charitable endeavours to settle funds for the easing the poor in such cases as these, and delivering them from the necessity of submitting to such extravagancies. If such endeavours are built upon a right foot, they deserve and cannot miss of encouragement, if we have really any disposition to render trade flourishing and make the poorer sort of our trading labouring people easy.

Secondly, the incredible swarm of the begging poor in South Britain, especially where there is so plentiful provision made for truly necessitous, and such strict, though ill-executed, laws to punish the vagabond mendicant poor. And here I cannot but put in a word in behalf of our North British poor, for whom no parochial provision is made, and to note that after all we can say of the poverty of Scotland, were the laws for maintenance of the poor the same in Scotland as they are here, or something like it, there would be fewer beggars there than in any part of England. But to have people beg in England, where wages for work is so dear, provisions so plentiful, established allowance to the really indigent so considerable, is a shame to our government, and declares we have the best laws the worst executed of any nation in the world.

Thirdly, the deficiency in spreading our manufactures in the most proper places of Britain, by which means the great circulation of trade, which is the health of our commerce, is obstructed, and the people drawn in unequal and ill-proportioned crowds from one part of the nation to another. This has a great many ill consequences, both on the rates of provisions, the price of wages, and indeed on the manufacture itself—but much more upon the improvement of lands and the peopling the nation. This head, when I come to treat of it in particular, will lead me to show you a little in England how much it is your concern to promote and extend trade manufactures, and a full employment to the people of Scotland—who are and ought now to be esteemed a part of yourselves,[4] and who by an increase of commerce would grow rich in produce; the rates of labour increase, for want of which their people fly from home; their lands would be improved, the rents and value rise, the price of provisions advance, and that nation soon be made as populous, and consequently as rich, as yourselves. Whether you will like to hear of this or no, I know not, nor shall I forbear to tell it you upon that apprehension.

Vol. VI, No. 42 Saturday, July 9, 1709

CIRCULATION IN TRADE, AND A SUIT OF CLOTHES[1]

WHEN WE TALK of people, and planting them in a nation,[2] we are to consider this nation as concerned in trade; trade, which is now the consequence of peopling a country. And this trade is to be considered in its full circulation, by which it employs perhaps ten times the hands which the same things produced in another manner would employ, and which circulation is the life of general commerce. 'Tis for want of this distinction that most of our vulgar errors about trade are midwifed into the world.

For example: I wear a suit of clothes. They are made of cloth, lined with shalloon, stitched with silk; the buttons are of one work, the buttonholes of another; the pockets are of leather, the waistcoat is lined with flannel, the breeches with dimity, and the like.

[4] The union of Scotland and England dates from March 6, 1707. See below, p. 153, n. 2.

[1] The first four paragraphs have been omitted.

[2] This is a continuation of Defoe's plea on behalf of the refugee Palatines.

I will make it appear that from the first principles of the clothes to my wearing them, 100 families have a part of their subsistence out of this one suit of clothes as the things are handed on in the course of trade, and as they circulate from one place to another. The farmer bred the sheep, part in Leicestershire, part in Lincolnshire, part in Kent, part in Wiltshire, &c., where, the wool being shorn, he sold it to the staplers, who carried it to London, or to Sturbridge Fair, or to Gloucestershire, for sale. Of him the clothier bought it that made the cloth, and a multitude of hands it runs through there too. The shalloon-maker dwelt in Northamptonshire, perhaps at Kettering; he bought his wool at London, had it spun in Bedforshire, dyed it at Coventry, wove it at Kettering, and it was sold three times after it was made before I bought it for the tailor. Thus again, the cotton, that occasioned manufactures here to be shipped to Jamaica, from whence it comes, then ships to carry them, factors there who exchanged them for it, ships to bring it home, merchants to do all this, factors to buy it, carriers to carry it 150 miles from London to Manchester. There it runs through ten or twelve operations, and being converted into fustians comes back again to London to line waistcoats, breeches, pockets, and such trifles—and thus of all the rest.

Now, it is true that all these things may be done in every little village in England. And a worthy member of Parliament, by name Sir H—— M——,[3] did us once the favour to propose for the settling and employing our poor people, that every parish should thus manufacture for themselves—a project, saving our respect to the author, as fatal to the being of England in trade as a plague would be to the increase of our people. For this would be nothing but reducing us to our primitive state, and making every village be a colony within itself, independent of all about it. In this case, five farmers and one of every general occupation shall feed and clothe the whole parish; and where is the thing you call trade when this is done? You would by this method leave two millions of the people we already have, without employment. The very carrying, driving, and re-carrying our goods from one part of the nation to another employs in England an incredible number of people and horses. The circulation of trade in England is the

[3] Sir Humphrey Mackworth, whose plan to develop collieries and smelters in Wales was voted fraudulent by the House of Commons in 1710. See above, p. 112.

life and being of all our home trade. By this means one man employs a thousand—and all the thousand employs him. And the wealth that rolls from hand to hand, insensibly growing as it goes, is inexpressible. There's not a suit of clothes on your back, and a dinner you eat, but has employed somebody or other, or some part of the land in every county in England. This is the event of the manufactures being extended and spread over every part of the nation, and the farther they are spread the better, and of the tradesmen living in populous cities from whence by correspondence trade is made to circulate round the nation as the blood in the body. The roads are the arteries that convey, and the manufactures, provisions, and produce of the whole flow through them to the general supply of every part.

This is the foundation of our argument. This proves that a number of people planted anywhere in England, where they may improve land that was not improved before, shall be necessarily our advantage; since everything they want but bare meat and drink, nay, and the very produce of the land they cultivate, circulates through so many hands and affects so many branches of trade that a hundred of the poorest of these Palatines, after being put in a posture but to eat their own bread, shall assist in employing a hundred thousand other people.

I cannot but reflect with some astonishment on the prepossession of our people here that will not apprehend the advantages of peopling this nation, for fear of wanting work, when 'tis so evident that by the circulation of trade every single person in this nation makes ten times more work than he can do. And all this is owing to the several branches of manufacture, the several little fountains from whence supplies of provisions come, and from whence every part of Britain helps and assists one another, corresponds and barters with one another for what they want, just as the distinct nations of the world do in the more general commerce. Norwich sends stuffs to London, and buys there all her other manufactures, as cloth from Leeds, stockings from Yorkshire, serges from Exeter, finer cloth from Wiltshire, cotton ware from Manchester, flannels from Wales, and the like, all by way of London—all these places again being employed in their other respective manufactures which universally go to London, buy their stuffs there from Norwich. And for this reason, I say, if Norwich trades with Exeter, if Exeter trades with Leeds, if Leeds trades with

Canterbury directly, and not by London, a model too much practised, it is an invasion made upon the circulation, and a lessening our trade; because the manufacture passes through the fewer hands, and the rest are left destitute of employment.

From all this it is evident that numbers of people must increase trade, because the circulation is the greater which is of itself the being of that trade. Increase of trade, all men will allow, is an increase of employment for the poor; increase of employment to the poor must be a raising of wages, rather than lowering it. Where then is the grievance of these poor people coming hither, and what do we complain of? Indeed nothing that I know of, but according to our old custom of railing at our benefactors, and despising our blessings.

Let any man go but into Scotland and he may see—and I hope that wise people will both see and rectify it—what is the reason of their want of a home trade there? but because the poor people make their own clothes, card, spin, and weave their own wool in every village; and the circulation of trade is anticipated. The wool grows, is wrought and worn in the same place, perhaps in the very same town. But if ever the poor people there are encouraged in their own manufactures, as I hope they will, and we are distracted if they are not, when they come to have work from others, and good wages, they will stick to that work and buy their own clothes in other places. Then the several shires and burghs will fall into their several works; the wool, the flax, the yarn, the cloth will pass and re-pass from place to place, and the same number of people clothed, but in the same manner and with the same expense, shall yet employ twice the hands in the work, and the trade shall increase itself by its circulation.

It might be a farther explication of this to examine from whence it comes to pass that we send so much of our produce abroad, and of the labour of our people. Those that work on the goods exported do not work on the home consumption. They must necessarily then have others at home at work for them. When Scotland shall, by improving her linen, as she may well do, employ her people so as to take off the commons from making their own woolen[s], those woolens must be made then by some who are not employed in those linens; these, when made, must be bought, bartered, carried and fetched; and all this makes trade. I speak this respecting the present state of Scotland, as I would be daily opening your eyes to the advantages you may reap by employing the poor in Scotland, and encouraging trade there—which is your debt to the Scots by promise, and to yourselves by interest—of which hereafter. . . .

Vol. VI, No. 56 Thursday, August 11, 1709

DEFOE'S PLEA FOR THE REFUGEE

I AM NOW turned beggar and am prompting you to charity to the Palatines.[1] I shall make no harangues upon the nature of charity, or the duty of charity. I see but little force in the arguments, either of philosophy or religion, to influence this generation. We are got so many degrees above both that to talk that way would be *so* out of fashion, *so* odd, *so* bizarre, *so* ungenteel, nobody would mind me. Tell this age of giving to the poor, and its being lending to the Lord, who will certainly repay it! 'Tis good divinity, but it won't do in Exchange Alley. I never found any of that stock would sell there. The fund is not good, in their language, for though the promise mentions payment of the principal debt, they say there's nothing mentioned of paying the interest, nor any time fixed for the demand. The Bank of England bears a better price there than the Bank in Heaven. One rises to 30 per cent advance, and the other is fallen to just 100 per cent discount—no buyers.

'Tis hard indeed it should be so, and it seems the only fund that is left us clear of stock-jobbing, but the reasons are plain—the stock does not rise, (1) because the value is real, not imaginary, and (2) because the seller cannot transfer, having nothing but bearskins in the case, I mean a pretense to the interest, but no real stock in the bank. I shall therefore leave the allegory; when the stock-jobbers get any

[1] Defoe further argues on behalf of the Protestant refugees from the Rhine area. See above, pp. 134 ff.

interest in Heaven, there's no doubt but they'll sell it, if they can get money by it. But at present they have nothing to do with that fund, so I have nothing more to say to them this time. But when I am moving you to charity, 'tis not with pulpit oratory, or arguments from Scripture, sense of duty, and the commands of God—your ministers have room to say enough to you on that head, and I doubt not but they do their part—but this age values themselves mightily upon their honour, the generosity of the English nation, their humanity, their compassion to the miserable, and their pity to people in distress. And this is the handle I would take hold of you by.

It has been a long and deep-rooted scandal upon our nation, I mean the south part of it, that we are surly and unhospitable to strangers—and I dare not undertake to defend you in it. The misfortune is, there is too much truth in it. But give me leave to tell you, you seem now to have an opportunity put into your hands to wipe off that reproach and to clear yourselves effectually of the charge. Here's an occasion to remove the scandal, to fill all Europe with a report of your generosity, and tell the world that the reproach Englishmen have so many ages laboured under has been a mere slander, or at least that the nation has reformed the vice and, contrary to the practice of their ancestors, are become the sanctuary and relief of the distressed foreigners. Really, gentlemen, this unhappy temper has been too visible among us—to abuse, affront, and insult strangers. And if now you should put a new spirit of courtesy and charity upon your actions, you will retrieve that reputation you lost when the Dutch that came hither to bring over your deliverer, and indeed your deliverance

Were paid, and cursed, and hurried home again.[2]

I am not for raking into our own laystall, nor exaggerating national crimes; but sure hitherto we have the worst name among the nations of Europe for behaviour to strangers, and our contempt of foreigners. It has been bad enough in former days—but the last age has clinched the charge upon us too firmly, and when any offers to deny it, I need give them no other answer but King WILLIAM. However, I am not now writing a satire; I name it only to put the thing in a method of

[2] From Defoe's poem, *The True-Born Englishman.* William III of Orange was invited by disaffected Englishmen to supplant James II. To effect this, he brought some of his own Dutch troops with him.

conviction, but now is your time to retrieve your honour. Now, gentlemen, you may secure about ten thousand witnesses [3] to testify to the ages to come, your generosity; that may prove by the force of undeniable demonstration that you are changed, and from the most surly, unhospitable people in the world, are become the kindest, most charitable, and open-handed nation in the world. Relieving these poor people, and opening your hands and hearts to them will stop the mouth of raillery and satire upon the nation; 'twill give the lie to the reproach of your being cruel and hard-hearted to strangers, and be an eternal honour to the name of Britain in the ages to come. The blessing of him that is ready to perish will come upon you; the affections of all the men of wise, honest, and pious principles will be knit to you, and you'll be a pattern to your posterity, to increase the good character you shall leave them. Shall I use another argument or two with you? And whether you will please to believe it to be of consequence or no, I know not, that is as you please; but there are thousands among us that have felt it, and may feel it, either for good or for evil in foreign parts. As you will have the memory and reputation of your usage of these poor refugees influence such of your own nation as happen to fall into misery and distresses abroad, so deal with them that are the objects of your compassion and charity at home.

And here give me leave to tell you that many an Englishman has perished abroad and been refused the relief that otherwise would have been shown them, because of the bad treatment other strangers have met with when they have fallen in distress among us. And I'll tell you two cases within my own little knowledge which ought to move you in the case before us. A ship I had some concern in myself,[4] in a violent storm comes ashore on the coast of Biscay, and stranding, the men made signals of distress to a Spanish vessel that lay at an anchor under the shore, the captain of which would not take the least notice of them—though had he manned out his boat, he might have saved the whole crew. At last, upon repeated signals, two boats from the shore went off and saved the master and five men, the rest perishing

[3] Ten thousand Palatines were offered refuge by England.

[4] For the most part, Defoe's business ventures still remain enshrouded in mystery. We are here to conclude that he had either bought a share in a trading venture, or that aboard the ship referred to were goods under his name.

before they came. The master afterwards meeting the captain of the Spanish ship, asked him why he would not afford his succour, as he might have done? The Spaniard answered with an oath that if he and all his men had swam to his ship side he would not have taken one of them up, though they had been to be drowned in his sight, and he gave this reason for it: that having been shipwrecked somewhere on the coast of England, the people, instead of saving him and his ship, came off and robbed him, tore the ship almost to pieces, and left him and his men to swim ashore for their lives, while they plundered the cargo—upon which he and his whole crew had sworn never to help an Englishman in whatever distress he should find them, whether at sea or on shore. If our cruel coast people do not believe that many an Englishman has been sacrificed abroad to the resentment of their barbarities, in the case of shipwrecks and distresses on our coast, they are very much mistaken.

On the other hand, acts of kindness done to strangers in England shall oftentimes turn to the advantage of our own people when they come abroad and fall into distresses in other countries. If, then, you will be well treated abroad, if you will be taken up when shipwrecked, if you will be clothed and fed when you may be found naked and starved abroad—as many of our people come daily into such circumstances—begin at home and show yourselves a nation of pity and compassion to miserable strangers, that others may show your distressed friends the same beneficence.

Politics: Britain's Glory and Shame

Defoe's Part in the Union of Scotland and England[1]

I have a long time dwelt on the subject of a Union;[2] I have happily seen it transacted in the kingdom of Scotland; I have seen it carried on there through innumerable oppositions, both public and private, peaceable and unpeaceable; I have seen it perfected there, and ratified, sent up to England, debated, opposed, and at last passed in both houses, and having obtained the royal assent, I have the pleasure, just while I am writing these lines, to hear the guns proclaiming the happy conjunction from Edinburgh Castle. And though it brings an unsatisfying childish custom in play, and exposes me to a vain and truly ridiculous saying in England, "as the fool thinks, &c.," yet 'tis impossible to put the lively sound of the cannon just now firing into any other note to my ear than the articulate expression of UNION, UNION. Strange power of imagination, strange incoherence of circumstances that fills the mind so with the thing that it makes even the thunder of warlike engines cry peace; and what is made to divide and destroy, speaks out the language of this glorious conjunction!

I have hardly room to introduce the various contemplations of the consequences of this mighty transaction; 'tis a sea of universal improvement, every day it discovers new mines of treasure, and when I launch out in the barque of my own imagination, I every minute discover new success, new advantages, and the approaching happiness of both kingdoms. Nor am I an idle spectator here; [3] I have told Scotland of improvements in trade, wealth, and shipping that shall accrue to them on the happy conclusion of this affair, and I am pleased doubly with this, that I am like to be one of the first men that shall give them

[1] The first paragraph has been omitted.

[2] Beginning early in December of 1705, Defoe wrote copiously in the *Review* upon the Union of Scotland and England. During 1706 (Volume III), when negotiations were under way, the Union probably got more space than any other single topic. See p. 172.

[3] As confidential agent to Speaker Robert Harley, Defoe labored in Scotland for about sixteen months during 1706 and 1707 to help swing Scots opinion in favor of the Union.

the pleasure of the experiment. I have told them of the improvement of their coal trade, and 'tis their own fault if they do not particularly engage 20 or 25 sail of ships immediately from England on that work. I have told them of the improvement of their salt, and I am now contracting for English merchants for Scots salt to the value of about ten thousand pounds per annum. I have told them of linen manufactures, and I have now above 100 poor families at work, by my procuring and direction, for the making such sorts of linen, and in such manner as never was made here before, and as no person in the trade will believe could be made here, till they see it.

This has been my employment in Scotland, and this my endeavour to do that nation service, and convince them by the practice that what I have said of the Union has more weight in it than some have endeavoured to persuade them. Those that have charged me with missions and commissions from neither they nor I know who, shall blush at their rashness, and be ashamed for reflecting on a man come hither on purpose to do them good. Have I had a hand in the Union, have I been maltreated by the tongues of the violent, threatened to be murdered, and insulted, because I have pleaded for it and pressed you to it—gentlemen, in Scotland, I refer you to Her Majesty's speech: there's my claim, and you do me too much honour to entitle me to a share in what Her Majesty says shall be their due that have done so. Hearken to the words of your sovereign: "I make no doubt but it will be remembered and spoke of hereafter to the honour of those that have been instrumental to bring it to such an happy conclusion." (QUEEN's Speech to the Parliament, March 6, 1707.)

Pray, gentlemen, have a care how you charge me with having any hand in bringing forward this matter *to such an happy conclusion,* lest you build that monument upon me which Her Majesty has foretold, and honour the man you would debase. I plead no merit, I do not raise the value of what I have done; and I know some that are gone to London to solicit the reward of what they have had no hand in—I might have said, are gone to claim the merit of what I have been the single author of—but as this has been the constant way of the world with me, so I have no repinings on that account. Nor am I pleading any other merit than that I may have it wrote on my grave that I did my duty in promoting the Union, and consequently the happiness of these nations.

I know nothing remains for me to do but to sit down pleased and thankful, though I am like to be among those who are like to enjoy the least share of the blessing by the Union. One thing, however, I must acquaint the world with, and which I am confirmed in Her Majesty's speech—I cannot quit the subject, nor go on in the history of this Union, which God willing I purpose to write,[4] till I have, as I lately promised (*Review*, No. [153] of Vol. III) undertaken to show these nations their reciprocal duty and obligation one towards another. In pursuing which, if they will not make this Union the foundation of greatness, wealth, strength, and all sorts of happiness to both kingdoms, it shall be their own inexcusable negligence, diffidence, sloth, and perverseness; and even this paper, though not like the blood of Whitney's horses [5] to a late worthy of the law, shall rise up against them, and be a standing monument and witness against their most unaccountable folly.

Vol. VI, No. 7 Tuesday, April 19, 1709

A UNITED NATIONS FOR 1709

IN MY LAST I brought my scheme of the rise and growth of exorbitant power in France to the point I designed it for; viz., to prove the necessity of reducing it. And I cannot but note here that this fetching the reason of its being so needful to pull it down from its original is the best way to come at an answer to the objections started of the possibility of making the house of Austria exorbitantly great.

[4] Published, after much delay, in 1709. Still one of the best.

[5] A reference to an incongruous figure of speech made by the "hanging judge," Sir Salathiel Lovell, in 1693, and still current in 1707. The judge, who liked to indulge himself in speeches to the condemned, declared that on Judgment Day the blood of the horses that highwayman Whitney had killed would rise up in judgment upon him.

I confess I have read and known so much of the terrible effects of Austrian exorbitance that I was not without some anxieties lest the present run upon France should blindly carry us into building that power again, which once was more formidable to the Protestant interest than ever France was, and cost a great deal more to pull it down. But when I come to examine the present state of the Austrian monarchies, and of the rest of Europe, I do acknowledge to me it appears plain that an effectual reduction of French power to its proper bounds is the best security against the future greatness of the house of Austria. For as the power, vigour, discipline, and goodness of the French troops are now in the world what they never were before, and the Spanish and Italian infantry, that were then the glory of Europe, are now entirely sunk, France reduced to a pitch of safe equality is the best trump you can play upon Spain if ever they should come to lead the game of power again in the world.

And this is the true foundation upon which the late glorious King William said to Sir William Temple, that if we were to go beyond the Treaty of the Pyrenees,[1] he should be as much a Frenchman as he was then a Spaniard. Why was it that Q[ueen] Elizabeth always aided the French and the Dutch against the Spaniard? Even for the very same reason that King William aided the Spaniard against the French. THE CHASE is exorbitant power. All the powers of Europe are the hounds; bring but France to run true, she will be the best and most stanch hound in the pack; and wherever exorbitant power comes in her way, she will run it down in view.

This brings me back to the original of this war. We do not fight against France as a kingdom, or against the King of France as a king, no, nor as a tyrant insulting the liberties of his own subjects; but we fight against France as a kingdom grown too great for her neighbours, and against the King of France as an invader of other nation's rights, and an oppressor of the common liberties of Europe. And we fight to reduce him to a condition that he may be no more dangerous to his neighbours. In short, we fight to reduce his exorbitant power; and this consists in that little understood but very popular and extensive

[1] Of November 7, 1659, whereby Spain ceded to France frontier fortresses in Flanders and Artois, and also Roussillon and Cerdagne. William here seems to have meant that further concessions would alter the political complexion of the Netherlands.

word, *a balance of power*. This balance is nothing but a keeping all the powers of Europe in such a posture, so leagued and so separated, so jointed and so disjointed, as that no one or no united interest may be able to subject the rest. To preserve this balance, 'tis as necessary France should remain a kingdom as it is necessary Spain should not be annexed to it. But take it with you also, it is as requisite that France should possess no additions of power as it is necessary she should remain a kingdom.

Now to make this out, let us examine the present state of France, view it in miniature, and compare her with her ancient state. Were France entirely stripped of all her conquests and encroachments, and bounded as she was at the Peace of Vervins, when the Meuse and Moselle was her extent on the side of Germany; when she had neither Lorraine, Barrois, or Burgundy; when Amiens was her frontier, and Dourlans belonged to Spain on the side of Picardy; when Dunkirk was Spanish, and the Sambre knew no French fortifications—yet even then she would be twice the kingdom in wealth and strength that she was in those days.

The naval power of France also is an entire acquisition of this very reign; and the improvement in military affairs such, that we have seen the French infantry, which in those days was but a very mean sort of thing, behave very well, and overmatch the Spaniards and Italians, to whom they were once so contemptible. The foreign commerce of France, and their manufactures at home, are ten times as great as then; and as their trade has increased, so has their wealth. What then is not France able to do? This makes the necessity of reducing her most evident, and is an invincible argument for carrying on this war till she is reduced, especially considering the rational prospect we have of it at this time.

This alone should cure us of all our impatience at the continuance of the war. This should prevent our being in too much haste for peace. It is true we want peace, but we do not want a truce; we do not want a peace of two or three years. We can much better carry on this war if it were seven years longer, though it would fall very heavy, than we can begin another war seven years hence. Our enemies would gain strength, and we should lose strength by such a breathing-time; the war may hurt us, but an uncertain peace to revolve into a war again would kill us. We shall be impoverished if the war continues, but we shall be ruined if it returns; therefore this war must not end but with a security that it shall not return. And this security consists in two things.

1. *In an entire reduction of the exorbitant power of France,* explained as before.

2. *In a continued cement of the Allies,* keeping alive the Confederacy; [2] so that France may never be able to take them apart, and revenge the mortification of this war upon the several branches which he cannot do when united.

This I argue from the condition of France, supposing, I say, she should come to a peace even upon our own terms. If she can find a way to terminate this alliance, she may unravel the whole work again. France, even in the condition as above, stripped of all her conquest and of all her usurpations, will yet be the greatest, the richest, and the most powerful monarchy in Europe, and no single power of Europe could hold out against her; nay, to carry it farther, not any two of the present powers of Europe could stand against her, not England and Holland, not the Swede and the Empire, not any private league would do it, nothing but a concert, a grand alliance—and it is but too evident how hard that is to be brought together. Nothing then can be a sufficient guarantee for the present peace, but the whole Confederacy, the body of powers that have now acted, being formed into a politic frame or constitution, upon which they can again act in case of an invasion upon any of the branches. Call this what you please, and let the difficulties be as great as you can propose; if this be not done, France may attempt hereafter to oppress some or other of the Confederacy, and find out new tricks to ground such invasions upon; but if a constitution be formed by which the whole Confederacy may resume and act as a body, then the peace will be always under the protection of the same power that has procured it.

Not France only, but no other power of Europe can ever encroach upon Europe's liberty; all the suggestions of Austrian greatness would die here if this Confederacy now formed are continued in a body to

[2] A coalition of Austria, some of the German states, England, Holland, Denmark, and Portugal against France, Spain, Bavaria, and Cologne.

act under such constitutions, and by such congress as may be settled. They will be an effectual security to Europe from being ever subject either to the encroachments of France, or any other prince whatever. Nay, what if I should say that it is now in the power of the present Confederacy forever to prevent any more war in Europe. It is in their power to make themselves arbiters of all the differences and disputes that ever can happen in Europe, whether between kingdom and kingdom, or between sovereign and subjects. A congress of this alliance may be made a court of appeals for all the injured and oppressed, whether they are princes or people that are or ever shall be in Europe to the end of the world. Here the petty states and princes shall be protected against the terror of their powerful neighbours; the great shall no more oppress the small, or the mighty devour the weak; this very Confederacy have at this time, and if they please may preserve to themselves, the power of banishing war out of Europe. They are able from henceforward to crush the strongest, and support the weakest.

If they send the King of Sw[ede]n notice to forbear pushing the Muscovite, and end a war that few know to what end it is continued; if they command the King of Poland to resign his crown as an usurpation, restore Poland to her liberties, and submit to a fair un-influenced election; if they demand liberty and the re-establishment of religion to the Hungarians; if they demand the Muscovite to quit the Baltic, lay down his naval improvements, and demolish the impregnable fortress of Petersburg, from whence he bids fair to be one day master of the sea on that side of the world—if these things are commanded by this body, they will not be disputed, nor indeed any just thing, by the greatest power in Europe.

What a blessed day of peace to Europe would this be! What seas of blood would this prevent in the world which the lust of tyrants has hitherto made nothing of! I might give some late instances where the powerful interposition of neighbours has prevented bloody wars and maintained peace; when nations and states, governed by their passions and prompted by their advantages, have been running headlong into confusion and destruction. Thus the English in King William's time protected the peace of the North, and held the hands of the Dane and Swede till they thought fit to submit to such terms as preserved the tranquillity of Europe. Thus the princes of the Lower Saxony formed the Treaty of Travendal [3] and prevented the ruin of the Duke of Holstein; and thus the Lüneburgers and the Prussians hold the balance now between the Imperial Commission and the city of Hamburg.

In the same manner, when this war shall end and France be brought to a condition to give Europe no more disturbance, a just constitution formed upon the foot of this Confederacy might forever answer for the peace of this part of the world. They may give laws to all the powers and states of Christendom, for they will have a superior power in their hands to enforce those laws. Perhaps this may pass for a wild thought of mine, and I confess it is new and undigested; but I refer it to the consideration of those in whose hands the power of better modelling this thought lies, whether they have not now the only opportunity that ever Providence entrusted with mankind to make sure the peace of all this part of Europe, as long as the world shall last; and if it be neglected, let them answer for it that ought to have improved it.

Vol. V, No. 62 Thursday, August 19, 1708

The War Makers [1]

O THE MISERABLE state of mankind, who on so many occasions becomes a prey and is exposed to the rapine and voracious temper of his own kind! What do nations and people suffer for the lust, and to gratify the insatiable ambition of you, O tyrants, you the destroyers of the world, the firebrands of nations, the plague

[3] Frederick IV of Denmark, disregarding a treaty of 1689, attacked the Duke of Holstein, who had married a sister of Charles XII of Sweden. Charles quickly made Frederick sue for peace, and a treaty was signed at Travendal August 5, 1700.

[1] The first three paragraphs and a section at the end have been omitted.

of your fellow-creatures? What has France and Spain to lay to the charge of the ambition and unbounded pride of usurping monarchs? What blood, what destruction, what ruin does poor Spain feel to determine that mighty insignificance—which of two boys [2] should govern them? Well might the king of France say at the news of the battle of Audenarde,[3] O Spain, what blood you cost! He should rather have said, O tyrant, O invader, what blood you spill! What seas of blood do you sacrifice to the glory of the house of Bourbon? Mighty sham! The glory of ambition, the glory of mighty robbery and rapine, the glory of unsatisfied avarice, and lust of rule—is this the glory of man to ruin and destroy his fellow creatures, and lay waste the creation? Such glory will end in destruction; and though God in His infinite wisdom may permit such monsters as these to ravage His own glorious works, and in judgment let them loose like wild beasts upon the earth, yet He always brings them down at last, and they end in stench and abhorrence. Nor can it indeed be otherwise, the very nature and being of God, who is infinitely good, is directly contrary to the wicked and ambitious projects of an exalted tyrant—an excellent and useful reflection for those who sanctify all the villainous excursions of such beasts of prey, purely upon the article of their wearing a crown, as if such monsters as these were sacred by office, and fiends incarnate grew saints by the sanction of a scepter. Hear the censure of a true satire on that subject.

> To say such kings, Lord, rule by thee,
> Is most prodigious blasphemy;
> If such kings are by God appointed,
> The Devil may be the Lord's anointed.
>
> And. Marvell

[2] Philip, grandson of Louis XIV, the Bourbon claimant, who became Philip V of Spain; and Charles, son of Emperor Leopold I, who became Emperor Charles VI. The alliance of England, the Holy Roman Empire, and the Dutch against Philip's succession to the Spanish throne precipitated the War of the Spanish Succession.

[3] At Oudenarde, near Ghent, Marlborough and Prince Eugene of Savoy defeated the French, inflicting losses of six thousand killed and wounded, and nine thousand taken prisoner. This battle established Marlborough's fame as one of the greatest generals of the age.

Vol. IV, No. 20 Thursday, March 27, 1707

A TOAST TO KING WILLIAM

IT MAY perhaps be thought by some people a digression too remote to my present pursuit of the union of nations, when I launch out too far into the crimes of a party; but if I am carried into extremes when the memory of King William is touched, I am altogether careless of making an excuse, and I acknowledge myself less master of my temper in that case than in anything I can be touched in besides. The memory of that glorious monarch is so dear, and so valuable in the hearts of all true Protestants that have a sense both of what they escaped and what they enjoy by his hand, that 'tis difficult to retain any charity for their principles that can forget the obligation. His name is a word of congratulation, and the immortal memory of King William will be a health as long as drinking healths is suffered in this part of the world.

Let the ungrateful wretch that forgets what God wrought by His hand look back upon popery coming in like a flood, property trampled under foot, all sorts of cruelties and butcheries fell in practice in Scotland, and approaching in England! Let them review the insolence of the soldiery, the inveteracy of the court party, the tyranny, perjury, and avarice of governors, and at the foot of the account let them write, *Delivered by King William*. Then let them look back on the prince, how great, how splendid, how happy, how rich, how easy, and how justly valued both by friends and enemies. He lived before in the field glorious, feared by the enemies of his country, loved by the soldiery; a vast inheritance of his own, governor of a rich state, blessed with the best of consorts, and as far as this life could give, perfectly and completely happy.

Compare this with the gaudy crown we pretend, we gave him a trifle; had there a visible scheme lay with it of all the uneasinesses, dangers, crosses, disappointments, hurries and dark prospects which that prince found with it, no wise man would have taken it up off of the dunghill, or come out of a jail to be master of it. In council how was he constantly betrayed, in treaty bought and sold, in action abandoned, in treasure disappointed, in reputation slandered, in expeditions delayed, in his trusts abused, in recommendations imposed upon, and in expectations deceived? How were the funds we furnished him with scandalously deficient, their time late, the end base, and the means ridiculous? How was he sent to war without armies, and his armies without pay? How was he continually balked and trepanned in all his measures by foolish, false, ignorant or treacherous friends, more than powerful enemies? How did he fight for us, and we rail at him? How did he waste his own patrimony in the expensive war he undertook in the defense of religion and liberty, and yet we murmur at him as if all the money had been given to himself? What ill language! What daily rudeness did he receive here from those that durst not show their faces with him or venture like him on a country that indeed he was no way in debt to?

Who can look back on these things without regret when they hear insulting devils affront the memory of a man that lived but for them, and for thirteen years lived in torture under their constant murmurs and ungrateful reproaches; that were saved by him, and then like a snake hissed at and spit in the face of their benefactor? Unhappy Englishmen! Is this the man you reproach? Had he any failing but that he bore too much with the most barbarous usage in the world? Had he not the most merit and the worst treatment that ever king in England met with?

And now to come to the particular. See, ingratitude pursues him beyond the grave, not content to have given a mortal stab to all his enjoyments. Here they are for carrying on the murder to his good name, in which I can see no flaw save that he had the misfortune to find more Judas's than one to every twelve that attended him. Is a man knighted and then made a lord, is he loaded with honours, put into places, has he the king's ear, and eats his bread? Expect this shall be one of the first that shall fly in his face. Expect this shall tell you who was not requited for their extraordinary service at Londonderry; [1] but

[1] Reverend George Walker, leader of the defense of Londonderry, Ireland, in a 105-day siege by troops of James II in the summer of 1689, was feted by London and awarded £5,000 by William III. The widows and orphans of his soldiers, at Walker's

never a word who were over-rewarded for the same occasion. Expect their own crimes at the time of his government all laid at his door, and his injured reputation making amends for the seeming loss of their own. Prodigious ingratitude! Can'st thou not, O man, be content to be advanced without merit but thou must repine at them that another time have merit without reward? To such I would recommend to consider their own value as not the least instance of the king's misfortune; how he had honest men misrepresented, and knaves mis-commended.

Who can look back on those days without horror when we consider even those that he hazarded all to defend, flying in his face because they are not sufficiently rewarded, and their fancied merit not enough taken notice of, or, in English, because he did not give them the wealth and blood of the nation, satisfy their avarice on one hand, and their revenge on the other? I am loth to bring to memory what I wish had never been true; and what to say is a satire upon the very English nation; but *Difficile est satyram non scribere.* (Juvenal, Lib. 1.)

I confess my blood boils at the thoughts of it, and I can less contain the just resentment in this than in anything before me. Who can hear men tell us they helped to make him king, and were not considered for it? You helped to make him king! Pray, what merit do you plead, and from whom was the debt? You helped to make him king, that is, you helped to save your country, and ruin him! You helped to recover your own liberties and that of your posterity, as you ought to have been blasted from Heaven if you had not; and now you claim rewards from him! I'll tell you how he rewarded you fully; he rewarded you by sacrificing his peace, his comforts, his fortunes, and his country to support you; he died a thousand times in the chagrin, vexation, and perplexity he had from the unkindness and treachery of his friends, and the numberless hazards of the field against the enemy.

And yet all would not satisfy a craving generation, an insatiable party who thought all the taxes raised for the war given not to the nation but to the king, and endeavoured to blot the best character in the world with the crimes of those they themselves recommended to him to trust. Who could read a poem called *The Foreigners* [2] written on pur-

---

petition, were voted £10,000 relief. But as to who was not "requited," I cannot determine.

[2] Written by journalist John Tutchin in 1700, this anti-King William, anti-Dutch

pose to insult his person without a just indignation; wherein not his person only, and nation, but his character and morals are insolently abused? Who can hear printed speeches reproach him with breach of faith, without just reflections on this, that he only too much favoured the wretches that abuse him? Is this a short essay? Expect, gentlemen, to be more surprised in my next, when I may give you the history, who he trusted, who betrayed him, why he employed Tories and High Flyers, and the like, for which these people abuse him; meantime accept of the following repetition of what, in the sense of these things, I told you long ago.

With what contempt will Englishmen appear,[3]
When future ages read his character?
They'll never bear to hear in time to come,
How he was lov'd abroad and scorn'd at home.
The world will scarce believe it could be true,
And vengeance must such insolence pursue:
Our nation will by all man be abhorr'd,
And WILLIAM's juster fame be so restor'd.
Posterity, when histories relate,
His glorious deeds, will ask, What giant's that!
For common virtues may men's fame advance,
But an immoderate glory turns romance.
Its real merit does itself undo,
Men talk it up so high, it can't be true;
So William's life increased by doubling fame,
Will drown his actions to preserve his name.
The annals of his conduct they'll revise,
As legends of impossibilities:
'Twill all a life of miracles appear,
Too great for him to do, or them to hear.
And if some faithful writer should set down,
With what uneasiness he wore the crown,
What thankless devil had the land possessed,
This will be more prodigious than the rest:
With indignation 'twill their minds inspire,
And raise the glory of his actions higher:

---

poem stirred Defoe to write his most famous poem, *The True-Born Englishman* (1701), a ringing celebration of England's immigrant forefathers.

[3] From Defoe's poem *The Mock Mourners* (1702).

The records of their fathers they'll deface,
And blush to think they sprung from such a race;
They'll be asham'd their ancestors to own,
And strive their fathers' follies to atone.
New monuments of gratitude they'll raise,
And crown his memory with thanks and praise.

Vol. V, No. 31 Tuesday, June 8, 1708

ELECTIONEERING, ENGLISH STYLE

WELL, GENTLEMEN, I have done with my exhortation about your choosing Tories. Your elections are near over, and if you have been mad, you must reap as you have sown; if you have done well, you will fear no envy; if you have done ill, you will deserve no pity. The issue must determine the thing. But I cannot quit this affair of elections before I take notice a little of the general behaviour of the gentry and persons of quality, in order to their election. What is become of all our comedians? Ah, Rochester, Shadwel, Otway, Oldham, where is your genius? [1] Certainly no subject ever deserved so much to be exposed; nothing can be so fruitful in banter, or deserved more to be ridiculed.

Here's a knight of the shire, and he rides round the country to get votes; and he is to be at such a town on the market day to meet with the country freeholders. Two countrymen are going to that market, and they hear the great man will be there, and they fall to talk of it as they go along. One's a grazier, and has a cow to sell, the other's a farmer, and he has a sow and pigs; and they fall to dialogue it as they go along.

Grazier. Neighbour J., what, they say Sir Thomas will be at the town today.

[1] Contemporaries of Dryden whose poetical satires (particularly those of Rochester) Defoe held in high esteem.

Farmer. What, to speak about his election I warrant ye, isn't it?

Grazier. Ay, ay, zooks, we mun all vote for him, they say, his bailie was with all the tenants t'other day, and kissed all our wives round and said my landlord sent him; but they say he shall come and kiss 'em himself before they'll speak for him, they won't take it at second hand.

Farmer. Your good wives know their landlord well enough. Was it not he that kissed Farmer M.'s wife, and put two guineas into her mouth which served to stop her mouth, and make her husband speak?

Grazier. My landlord does all he can to get in, and yet he never could get half his own tenants to vote for him.

Farmer. He's too close-fisted. He does nothing for poor folks all the time, but just when he wants to be chosen.

Grazier. Well, well, we must make him pay for it then, and he shall pay for it, if he gets my vote, for all I am his tenant. I pay him rent enough for his farm, and if he don't like it I have a little farm of my own—I cannot [can] live without him. If he comes to speak to me, I'll be very plain with 'n.

Farmer. In troth, so will I too. But what shall we say to him, will he give us any money?

Grazier. I can't tell. But if he won't, Sir William will, and he sets up against him. The Greyhound is his house, and he spends his money like a prince. I'm resolved to go there; I know his steward Jeffery.

Farmer. Nay, I'll go to them both. A body may get drink enough at both houses, and money, too, they say. I'll e'en get it of both of them as long as it is to be had.

Grazier. No, no, M., that is not fair.

Farmer. Fair! They are rogues to give money at all. If they will give their money away anybody may take it, mayn't they? I don't steal it from them.

Grazier. But they give it to get your vote, and you promise to vote for them, and you must cheat one of them.

Farmer. That's your mistake now, neighbour. For Jeffery was with me yesterday, and I am to have two guineas of his master's today, and I made him no positive promise, but put him thus: Why Mr. Jeffery, Sir William knows I won't be against him. Leave the rest to me. He pretends to understand me, and I shall promise just the same to Sir Thomas today if I can get two guineas more. And then when the day comes I'll e'en stay and home and vote for nobody, and a'nt I as good as my word?

By this part of the story gentlemen may see how they are used when they go underhand to bribe and buy voices from the country; they debauch the very morals of the people, gull and cheat themselves, see themselves bubbles to the poorest clown, and are bound to stand still, and though they know it, say nothing.

Here are two gentlemen in a town on the market day, there they take up each of them a public house; first the alehouse keeper, he bamboozles them, and charges all the ale he has in the house twice over, so much a barrel, whether 'tis drunk out or no. If his worship does not like it, he does him wrong, for he has brought in all his customers to vote for him; and Sir William sent his gentleman to him and would he but have espoused his interest he offered him all that, and ten guineas for the use of his house. Well, there's no disputing, there's 150£ to pay and there is no remedy.

Well, then here sits Sir Thomas all the market day. The rooms are all full; here's two or three butchers, there half a dozen farmers; in another a gang of such townsmen, and upstairs a parcel of their wives. Sir Thomas has his servants up and down the town, and in every gang among them, fishing for votes and drinking with them. Now he goes into this room, then to that; here a drunken butcher, gorged with his ale, spews in his worship's presence. There a clown belches in his face; here Farmer Q.'s wife huffs his steward because Sir Thomas was not civil to her—that is, spoke to her to have her husband's vote but did not put two guineas into her hand—and tells him her sons are both freeholders, and what does Sir Thomas mean? There's an old woman —she's out of humour and a going away; and what's the matter? No, nothing's the matter, but my dame goes away and won't promise the steward anything. Well, she's quite lost, and the reason is never known till it comes out among the gossips in the neighbourhood and the steward hears of it—that Sir Thomas spoke to her in the street, and did not salute her gentlewomanship, whereas he had kissed all the goodies and gammers in the upper room. This scene is at the sign of the Red Lion, Sir Thomas ——— knows where.

Shall we go over the way now to Sir William ———? He is at the Greyhound, as the farmer told us just now; and pray, friends, take it with you as you go that this farce now has the misfortune to be so true a jest that really I can hardly find in my heart to laugh at it. Sir William is a jolly, frank, open-handed gentleman, whether Whig or Tory, I don't examine—that is not to the purpose here. The lesson is to them all, and either may make use of the moral, while it would be their wisdom to let alone the fable. Coming into the Greyhound Inn at ———, you find it a large house built on all sides of a square yard, or in our common dialect, all round the square. The rooms and galleries are full of the country people, and several tables in the yard, some quite drunk, some three-quarters speed, all drinking, stinking, roaring, swearing, sleeping, spewing, &c., and all for Sir William. At a table on the right hand under a shed on the northeast corner of the wall, just by a kennel where the fox is chained (I am the more particular because perhaps Sir William may want those directions to remember it by, though one would think he should not neither)—at this table sits about half a dozen country fellows, butchers, tanners, farmers, and sike-like, drunk enough, you may be sure.

Sir William, as he visits the rooms where his freeholders are drinking, comes out into the gallery, and they spy him. Then first "Huzza!" and all upon their feet shouting "a ———, a ———!" naming his name. Sir William salutes them from the gallery, and down they sit to it again. By and by, one drunker than the rest, he calls out to Sir William that he drank his health—then there's another bow due from Sir William. "But, Sir William," says the clown aloud, "Won't you come and drink with us?" And then he wraps out a great W——ds. "Won't your worship come and drink one cup with your honest freeholders? We are all freeholders," and swears again by his Maker, and again, "All freeholders, B—— G——d, yea, Sir William, all freeholders; won't your worship drink with us?"

Well, Sir W., honest gentleman, he does not care for it; but he says, "Ay, ay, gentlemen, I'll come to you presently," and then he sends one of his stewards or agents, bids him go to them. "Who a p—— sent you to us, goodman gentleman? You are a steward, you are a slave. Bring us Sir William or the young esq[uire], d—— ye, we scorn to drink with anybody but your master, sirrah." "Well, gentlemen," says the steward, for he must not offend them, "My master will wait on you." Then another begins with two or three hiccups and belches, "Why look you, Mr. ———," to the steward, "We are all men that have something of our own, man, and if Sir W. won't drink with us, look ye sir, d'ye see, and ye won't drink wy us, that is, and if Sir William, that is, thinks himself, d'ye see, too good to drink, that is, with poor country folks, d'ye see, why then I'll tell ye, that sir, d'ye see, we'll vote none, that is, come Tom, we'll be gone." "No, pray gentlemen, pray gentlemen, my master is coming." Away he goes, and tells Sir William they are going away if his worship does not come down.

Down comes Sir William, and O then they are as joyful as drunkenness and oaths will let them be, and his worship must sit down; and could I but give you a picture now of the baronet among the boors! On one hand of him sits a butcher greasie as the master of the company, fat as a bullock of 12£ price, drunk as a drum, drivelling like a boar, foaming at mouth with a pipe in his jaws, and being in the open yard, holds it so that the wind carries the smoke directly in Sir William's face. On the other hand sits a tanner, not so fat, but twice as drunk as t'other; every now and then he lets a great fart, and first drinks his worship's health, then spews upon his stockings. A third gets up from the lower end of the table to make a leg and drink to his worship; then comes so near him to give him the flagon that, making his reeling bow, he spills some of the beer upon him, gives a great belch in his face, and so scratching his head waits till his worship must drink after him and give him the pot again. And making his leg again, a little too low, runs forward, being as the sailors call too much by the head, and oversets Sir William's chair and all and falls upon him. The rest get all up to help him up; and two or three of them dragging their brother beast off him, Sir William gets up himself, and his man is fain to help them up one after another. Well, then his worship sits, there's no getting away from them. If he offers to stir away—"What, your worship, drink with us, we'll all vote for you." Then a hiccup and an oath by their Maker, and every word interleaved with damnation and curses. Well, at last comes in the farmer we talked of with his sow and pigs. "Ho, M., M., you dog, you," cries the butcher, for belike he was a chairman, "Here, come hither! Here is Sir William ———" (I cannot foul my paper, nor your mouths, readers, with their oaths and blasphemies, but your imagination will suggest them).

"Come hither, M., you dog, come hither!" Then the tanner begins with an oath to Sir William, "That's a freeholder, an't like your worship, we'll make him vote for your worship, and he was always for Sir Thomas. We'll make him be for you. Come hither, M., you dog, won't ye drink with Sir William? Huzza, a Dottrel, a Dottrel," or a anything, that's instead of his worship's name, by the way.

Well, M. comes and makes his leg, and Sir William speaks to him for his vote. "Ha, ha, an't like your worship, I han't promised anybody yet; I am as like as another not to be against your worship, ha, ha." "And what hast got there, Goodman M.," says Sir William, "What hast brought to market?" "A sow and pigs, an't please your worship to buy them, it will do me a kindness." The butcher whispers Sir William, "Buy them, buy them, your worship shall be sure of him then." "Well," says Sir William, "buy them for me. If you give him a little more than they are worth, you understand the thing." Up gets the butcher. "Let's see them, M., what shall Sir William give you for them?" M.: "Why, I'll have three mark for them." "No, no, look you M., that is too much; but you know Sir William stands for our shire, you shall vote for him, and he shall take the sow and pigs and leave the price to us." "Well, well, I an't against him, I'll give you my word for that." So they make the bargain. The butcher come back, "Sir William, I have bought the sow and pigs, and he promises; your worship must give him three mark for them." Sir William orders the steward to pay the money; the sow and pigs are worth about half the money, the fellow promises he won't be against Sir William, but never promises to vote for him; goes away after that to Sir Thomas, gets ditto of him and keeps his word with both by voting for nobody.

I could carry this scene on to the most sordid monstrous excesses, to which I have been eyewitness; but I leave the gentlemen yoked with boors stooping to all the meanest, and vilest, and most indecent things imaginable, nay, till one of the brutes calls him to reach the chamberpot over the table to him. But this beastly doing is enough to show the gentlemen their own picture in little, when their interest guides them to seek an opportunity of getting into a Parliament house. What men that can stoop to this are fit for when they come there is a question admits of a farther enquiry.

Vol. V, Preface [April (?), 1709]

THE UNION FOREVER

THE FIFTH VOLUME having now run a full year, two reasons oblige me to put an end to it: (1) the usual bulk of the book requiring it, and (2) the request of some gentlemen in Scotland who have by own voluntary subscription encouraged the reprinting it at Edinburgh, and being to begin at this quarter have desired the volume and their subscription may go on together. It has been customary to add a preface to every volume which though placed at the beginning, is written, as this is, at the end of the work. The great variety this work has gone through gives indeed room for a large preface, but I shall reduce it to a shorter compass than usual.

The author having been in Scotland at the time of finishing the Union [1] there, the last volume and this are taken up in many parts of them with that affair. At first the novelty of the Union took up everybody's thoughts, and the town was delighted to hear of the disputed points as they went on. But novelty, the age's whore, debauching their taste, as soon as they had fed on the shell of the Union, they were satisfied, and the *Review* entering into the substance of it, they grew palled and tired, like an honest country gentleman who, hearing his minister preach most excellently upon the subject of eternal blessedness, applauded him to the skies for his first sermon. The good man, thinking it was useful as well as acceptable, or indeed thinking it would be useful because it was acceptable, went on with the subject—but the gentleman was observed to sleep all the while. It happened that a stranger coming to his house, and going to the church with him, was exceedingly taken with the admirable discourse of the minister, and praising him to the gentleman, asked him with freedom how he could sleep while he was upon such a sublime subject and handled it so admirably well? "Why truly," says he, "I was mightily pleased with

[1] The political union of Scotland and England, effected in 1707, was a cause to which Defoe devoted much time and much space in the *Review*.

it for the first sermon or two—but I hate a story that's long a-telling." And indeed, gentlemen, it is too true in practice; one reason why your ministers are no more acceptable, and their preaching no more minded, is this very thing: this story of Heaven is so long a-telling, you hate to hear of it. But that by the by.

And just thus it was with the *Review*—the people would take up the paper and read two or three lines in it and find it related to Scotland and the Union, and throw it away. "Union, Union! this fellow can talk of nothing but Union. I think he will never have done with this Union; he's grown mighty dull of late." And yet, gentlemen, give me leave to tell you, you have hardly learned to understand the Union all this while; the truth of the case is this: the story is good, but 'tis too long a-telling. You hate a long story—the palate is glutted; novelty is the food you lust after; and if the story were of Heaven you will be cloyed with the length of it.

Now, gentlemen, the author takes the liberty to tell you he knew, though distant, your general dislike, and he knew the disease of your reading appetite. And though at other times he has laboured to please you by variety and diverting subjects, yet he found this affair so necessary, so useful, and with some few good judgments so desirable, that he chose to be called dull and exhausted, he ventured the general censure of the town critics, to pursue the subject—and ventures to tell you that among those people whose opinion is past any man's contempt, these two volumes pass for the most useful of the five; and I cannot but join my assent to it.

The bookseller also gives a testimony to the truth of this by an observation particular to the trade, viz., that of these two volumes fewer have been sold in single sheets, but twice the number in volumes, of any of the former. Nor has it been without its testimony abroad, since the application of the author, in this volume especially, to the real work of uniting the hearts of these two nations who have so lately joined hands, has been received by our brethren of North Britain as so profitable, so honest, and so needful a work that they have desired the re-printing it at Edinburgh, in order to its being seen throughout Scotland, and have voluntarily subscribed a sufficient sum for the expense of it.

Unhappy to you in England is the inference I draw from hence, viz., that it seems you gentlemen in England were more solicitous to bring the Scots into a Union than you are to pursue the vital principles of that Union now it's made; I mean, union of affection and union of interests, in which alone the happiness of both kingdoms consists. I must confess, and I speak it to your reproach, the temper you showed of uniting when first you put the wheels to work to form the Union seemed to me quite different from what you show now it is done—as if your politic ends being answered, you were diligent to discover that you did not unite from any true design of general good, but for your private advantage only. Thus you seem now united to Scotland, but not one jot more united to the Scots nation. And do not call this a slander, gentlemen, for I can give you but too many instances of it, though I spare you for the present, my desire being to heal, not exasperate. But this I cannot omit, how have you permitted insolent scribblers to abuse, reproach, and insult the established Church of Scotland, slander the very nation, and insult her judicatories in print—even while the very Parliament of Britain is sitting, and yet the laws have not been executed in that behalf, nor the legislative authority been pleased to give that discouragement to it that in case of the established Church of England being so treated has frequently been done, and, I believe, would have been done.

I speak not to prompt any private man's persecution; my design is not to punish persons, but to prevent the practice. But with all humble deference to the Parliament of Britain now sitting, and whose care and concern the Church of Scotland is, and ought to be, equally with the Church of England, I crave their leave to ask this question. If the government and discipline, if the doctrine and worship, if the judicatories and authority of the Church of Scotland, which by the Union are legally established, and are the care of the whole nation to support, shall be trampled under foot, reproached, slandered, and insulted, be libelled and falsely accused in public and in print, without due resentment and legal prosecution—and at the same time the same liberty with the Church of England is not taken, or if taken, is not allowed, but censured and prosecuted—how then do the subjects of both kingdoms enjoy equal privileges? And if you do not permit the subjects of both kingdoms to enjoy equal privileges, how then is the Union made more and more effectual, as has been frequently proposed to be done in our British Parliament? I hope there is nothing bolder in this than may consist with reason, with truth, with justice, and with due respect.

I may seem by some to reflect in this on the Parliament's treating a late paper concerning the Sacramental Test [2]—but I have not my eye that way. I doubt not but when God's time is come, when Dissenters are less easy in compliance, and the Church of England charity less straitened in imposition, I doubt not, I say, but even the church herself will take that yoke off from the necks of her brethren and cast it away as too unchristian, too near a kin to persecution, and too much a prostituting the sacred to the profane, to consist either with her reputation, her interest, or her principles.

We have a great cry here, in matters of trade of late, against monopolies and exclusive companies: I wish these gentlemen who are making an exclusive company of the church, and a monopoly of religion, would remember that these things are what they themselves will one day cast off as a deformity in practice and a deviation from the great rule of original charity; but of this hereafter.

I shall end this Preface with this short remark on the work in general. The title is *A Review of the State of the British Nation.*[3] I cannot pursue this title and make the outside and the inside agree unless I always plainly animadvert upon everything on either side which appears inconsistent with you all as a *British* nation. That is, an united nation. I have been a witness to the great transaction of the Union; I know the warmth with which England pursued it; I know the difficulty with which Scotland complied with it. I acknowledge it lies upon

[2] The Test Act of 1672 required all office holders, civil or military, to take the sacrament of the Lord's Supper according to the rites of the Church of England. Variously amended, it was finally abolished in 1828. With modifications, it was in effect in the English universities until 1871.

[3] Through Volume I, Number 7, the title was, "A Weekly Review of the Affairs of France," the word "weekly" being dropped with No. 8 and the title thus modified continuing through the end of Volume II. As Professor Secord says in his Introduction to the facsimile edition, "to Defoe's contemporaries [during the War of the Spanish Succession] the affairs of France were the affairs of England" (p. xvii). "With Volume III, it became 'A Review of the State of the English Nation,' and, in Volume IV, No. 12, in recognition of the Union [of Scotland and England], 'A Review of the State of the British Nation'—the form used continuously thereafter until abbreviated to the one word 'Review' in Volume (IX)" (*ibid.*, p. xviii).

England to convince the Scots that when they opposed it they stood in their own light, and opposed their own wealth, freedom, safety, and prosperity; and this can only be done by endeavouring to assist them in trade, encourage them in improvements, support them in their just liberties, and taking off their ancient chains of bondage. And if this be omitted, you must expect to be told of it by this author as long as he has a tongue to speak, or a hand to write, whether it shall please or provoke you.

D. F.

Vol. IV, No. 101 Saturday, October 4, 1707

ENGLAND NOT IMPERIALIST [1]

I AM AT PRESENT diverted by the clamour of a sort of people that are for engrossing lands and dominions, and that cannot see through this paradox, that England may, and in great probability will, be infinite gainers by this war without adding one cubit of earth, or the smallest tittle of possession to what we already enjoy. Nay, it is the happiness of our national constitution that the accession of larger dominions will rather injure than profit us.

It is a common question among some of our people— Ay, ay, you are always getting this town and that town from the French; the emperor gets, the King of Spain gets, the Dutch get, but what does England get—what additions to Britain by all your victories? When you made peace before, we had nothing for our share in your Treaty of Partition; [2] we got nothing but the Canaries, when others got whole kingdoms.

[1] The first few sentences have been omitted.

[2] In 1698, and again in 1700, England, Holland, and France signed a Treaty of Partition whereby the disputed claimants to the Spanish throne, the dauphin of France, Archduke Charles of Austria, and the electoral prince of Bavaria shared the colonies and domain of Spain.

The French does not serve his neighbours at that price. 'Tis plain he takes more care of his subjects, and of their interest. In setting his grandson upon the throne of Spain he has given his own merchants an inlet into the trade of America, and he never fails to make room for the gain and advantage of his subjects in everything he does. The golden trade the merchants of France have made to the Spanish West Indies has been an incredible wealth to them; but what do we get by all this—we have had about seventeen years' war, and though at last we should get the better, and our enemies be brought to the necessity of begging a peace, pray, where is our share of the gain? This specious outside of a question has really a great weight in the mouths of some of our most forward gentlemen.

But here, I say, lies the happiness of England; and the glory of Britain is made evident by it, that we not only seek no accession of dominion, but if we were to possess the territories of our neighbours, it would be no addition to us. If we were now to pull France to pieces, and re-possess the duchies of Normandy and Aquitaine, the provinces of Gascogne and Poitou, as formerly we did, it would be so far from an advantage to us that it would really hurt us. The wine and brandy trade, which is now prohibited and which must then be open, for we could not bar our own subjects, would be our destruction, as to trade. If we were to possess the silver and gold of Peru, and the wealth of Mexico, the scattering our people and the bringing our manufactures to be wrought in those populous countries would make the gain of them be less to us than they are now—that is, in an open trade to Spain.

We want not the dominion of more countries than we have; we sufficiently possess a nation when we have an open and free trade to it. We know how to draw wealth from all nations if we can but trade to them; the value and bulk of our own manufactures have found the way to make themselves necessary to all the world, and they force the wealth from the best and richest countries, be they never so remote; our trading to Old Spain has been a full trade to New Spain,[3] and a trade by which England has always drawn as much money from America as Old Spain itself.

It is too long a story to enter into here; but I think I may be very

[3] Those portions of South America, Central America, and southern North America under the dominion of Spain.

free to say to you that we get more money by our trade to Old Spain, even from America, than we should do if we had a free trade to their plantations in America directly. I do not say but for a few years at the first of that trade we should, by the exceeding prices they now give, make more of it—but when the staple was fixed, and the market glutted with goods, and the country become known, they would give no more for goods there than other nations do; whereas now Spain keeping the trade prevents great gluts of goods going thither, maintains the prices to their own advantage, and we have equal benefit from the trade as if America were laid open to all the world.

I could run the same length in other countries; 'tis evident the best possession we can desire of any country in Europe, Asia, or Africa at this time is to have a free trade thither. This carries our goods to them, brings their money to us, and our subjects go and return again; if you were to have those countries for your own, your people would go and not return; their produce must flow in upon you *ad libitum*, and you would lose both your money and your people. What would the kingdom of Naples or Sicily, what the duchy of Milan, what, I say, would these kingdoms signify to us if we were by right of conquest, or by any partition, to possess them? You could have no greater trade to them than you have now, and all the rest would rather draw from you than return to you.

Upon the whole, the greatest blessing Britain can enjoy is to have peace, a quiet possession of that part of the world they do enjoy, and an open uninterrupted commerce with the rest. Give them but peace, and let them alone to make themselves rich; give them but PEACE, they must have trade. This keeps their people at home, and brings the wealth of all the world to them; they covet no share of other princes' dominions, they are abundantly happy in the possession of their own. And in this they differ from all the world, that when of other nations a man gets an estate in a foreign country, he settles there, establishes his family, and his posterity become natives of that country—he is lost to his own country. But if you speak of England, if any of her subjects grow rich abroad, whether in East or West Indies, Germany, France, Italy, or Spain, he always depends upon coming home to enjoy it. All their earthly heaven is there, and then their native climate is sure to possess their wealth, and their posterity are restored to their country.

The Spaniards go away to Mexico and Peru, the Dutch to Batavia, and the Portuguese to Brazil, where the ease, the plenty, the climate, and the convenience of living so much excel their own that they care not to return. They go home no more, and their posterity grow natives and seek no farther. Thus the Dutch, some tell us, are as populous in the East Indies as in Holland; the Portuguese as numerous in the Brazils as in Europe, and the Spaniards much more in Mexico than in Castile. But England is the true center of all her own people; the rich stay at home because they can nowhere live more deliciously, pleasantly, and agreeably than there. The poor stay at home because they can nowhere gain so much money, or get so much wages as at their own doors.

And this is the reason why there are fewer English in foreign parts than of any other nation, and fewer soldiers, and harder to be raised than in any other nation. What should they go abroad for, that live so well at home; what should make the soldier fight at 3*s.* 6*d.* a week that can work at home and get near that in a day? 'Tis poverty makes nations scatter, and want of bread drives men into the army. But England, happy in herself, seeks no living abroad, nor dominion abroad; give her peace and trade, she is the happiest, and will be the richest, and in time the most populous, nation in the world.

Vol. VIII, No. 165 Saturday, April 12, 1712

A PUN UPON PEACE MAKERS

Difficile est Satyram non scribere.
Juven. *Sat.* 1

WHAT PEN is able to refrain, when we hear our accounts from abroad, and compare them with things past, and the prospect of things to come? Our peace-jobbers at U[trech]t [1] having brought the world to gaze at them, and themselves to a full stop, what

[1] The War of the Spanish Succession (1701–1714) was formally ended for England when the Treaty of Utrecht was signed in April, 1713. Louis XIV recognized the Prot-

are they doing now? Why now scolding, and then recriminating, Billingsgate-like, takes up the time on both sides, while the plenipo's gravely meet, and part with this wise result of their weighty assemblings. U[trech]t March 27. U[trech]t April 1. U[trech]t April 3. U[trech]t April 8. U[trech]t April 12. "This day the ministers of the Allies met in conference as usual, but nothing material was offered." Again, "This day the ministers of all the powers met in a general conference, but nothing material was entered upon." Yet again, "This day was a general conference, but nothing more was offered than before," and the like.

Blessed doings is this indeed! Are the wounds of Europe to be thus healed? Will the fatal breaches of nations be stopped this way? When the Christian interest is bleeding to death, is this the haste her doctors make to stop the blood? When the Protestant interest is on fire in the world, is this the dispatch they make to quench and throw water upon it? And after all, what can be the meaning of this jargon, these new-fashioned words, plenipotentiaries, treaty, congress, negotiation, meeting-together, conference, general-conference, specific-demands, and the like? Or have these words no meaning in them? What is the meaning of sending men at an infinite charge to meet? Was it to scold and quarrel? Represent and misrepresent? Or was it to confer together in order to accommodate matters, and stop the effusion of Christian blood in Europe?

Our plenipotentiary, the Bishop of Bristol,[2] told them at the opening the congress, *they were met together in the name of God;* I fear his lordship was mistaken in some of them. I doubt some of them are met there in the name of the D[evi]l. I shall explain myself immediately. If any men are sent thither with a design to break the just measures for a good peace, to confound and distract on purpose to break off the treaty, that embarrassing the rest, the war may go on of course—such, I say, let them be who they will, *are met there in the*

estant succession and agreed to give no further aid to the Stuarts. France ceded to England Newfoundland, Nova Scotia, the Hudson's Bay territory, and St. Kitts. The treaty, in which Matthew Prior had a hand, has been considered the most important, from the standpoint of colonial development, ever signed by England.

[2] John Robinson (1650–1723), formerly ambassador to Sweden, and latterly bishop of London, was one of three plentipotentiaries representing England at the drawing up of the Treaty of Utrecht.

Devil's name to promote his interest and do his work, for he is the author of confusion, and the evil spirit in the minds of wicked men, sent out to deceive them and hurry them by pride, ambition, and greediness of possession, to shed blood, commit spoil, and promote all sorts of disorder in the world.

They that meet in the name of God, meet for peace, for He is the God of peace, of order, and of government in the world; and were these men impressed with a sense of the wounds made in the general tranquillity by this bloody destructive war, they would labor to dispose their fiery ambitious masters to abate their fury, disgorge illegal conquests, abate of devouring expectations, and bless the bleeding world with rest. Would the French plenipotentiaries look back upon their exhausted country, their impoverished paisants, their waste vineyards, decayed manufactures, broken banks, bankrupt merchants, and ruined commerce, all the effect of a tedious war; immense taxes and depopulating armies; and these all owing to the lust of an ambitious tyrant who, heaping *Pelion sur Ossa & Ossa sur Pelion,* fights against Heaven and all his neighbours to engross government and make a monopoly of all the crowns of Europe—were they sensible of these things, and what a sea of blood France has lost, what a languishing is upon her vitals, and how one blow more must be her destruction, would they trifle, swagger and hang back upon the ceremony of giving an answer in writing, or proceeding by conference?

Would the German plenipotentiaries reflect how much it has cost their Allies, for I cannot say much of their own, to push on the interest of their master; would they remember sixty-two thousand Englishmen whose bones are now monuments of the bloody contest for Spain, and but very few inches of hold gotten for it neither; would they look back into the ravaged Empire, the flourishing countries of Swabia, the Palatinate, Bavaria, Wirtembergh, and the banks of the Rhine, and see how they lie waste, destroyed by the fire and sword; would they take a view of Italy, and see how the rich duchy of Milan is reduced; how the demolished fortifications of Pignerol, Cassal, Vercielle,[3] Ivrea, Montmélian and many others of the Duke of Savoy's dominions lie as sad remains of this terrible war—would they think it just to prolong the war, if reasonable terms may be had?

[3] Wittemberg, Cassel, Vercel.

And have these men spent two months now, and not begun the treaty, not entered into one conference? Did some of them come thither with reluctance and do manage now with measures, the consequence of that reluctance apparently determined to bring it to nothing? And is this in the name of God, or in the name of the Devil? How do they lie upon the catch at one another, dodging and cutting and turning to get advantages? one side to get advantages in the treaty, and the other to get advantages against the treaty. These would treat so as to make their market of the peace; those would break up the treaty, that they might make their market of the war. And both, for aught I see, are for making their market of us. They tell us of their making peace at U[trech]t. I think they are making war at U[trech]t, and the worst sort of war too, for it is a war under the pretence of peace—getting all the world with child of a peace in hope, and then like a wretched mother teeming a spurious birth, that stifles the fruit in her own body that she may bring an abortive bastard into the world.

Is this making peace? I think a natural pun produced by two honest countrymen upon this article t'other day gives us a good notion enough of the affair. You must know two west-country men met one day at a fair near Salisbury, and having sold their sheep, and taking a pot after it, John begins with his neighbor, thus.

John. Well, neabor William, what's the news shure?

Will. Nay, John, I doon's meddle with those vurdern things, not I, What doest ask me vor news vor?

John. Why, but William, thou doest live at Amesbury and there is ale the news shure. Prethee tell me the news. Wha' do volks talk o'?

Will. Indeed John, I doon't much mind what they do zea—but they do talk hugely o' th' peace.

John. And shall us have peace doest think, William?

Will. I doon't know, indeed, but soo they do zea, the volk be met about'n I do think.

John. Nea, William, and if they met about'n, shure they will end'n, I hope. Where be they a met shure?

Will. At a great vurdern place yonder, over the zee, I can't tell the name o'en.

John. What, tis'n Youtrich, is it, William?

Will. I belive 'tis, William, 'tis zome zuch name, I do think, it is

You-trik or We-trik, or zomething like that, but shure I doon't remember, vor I doon't use these outlandish words much.

I won't trouble you with the rest of the dialogue, gentlemen; for the jest is out. The poor country pun may have more in it than we are aware of. I must confess *You-trick* and *We-trick* is all that I see in the affair. The French and the Germans are at play at shuttlecock, English money and Protestant blood is the feathered bauble that flies between them, and every stroke they give to drive it from one to t'other speaks out just like honest Amesbury Will, You-trick and We-trick.

A learned etymologist, as I was writing this, said, he would prove the sounds were both High Dutch and French and that therefore they seemed to be something more suitable to it, if not prophetic in them, and that my honest Amesbury-man had spoke more learnedly than he knew of. For, says he, the vowel *u* in the old High Dutch original should be spelt out thus, *youu*. Then, says he, the *cht* is originally *k* as appears by the original spelling the word *kirk,* or church, which was spelt in the High Dutch tongue *chirch,* but pronounced the same as *kirk,* so that Utrecht in the German language should be spelt *Youutrich* and pronounced short *You-trick.* Then for the French, says he, they transpose the letters *you* thus, *ouy,* which in the French they pronounce *we.* So that *You-trick* and *We-trick* is the very natural etymology of the word Utrecht. Now as my friend is old dog at an etymology, and these things are above my reach, having never been much learned in the science of punning, I leave them to pun-master General T—— D——,[4] to examine. But whether the derivation be just, or the pun worth noting, I begin to fear the jest of it will be too true; and that You-trick and We-trick, at least between the French and Dutch, will be the end of the matter.

[4] Probably Thomas D'Urfey (1653–1723), playwright and poetaster. Defoe, in his poem *The Pacificator* (1700), initials several characters in the scribbling world, among them "Pun Master General D——y."

Curiosa: Britain's Manners, Morals, and Wonders

Vol. VIII, No. 159 Saturday, March 29, 1712

Mr. Spectator, Mr. Review, and Mr. Milton

The inhabitants of Mecca in Arabia, whither the Mahometans go annually in pilgrimage to the tomb of their great prophet in caravans of 50,000 people together, tell us that when Adam and Eve after the Fall were turned out of Paradise by the angel of God, and that angel placed with a fiery sword at the gate to keep them from returning, Adam was so afflicted at his loss that it turned to ill humour, and he fell out with Eve, reproaching her vehemently with being the cause of his ruin, and the like. Eve was so affronted that her husband should use her ill upon that account, that she took pet, and in a sullen humour turned away from him, and wandering in her melancholy fit she knew not whither, and to be sure out of the way. Adam not perceiving, or perhaps not caring, which way she went, and not imagining she would have gone out of his sight, as soon as he missed her immediately went in search of her. But guided by the same evil fate, fancying her gone a quite different way than that she took, the more eagerly he sought her, the farther he went from her, so that they quite lost one another. They say this misfortune was of a long continuance, and that it was forty year before they found one another again; when Adam one morning, having entered on a great plain, saw his wife at a great distance from him, who wandering westward towards the sea, and frighted with the sight of a monstrous fish, came running towards the place where he was, and that here they met with a great deal of joy. This plain, they tell us, is that famous and most beautiful plain between the cities of Mecca and Medina, in Arabia, on the banks of the Red Sea, where afterwards their prophet Mahomet lived, and where (in the latter days) he lies buried.

They tell us that Eve having conceived in Paradise, and being with child before the Fall, was near her time when this disaster of losing one another happened; and being delivered of twins, a son and a daughter, they being untainted with the sin of their parents, which was committed after their conception, begot a most holy sanctified race, which

Eve left behind her in her wanderings, and from whom came by a right lineal descent their holy prophet Mahomet.

I tell this story to introduce a critical observation which I have long since made on the famous Mr. Milton, and which, reading the late *Spectators* upon that great work, occurred again to my thoughts. If anything could heighten the imagination, or move the passions and affections in the subject which Milton wrote upon, more than reading Milton himself, I should think the world beholden to the *Spectator* for his extraordinary notes upon that sublime work; but as I think all comments on that text imperfect and far from raising the rate of the work, which is above all praise, so singling out sublime parts of a poem all sublime, beauties out of a work all beauty, and bright things out of a performance all bright seems to me to do no more than if many people should meet to tell us which part *they think* or *in their fancy*, exceeds another. And were this done by any number, I question not but every period, or perhaps every line in Milton would be set down by some or other for the best.

When I have said this, I cannot be supposed to detract from Mr. Milton in offering the following doubt to the world, illustrated from the story related above, viz., *Whether Adam knew his wife Eve before the Fall?*

I do not think it so fair to propose a doubt and then attempt to solve it; I therefore wait obsequiously the favour of other judgments, and shall only suggest some farther difficulties in the solution.

1. If the affirmative be assumed, she must have conceived, for barrenness seemed not to consist with the state of perfection.

2. If she had conceived in innocence, how could it consist that the taint of original corruption should have been conveyed to that seed, conceived before nature received that wound? And this would make room for the Mahometan delusion above.

3. If Adam and Eve did not come together, then it gives room to suggest that Eve herself was that tree of knowledge to Adam, as Adam was to her, which was forbidden, and that concupiscence was the forbidden crime, which in many things seems also consistent with the text as well as with the nature of the thing.

It is plain, Mr. Milton is for the affirmative in this question, and brings in Adam relating to the angel Raphael his consummating the marriage of his new-created spouse, even the first night he found her, and that with a great deal of ceremony, in his *eighth* book, and brings in Satan viewing the happy couple sporting together in the *fourth* book, to the infinite enraging the Devil with envy and malice. The first of those relations is so exquisite that I cannot but give it for the illustrating as well as confirming what I am upon.

Adam is here represented telling Raphael what he knew of his own original, and of his first finding Eve in the morning of her creation. And after telling him that when he first spied her, she fled from him, he pursued. Says Adam:

> Seeing me she turn'd.
> I followed [her]; she what was honour knew,
> And with obsequious majesty approv'd
> My pleaded reason. To the nuptial bower
> I led her blushing like the morn: all heaven,
> And happy constellations, on that hour
> Shed their selectest influence: the Earth
> Gave sign of gratulation, and each hill;
> Joyous the birds; fresh gales and gentle airs
> Whisper'd it to the woods, and from their wings
> Flung rose, flung odours, from the spicy shrub,
> Disporting, till the amorous bird of night
> Sung spousal—and bid haste the Evening star
> On his hilltop, to light the bridal lamp.
> Thus have I told thee all my state, and brought
> My story to the sum of earthly bliss
> Which I enjoy . . .

Mr. Milton, to leave no doubt of his opinion that Adam consummated his nuptials with Eve in the state of innocence, brings in the angel reproving Adam for his rapture, and placing so much of his happiness in the embraces of his wife, as a woman; and this in a most majestic manner, as follows:

> But, if the sense of touch, whereby mankind
> Is propagated, seem such dear delight
> Beyond all other, think the same vouchsaf'd
> To cattle and each beast; which would not be
> To them made common and divulg'd, if aught
> Therein enjoy'd were worthy to subdue
> The soul of Man. . . .

All this was before the Fall. So that either Mr. Milton was quite mistaken in all this most beautiful scene drawn with a most exquisite judgment, and with a fancy like himself, or Adam consummated being barren, Eve must be supposed certainly to conceive with child in the state of innocence. And how then was that seed corrupted?

I should think the world would be exceedingly obliged to the justly approved *Spectator*, or any other capable pen, for a clear solution of this difficulty. I know my own notion of it, and I know it to be orthodox, but I am not arrogant enough to advance my opinion, till I have thus bespoke others to go before me in it; nor shall I venture my thoughts alone in a thing of such moment, and on which so many points of divinity depend.

Vol. V, No. 114 Saturday, December 18, 1708

THIEVES AND TYRANTS OF MERRY ENGLAND

I AM NOT very forward of late, gentlemen, to tell you when you do well, for you are apt enough to think you do so always; but when you push at extraordinaries, I must do you justice. And though this is a farther parenthesis to the long story of Scots persecution, and Mr. Rehearsal[1] is heaping up materials for farther detection, which shall come in their course; suffer me, gentlemen, to say a word or two about a bill depending, or ordered to be brought into the House of Commons, to prevent the plundering the ships that happen in distress to be run on shore, shipwrecked, or otherwise miscarry upon our coast.

It would make a black story, should I pretend to give you an account of the barbarous treatment poor shipwrecked people meet with

[1] The *Rehearsal* (1704–1709), edited by Charles Leslie, was first a weekly and subsequently a semiweekly paper. Tory in sentiment, it was one of the *Review*'s chief opponents.

upon the coast of England when they happen to be in distress; foreigners would hardly think we were Christians if they should hear of the usage poor men in that miserable circumstance have met with, when the country cannibals have been so far from endeavouring to save the people in distress that they have rather taken care to have no witnesses of the rapine they were ready for. How many ships that might have been saved have been torn to pieces; how many men's lives that might have been saved have been willfully let perish, I will not say murdered, no man can pretend to give an exact account of. But I could have thousands of witnesses to prove the robbery, the cruelty, the barbarity of our people upon the coast of England when ships have come on shore in distress.

Let the town of Deal tell the world how in the great storm [2] their boats went off with the utmost hazard to save the wreck and get plunder, and how they let the poor perishing wretches that were standing on Goodwin Sands stretch out their hands to them for help in vain, deluding their dying hopes, letting them see these monsters pursue a piece of a wreck and leave the tide to flow over those miserable creatures without any compassion. It is true this was their negative behaviour only, and only shews their humanity, that when the men-of-war were driven by the violence of that horrible tempest on the Goodwin Sands, and lay beating there to pieces with the waves, the poor distressed mariners got upon the sands, which at low water ebbed dry. And from the shore several hundred of them were perceived walking dry on the sands in the utmost despair, running about like people out of their wits, wringing their hands, and making all the signals of distressed wretches just launching into eternity, for they were all sure to be overwhelmed upon the return of the tide—a sight that would have moved the heart of a Mahometan, and have made men of the least humanity have run any tolerable risk to have assisted them. The mayor of the town at that time, I have been told, did all he could to encourage men to venture, and was the means of saving

[2] On November 26, 1703, there was a storm of hurricane proportions which affected the entire southern half of England. Defoe immediately compiled a volume of eye-witness accounts, *The Storm: Or, A Collection of the Most Remarkable Casualties and Disasters Which Happen'd in the Late Dreadful Tempest, both by Sea and Land*, and he published with his *Elegy on the Author of the True-born English Man* (1704) a poem entitled "An Essay on the Late Storm."

a great many of them. But how other boats roving about for prey came almost within call of the poor wretches, and put them in hopes they were designed for their relief, and then tantalizing them in the very moment of death, turned away from them to pursue their sordid advantage of plunder, is a story too sad to relate, and lies as a melancholy remembrance upon the consciences of the persons—all the poor people being washed off into another world in a few hours after.

But to come from this to positive guilt. Let us look not far from the same place—I can tell you of my own knowledge, and not a little to my loss. When a ship has come on shore in the night, and in distress, and coming gently on shore has sat upright, and the storm abating, the cargo might have been saved, and perhaps the ship got off again; when these mountain thieves have not rifled the loading only, but torn the very ship herself to pieces before help could be had, and rendered that desperate which otherwise might have been saved. And in a smaller time than one would think it possible, a whole ship has been plundered and gutted, and the goods carried up the country and irretrievably lost.

Were an honest confession to be made by our Portland cannibals, and the Isle of Wight thieves, how many men they have drowned and knocked on the head, how many they have let drown that they could have saved, I believe I do them no wrong if I should say they amount to more than the first of these islands has now alive in it. Nor is this evil without its excursion against Heaven, too, for the abominable wretches to satisfy their rapacious consciences, and flatter themselves with the lawfulness of this kind of theft, plead a property in it, and call it "God's good." Mr. Rehearsal must pardon me if the similitude of cases almost makes it natural to call it by a name he is mighty fond of, I mean DIVINE RIGHT. These sort of thieves, and those he calls monarchs, but in right speaking tyrants, happen to be in the two extremes of wickedness that mankind is capable of, both claim from the same original, and I think it is easy to prove they do it with the same authority.

God in his judgments on the world, having thought fit to correct them in kind with their own follies, suffers them to put kingdoms into the hands of land monsters that, pretending their safety and prosperity, devour them they should feed, and murder those that put themselves under their protection; destroy them that they should preserve, and suck the blood of those they should nourish at the expense of their own. These things we call tyrants, a word of abhorrence, a sort of creature all the nations in the world have in their turn expelled as noxious to society, and not fit to be suffered among men—as wild beasts to whom no fair law is given; as mad dogs that poison with their teeth, and the very saliva of their mouths or nourishment they take, infects the world with equal madness; crocodiles that delude with their tears, or rattlesnakes that jingle the world into destruction; painted death that tickles the eye, and at the same time consumes the vitals of a people.

Tyranny! A composition of all human plagues, a bundle of deaths, a weed that grows upon the verge of the bottomless pit, cultivated from Hell and planted by the Devil. TYRANNY! A medicine for nations grown wanton with God's goodness, and kicking against their Maker; a drug which well dried by the heat of ambition, pulverized in the mortar that Solomon brayed fools in, decocted with a proportioned quantity of a modern plant called SLAVERY, in about a tun of a nation's tears; boiled up to a consistency by the slow fire of oppression, and administered in a hot draught of innocent blood. 'Tis a vomit for a whole nation which, rightly taken, generally works parliamentarily, and so the kingdoms heave and cast gradually or legally; but if it be given in a little too large a quantity, it works violently, and the whole nation grows sick, and sp[ew]s; then up come tyrants, ill gotten conquests, broken laws, and such stuff; just as people bewitched vomit crooked pins, old iron, glass, and anything the Devil supplies them with.

Just thus these mountain thieves, these shore devils, when God in his judgments upon particular persons sends storms and shipwrecks, and poor men in their distress commit themselves to the rocks and shores, and to their less merciful inhabitants for protection and safety. In this condition they find to their sad surprise that where they expected their safety, they find their destruction; and the people into whose hands they fly from death, devour them without compassion. So they find death in flying from death, with this difference, that they find it from rational creatures, from whose humanity they might hope for deliverance, and die with the utmost regret. Thus plunder and rapine is their employment; the safety of the distressed, or the recovery of the estates of those whose effects are ventured upon the seas, is none of their concern, but to make their gain of other men's disasters, and make them miserable whom God has afflicted.

I assure you, gentlemen of South Britain, in the North, as poor as you pretend they are, it is not so; and we have a late instance of it, which I can give you of my own knowledge, when six Dutch East India ships came ashore in distress on the coast of Angus or about Montross. The ships are stranded, and some of them lost; but all that could be preserved of the cargoes are carefully saved by the help of the country, and the very tackle and furniture of the ships saved and laid up in storehouses, the gunpowder carried to the public magazines; the very money, which we are told amounts to 600,000 guilders, is secured, and true accounts taken of everything for the owners—and the owners honestly vested in them, upon paying a moderate salvage to the then Lord Admiral of Scotland, whose officers took care of them. The poor men at the same time were industriously assisted to save their lives, and treated with all possible humanity and charity.

This is in our northern barbarous country of Scotland, as some that know it not are fond of calling it; whereas had these poor people met with this distress on the Goodwin or Portland Beach, or indeed anywhere upon our more Christian shore, the ships had been torn to pieces, the goods rifled, the money disposed of, having no earmark, and the poor Dutchmen turned adrift to feed herrings, that they might tell no tales. In short, if the Parliament can effectually suppress this abominable, scandalous practice, so dishonourable to the whole nation, so injurious to trade, so fatal to the poor distressed seamen, and so many ways hateful to all honest men, they will do the best action that has been done within these walls since the passing the treaty of Union, or that perhaps will be done by them for a hundred years to come.

Vol. VIII, No. 23 Thursday, May 17, 1711

MR. REVIEW AS CHANTICLEER[1]

I AM no dreamer of dreams, and yet I dare not say that all dreams are to be entirely disregarded, or absolutely conclude that no man is now warned of God in a dream, as has been formerly; and I humbly pray all serious people that call themselves Christians, and that have charity to judge impartially and judgment to distinguish between things idly suggested and things seriously debated, to hear me with calmness.

I firmly believe, and have had such convincing testimonies of it that I must be a confirmed atheist if I did not, [in] a converse of spirits, I mean between those unembodied and those called soul, or incased in flesh. Whether the first act in their pre-existent state or otherwise, I think (and am thankful for it) is as needless as it is impossible to know; but that such a converse of spirits is in nature, I say I am fully satisfied; from whence else come all those private notices, strong impulses, pressings of spirit, involuntary joy, sadness, and foreboding apprehensions, and the like, *of* and *about* things immediately and really attending us, and this in the most momentous articles of our lives. That there are such things, I think I need not go about to prove; I never yet found the man or woman of any common thought but would witness to them. And I believe they are, next to the Scripture, some of the best and most undeniable evidences of a *future existence*. It would be endless to fill this paper with the testimonies learned and pious men of all ages have given to this; I could add to them a volume of my own experiences, some of them so strange as would shock your belief; though I could produce such proofs as would convince any man. I have had, perhaps, a greater variety of changes, accidents, and disasters in my short and unhappy life, than any man, at least than most men alive; yet I had never any considerable mischief or disaster attending me, but sleeping or waking I have had notice of it beforehand,

[1] The reader will be reminded of *The Apparition of Mrs. Veal* (1706). The first seven and a half paragraphs have been omitted.

and had I listened to these notices I believe might have shunned the evil. *Let no man think this a jest.* I seriously acknowledge, and I do believe, my neglects of these notices have been my great injury, and since I have ceased to neglect them I have been guided to avoid even snares laid for my life, by no other knowledge of them than by such notices and warnings. And more than that, have been guided by them to discover even the fact and the persons.

I acknowledge that the very time, persons, circumstances, &c. of such things have been in this manner discovered to me. I have living witness to produce, to whom I have told the particulars in the very moment, and who have been so affected with them as that they have pressed me to avoid the danger, to retire, to keep myself up, and the like—whose advice, if I had not as well as the notice aforesaid, entirely neglected, I believe, as I said above, I had been safe; which omitting and slighting, I went on, and have fallen into the pit exactly as described to me. And to anyone that thinks it useful I shall descend to particulars which I avoid here only as, being a private case, I think it not so material.

What profitable inferences may be drawn from every man's experiences in those things I leave out here as having not room for them—such, I mean, as may confirm the existent state of the invisible world; the certainty of futurity, and above all, the government of Providence, the prescience, omniscience, and goodness as well as being of a God, and the like. These are subjects too great for this paper, but those that can improve the hint will, I hope, accept of it.

But I bring them down to my present case, thus. If such notices, &c. by whatsoever hand, or to whatsoever purpose are given us in our personal, private, and particular cases, as I believe nobody will deny—why may not the same Providence and power permit the like notices, call them what you will, or be they given by whatsoever hand, to be given to some persons in matters public and national? History is full of these, and were I not, at the writing of this, absent from books (being now travelling and at an inn on the road) I could bring a numerous roll of quotations. But by my memory I may refer you to some. First, the famous Mr. Wishart,[2] the first glorious martyr for the Reformation in Scotland, burned in the square of the palace or castle

[2] George Wishart (1513?–1546), Scottish reformer, friend of John Knox, was burned for heresy. Foxe's *Book of Martyrs* tells his story.

at St. Andrews; the archbishop coming out into his balcony to feed his eyes with the sight of his torment, and insulting him at the time of his death—when turning to the bishop, he told him from the stake that within a certain time he should be murdered in the same place, and his naked body be cast over that very balcony in which he then stood, into the pavement, which actually and literally came to pass as he had foretold. This I refer for, to the history of that time.

Mr. Bradford,[3] martyr in Queen Mary's time, had notice of the resolutions taken for his burning, the night before, and to the very particulars of buying the chain he was to be bound with, as may be seen in Mr. Fox[e]. Another of the martyrs we read of whose name I forget, who on the rack was made entirely senseless of any pain, and dreamed, if it be reasonable to call it a dream, that a man in white with a linen cloth stood by him wiping the sweat off from his face. Mr. John Knox, Mr. Calvin, Mr. Luther, and the famous Buchanan,[4] had all of them eminent passages of this kind, and yet we do not call any of them prophets or enthusiastics. I might mention here the notices given by such hints to many people: of the destruction of Jerusalem mentioned by Josephus; the like of the fire of London particularly foretold by Mr. Withers, then a prisoner in the Tower, six or ten year before it happened; and many other.

I might descend to dreams—but I am very wary and cautious of this, because of the other extreme, into which many, even good people are apt to run. We have in the Scripture several instances of men being warned of God in a dream; I say no more to it than this: we are not told that God has been pleased to cease giving any warning to men in their dreams, nor is that Scripture taken by expositors in any sense prejudical to such a notion as this (Job 33:15, 16, 17).

In a dream, in a vision of the night, when deep sleep falleth upon men, in slumberings upon the bed;
Then he openeth the ears of men, and sealeth their instruction,
That he may withdraw man from his purpose, and hide pride from man.

[3] John Bradford (1510?–1555), Protestant martyr, whose life is described by Foxe in his *Book of Martyrs* and by John Knox, his friend and biographer. He was one of six chaplains to Charles I.

[4] George Buchanan (1506–82), Scottish reformer, instructed Queen Elizabeth and was tutor to James I. He was author of a book of unsubstantiated charges against Mary, Queen of Scots.

Mr. Poole [5] in his *Annotations* says, this is meant of the warnings God is pleased to give men to keep them from executing those evil works which possibly they purposed to do.

Job in another case expresses his disturbances in his dreams to be from God. "Thou scarest me with dreams, and terrifiest me with visions" (Job 7:14). Joseph's and Nebuchadnezzar's dreams are without objection in this case. And Daniel's words to the king of Babylon are remarkable—"Thy thoughts, O King, came into thy mind, upon thy bed, and he that revealeth secrets, maketh known unto thee what shall come to pass" (Dan. 2:29).[6] Again, Joseph was warned of God in a dream, and the angel of the Lord appeared to Joseph in a dream; Pilate's wife suffered many things in a dream, because of the sentence going to be passed on our Lord. I might look into profane history, to the dream, for such I take it to be of Brutus at Philippi, the dream of Caesar's wife, and many others.

But I refrain this, purely on account of those poor distempered people who, running into the other extreme, are always dreaming and interpreting—and even dream that they are dreaming, till they disorder their heads, and the heads of those about them, whose errors, however I pity, yet I cannot from thence reject all the warnings God is pleased to give us in the visions of the night. I wish heartily I knew how far I might go between the extremes, and to set you a rule to walk by, between overmuch and too little regarding of dreams; then I should say much more than I dare do now, being afraid I should be accessory to any of the frequent mistakes about this matter. . . .

[5] Matthew Poole (1624–79), whose *Annotations upon the Holy Bible* (1683–85) was reprinted as late as 1852.

[6] Journalist Defoe, who as a youth copied out the entire Pentateuch in shorthand (see *Review*, II, 498a), frequently quotes the King James version of the Bible almost verbatim. His inaccuracies argue a faulty memory rather than careless copying. Thus the passage from Job should read, "terrifiest me *through* visions"; the passage from Daniel 2:29 should read, "As for thee, O king, thy thoughts came into thy mind upon thy bed, what should come to pass hereafter: and he that revealeth secrets maketh known to these what shall come to pass."

Vol. VII, No. 19 Tuesday, May 9, 1710

PETTICOAT GOVERNMENT

SINCE THE LATE famous trial of Dr. Sacheverell,[1] they tell us a strange turn has been given to affairs in this nation of ups and downs, and particularly by a transmutation of customs as they affect the sexes, viz., the women lay aside their tea and chocolate, leave off visiting after dinner, and forming themselves into cabals, turn privy-counsellors and settle the state. The men leave off smoking tobacco, learn plain-work, and to knit knots, play at push pin, *Anglice* picket; and leave the more weighty affairs of the nation to the newly assuming sex, whose business it is, they say (under a petticoat government, as they call it) more now than usual.

Pursuant to this mighty change, Madam the Countess of —— keeps her levees every day, and gives audience in state; my Lady L—— has her offices of several kinds for intelligence and correspondence. And every lady of quality has her head more particularly full of business than usual. Nay, some of the ladies talk of keeping female secretaries; and there is a sad cry already among the waiting-women; since none will be now fit to be entertained by a lady of quality, for her woman, but such as can speak French, Dutch, and, which is worse,

[1] On November 5, 1709, Guy Fawkes Day, in commemoration of the Gunpowder Plot against the life of James I in 1605, Henry Sacheverell, D.D. (1674?–1724) preached a sermon at St. Paul's which set England in an uproar. The sermon, which was printed ostensibly at the suggestion of the lord mayor, was entitled "The Perils of False Brethren." It plumped for passive obedience, an outmoded doctrine dear to the hearts of the extreme Tories; it warned against members of the dissenting sects in government, and denounced religious toleration toward dissenters. Since this latter was a slur upon Queen Anne's avowed policy of toleration, the Whig government felt obliged to prosecute for seditious libel. Tried before the House of Commons in February and March of 1710, Sacheverell was found guilty and was forbidden to preach for three years. The mob, reputedly urged on by Tory provocateurs and Tory money, championed Sacheverell, and demonstrated their indignation by raiding and pillaging dissenting meeting houses and homes. The Whig government was subsequently overthrown. Defoe had earlier suffered at the hands of Sacheverell, for his *The Shortest Way With the Dissenters* (1702) was in part a reply to a sermon by Sacheverell.

LATIN. Nay, my Lady G—— they say, talked publicly of turning away Mrs. Busye, that had been her woman this twenty year, because she did not understand High Dutch.

The head-dressers and mantua makers have already felt the fatal consequence of this great alteration; trade sinks, and general commerce feels the mighty convulsion; furbelow scarfs, mercy upon us! are quite lost upon it; the ribbon weavers are undone; the ladies have left off their knots, lower their high heads, look all like Quakers. All the thing called gallantry and gaiety is laid aside; nobody dresses, nobody drinks chocolate—business, the weighty thing called business, engrosses the sex; matters of government and affairs of state are become the province of the ladies, and no wonder if they are too much engaged to concern themselves about the common impertinences of life. Indeed, they have hardly leisure to live, little time to eat and sleep, and none at all to say their prayers.

Turn but your eye to the park: the ladies are not there as usual, the church is thinner than ever, for it is the mode for privy councils, you know, to meet on Sundays. The very playhouse feels the effects of it, and the great Betterton [2] died a beggar on this account. Nay, the *Tatler*, the immortal *Tatler*, the great Esq. Bickerstaff [3] himself, was fain to leave off talking to the ladies all the while of the Dr.'s trial, and turn his sagacious pen to the dark subject of death and the next world—though he has not yet decided the ancient debate whether Pluto's regions were in point of government a kingdom or a commonwealth.

All the fine walks and retreats which used to be crowded with ladies to shew the glory of England, fine faces, and fine clothes—behold the metamorphosis.

> *Parkai, Templi, Lincolnii atq;* Grays Innis
> *Cum Greenwalks, whoribus jiltaribusq; plena*

(N.B. The author says you must not be too strict with him, in point of quantity; and if you use him kindly, he may bestow some more on you.)

[2] Thomas Betterton (1635–1710) was an actor and manager in the Duke's Company, where he played leading roles until 1695, when he became a salaried actor in the new Haymarket theater built for him and his company.

[3] Isaac Bickerstaff, a name Swift used in pillorying Partridge the almanac maker. Steele borrowed it as the pen name of the author of the *Tatler*.

Mob, rabble, and tumult possesses the streets; whores, pimps, and cullies, the walks; the dressing, the powdering, the *beau monde*, and the impertinence is adjourned to the chocolate houses, and is all among the men; the ladies are otherwise engaged; even the little boys and girls talk politics. Little Miss has Dr. Sacheverell's picture put into her prayer book, that God and the Dr. may take her up in the morning, before she has her breakfast. And all manner of discourse among the women runs now upon state affairs, war, and government; tattling nonsense and slander is transposed to the males, and adjourned from the toilette to the coffee houses and groom porters.

This being the general state of the nation, you must no more wonder, that our wiser statesmen, and able ministry, totter in their high posts, and you are every day alarmed with changes at court. My Lady M—— and my Lady the Countess of —— in their everyday cabinet counsels, do they not settle, resettle, and unsettle the state? How do their female secretaries fly up and down to every corner of the town, nay even into the city—where it has been observed for some time that more chairs come into the inside of the walls than have done for some ages past. Nay, it has been [a] matter of family jealousy, as well as state jealousy, that such and such great men, and great magistrates, whether l——d m——rs or sh——ffs, al——n or dep——ties, p——rs or com——ners, authors do not yet agree about it, are usually visited by women, and strange she-faces from the other end of the town crowd about them. This I doubt will in time oblige them all to bring their wives into the secret too, *and then ye know all;* it will be safe kept, silence being the great peculiar talent of the city ladies.

But what at last shall we say is the end of all this; and why is it observed, may the inquisitive part of our readers say? Why really, gentlemen, there are a great many useful observations, which I shall take the liberty to make from the premises, besides what may follow of course to every reader.

First, I observe that this new invasion of the politicians' province is an eminent demonstration of the sympathetic influence of the clergy upon the sex, and the near affinity between the gown and the petticoat; since all the errors of our present or past administrators, all the breaches made upon our politics, and all the mistakes of our ministry, in past times, could never embark the ladies, till you fell upon the clergy. But as soon as you pinch the parson, he holds out his hands to the ladies for their assistance, and they appear as one woman in his defense.

Secondly, I observe that tyranny in government, and non-resistance in subjects, are doctrines more natural, more taking, and more suitable to the women, than the men. And this is manifest by several considerations, viz., first, that they are most apt to tyrannize themselves; and, secondly, feel less of the mischiefs of tyranny when it falls, than the men. I am not making comparisons, nor speaking of family tyranny; I do not know but some female government there might do us good; but I speak of the propensities of nature, and the temper of the sexes—and give this as a reason why the ladies are better pleased with the doctrines of passive obedience, and non-resistance, than the men. It would be too invidious to rummage history for female tyrants. But it may be illustrated from the surprising joy this nation appears in under a female reign so entirely free from tyranny, even in inclination, as well as practice, that it amazes the world, and adds to the wonder, when we examine the mighty celebrated history of Queen Elizabeth, who though compared to former times, she was a mild, and merciful queen, yet compared to her present Majesty was an arbitrary and unmerciful tyrant. . . .

Vol. VIII, No. 90 Saturday, October 20, 1711

A Digression upon Witches

THE AFFAIR I am upon of the public news, treaties of peace, proposals, and preliminaries, are like to take me up a great deal of time; but as I know you love some little intervals in all things of length, I have ventured to make this paper a digression about witches and witchcraft, and shall return to the subject again. It is not so much for any weight in the question before me that I enter upon a decision of this kind of doubt, or from the importunity of the sender, from whom I have several letters too long to insert here, and whose aim in it I do not foresee; as it is from the atheistical use which many people make of this difficulty, and which it is evident they wish should be a difficulty, by the pains they take to make it so.

The question is, whether there is any such thing as a witch?

The letter which the inquirer has sent me on this head, I published before (*Review*, No. 83) and need not repeat it here, it being too long for this paper and not useful in the repetition, farther than to tell you that the author desires my opinion against La Hontan, Webster, and others who ridicule the world for believing witchcraft, or that there was any such thing as a witch in nature.

It is true that it would be a very odd thing that our laws should empower the judges to condemn, and the civil magistrates to put people to death, for witchcraft, if there were no such thing in the world; and that, therefore, if it were really a doubt, it would be necessary to bring that difficulty to a sudden solution. The author has put me upon enquiring into the arguments on either side, between Glanvil, Webster, La Hontan,[1] and others, who object, answer, and reply, *ad infinitum*, about this matter; and one tells me with assurance enough that none but our Europeans are so weak as to believe anything about it. But throwing all these authors by, as reasoning against foundations and principles, confuting demonstrations, and the like, which is a part of logic I never was taught, I must cut the question short, thus.

1. What is understood by a WITCH?
2. What has the Scripture in it, towards the proof of witchcraft?
3. What demonstrations are there of the thing, in common experience?

(1) For it is most necessary to understand and explain the term, before we can begin to argue upon it—what is understood by a witch? All the commentators that I have read upon the word, as used in Scripture, agree: that it is one in covenant with the Devil, and uses his help to deceive or hurts others. See *Poole's Annot*[*ations*] *on Levit-*

[1] All three expressed themselves as not believing in witchcraft. Joseph Glanvill (1636–80) in *Some Philosophical Considerations Touching the Being of Witches and Witchcraft* (1666); John Webster (1610–82) in *Displaying of Supposed Witchcraft* (1677); and Louis Armand, Baron de Lahontan, (1666–c.1715) in *New Voyages to North America* (1703), the Appendix to which, "Voyages to Portugal and Denmark," Letter V, carries a strong attack upon a belief in witches and wizards.

[*icus*] *18, v. 10.*[2] I should think it were very absurd to ask me if there were ever any such, after God, in His original institutes to the children of Israel, by His prophet Moses, had told them expressly in that text, v. 10, "There shall not be found among you, &c. an enchanter, or a witch, or a charmer, or a consulter with familiar spirits, or a wizard, or a necromancer." See what follows, v. 12. "For all that do these things are an abomination to the Lord, and because of these abominations, the Lord thy God doth drive them out from before thee." Again, Levit. 19: 31. "Regard not them that have familiar spirits."

Does not this undeniably prove, 1st, *that such are;* because, such that are so, "are an abomination to the Lord"? Would God have expressed His abhorrence and detestation of such if there were not, or could not be, any such thing in the world? (2) That there were such among the Canaanites; for because they were such, the Lord had driven them out before the children of Israel. But I think we have a farther and undoubted testimony of the fact which puts this case yet farther out of dispute, viz., in the case of Menasseh, King of Judah; of whom, reckoning up his abominable crimes, it is said thus: "Also he used enchantments, and used WITCHCRAFT, and deals with a familiar spirit, and with WIZARDS." (2 Chron. 33:6.)

Will any man after this ask us if there is any such thing as a witch in the world? I think the question must first, of course, set aside all Scripture testimony; and this tends to abundant atheism, which is the true reason why I mention these things, which none but those who can invalidate Scripture and divine authority will dispute. But as such are daily to be found who, ridiculing all the accounts of things in the Holy Bible, take this for no argument; therefore I do not go on to New Testament evidence, such as to Simon the sorcerer, and to other evidences of that kind; but God is not without His testimony from the mouths of those who have been convicted of witchcraft in all ages, and have confessed that they have had a familiar, or personal converse with the Devil, with whom they have entered into hellish compacts, covenants, and combinations, for the hurt and delusion of themselves and their fellow creatures. And these I take to be good evidences against the Devil in this case; it would be endless to enu-

[2] Matthew Poole (1624–1679) compiled a learned collection of annotations on the Bible.

merate these, and bring instances; but the records of justice are full of instances in all nations of the truth of this, particularly in England, New England, and in Scotland; and this, I reckon, amounts to demonstration, as far as we are able to obtain demonstrations of so dark a matter. For the confessions of many of these wretched creatures have amounted to giving evidence against others, and to bringing such particulars as they have not only convinced the hearers, but the persons themselves, nay, even the Devil himself has been obliged to give his concession and acknowledge the fact.

It would fill this paper full of a vast variety of stories to amuse and amaze the reader to go on to particulars in this case, but as I am only inquiring into the general, it is not the business of this paper; it is enough that there is abundant testimony, both from Scripture and from criminal process of the truth, of it: that there are and ever have been such people in the world who converse familiarly with the Devil, enter into compact with him, and receive powers from him, both to hurt and deceive, and these have been in all ages called witches; And it is these that our law and God's law condemned as such; and I think there can be no more debate of the matter.

Vol. I, No. 85 — Tuesday, December 26, 1704

ON THE REFORMATION OF MANNERS

THE DIGRESSION of the last two *Reviews* had ended with them, had not some new advocates appeared to vindicate our workhouses as useful steps to our reformation of manners, by being houses of correction and punishment to strollers, rogues, whores, and all sorts of vagrants. I would be very forward to yield up any point in their favour, and shall, I hope, never be guilty of saying anything to dishonour or discourage the needful work of reformation of manners. But it has been long in vain that I have been an impertinent fellow in preaching this doctrine, viz.:

For shame your reformation clubs give o'er,
And jest with men, and jest with Heaven no more:
But if you would avenging Heaven appease,
Avert his plagues, and heal the vile disease:
Impending ruin avoid, and calm the fates,
Ye hypocrites, reform your magistrates.

Reform. of Man., a Satire, p. 42 [1]

The punishing vices in the poor which are daily practised by the rich, seems to me to be setting our constitution with the wrong end upward, and making men criminals because they want money. 'Tis now eight years since I first had the misfortune to anger my masters the magistrates by writing a little book, called *The Poor Man's Plea*,[2] against all proclamations, or acts of Parliament for reformation, wherein the honest poor man protests against being set in the stocks by a drunken justice; or fined for swearing by a magistrates with a "G——d d——n him, let the dog pay for it!" Nay, and though an honest, learned, and judicious clergyman was pleased to do that book more honour than its author deserved, by taking it into the pulpit with him, 'tis plain he has been censured for the sermon and is hated to this day by all the leading men of the parish of St. J——, not far from the city of London. And yet I must still take the liberty against the rule of authors, to quote myself, and say to our gentlemen of justice and correction:

Our modes of vice from high examples came,
And 'tis example only, must reclaim.
You'll eas'ly check the vices of the town,
When e'er you please but to suppress your own: [3]

From hence, I confess, I have long ago left off complaining of the profaneness and immoralities of our people, and the lewdness, drunkenness, and ill language of our streets; and if ever I meddle with our vices, I place it chiefly on those who practice it in the very chair and bench of authority where they have (heavens regard their impudence) not stuck to punish with one hand the crimes they commit with the other. For this I am ill treated by the guilty, or their friends, as a

[1] *Reformation of Manners*, a long poem written by Defoe in 1702.

[2] *The Poor Man's Plea for a Reformation of Manners, and Suppressing Immorality in the Nation* (1698). Defoe is in error about the number of years elapsed.

[3] He incorrectly quotes from *Reformation of Manners.*

reproacher of magistrates, a reviler of the rulers of the people, and a meddler with what is not my business; and a certain noble person descended so much below the honour of his quality, as well as office, as to tell me in defense of these things, that if I saw a man lie with another man's wife, in the middle of the street, I had no right to publish the scandal, nor, unless I was a magistrate, to meddle with the matter. Had his lordship told me, if I saw my neighbor's house on fire, I had no right to cry out, because it would raise a tumult, I might have given credit to it, but to the other I can never agree.

Every man who is subject to the law, and punishable by it, has a right in the execution of the law upon all offenders equally with himself; and if one is punished for a crime and another goes free, the first man is injured because he has not equal justice with his neighbors. Again, I have a right of complaint when any offender is not brought to justice, because it is an encouragement to the offence, and I may one time or other find the effect of it. But to avoid these reasons, the reproach to justice, the scandal to the nation, the encouragement to vice by example, is what we are all concerned in; and I am, and ever shall be, concerned to hear us talk of reformation when those who should reform us practice all the crimes they ought to punish.

What a noise has a poor author about him if he tells a story of a drunken justice! All the drunken justices in the town, and Lord, how many are they! think themselves concerned if a poor author tells of a magistrate bound over to the peace for fighting, throwing brickbats and the like, and fined for swearing; all the fighting, swearing justices that stand bound over to the peace, of whom our records can easily tell the number, are abusing me for calling it to mind. What had I to do, say they, with swearing mayors, drunken aldermen, and justices keeping the peace? Why, that's true, gentlemen, but then pray don't talk of reformation societies that can't bear a sermon because 'twas preached in plain English. Talk no more of well governed cities with aldermen, and great folks in 'em, amongst whom are crimes black as the robes they wear; whose feasts are debauches and drunkenness; whose houses are filled with all manner of excesses; their heads with wine, in their hands is bribery and oppression, and their mouths are full of cursings and blasphemy.

Shall fear of the powerful injury of man stop the just exclamation of my pen at the flagrant abuses of the nation's laws! May these writers be forever d——d to silence who seeing the laws broke, good manners invaded, justice abused, the innocent punished, and the guilty sit in the chair of authority, [yet] are afraid to let the world know who is the villain, that the honest man may be distinguished. I am charged with promoting scandal, say some of my friends and well-wishers; I boldly affirm I never charged person, party, members, or body of high or low quality, or degree, with one fact, either obliquely or directly, which I was not able to bring untainted undeniable testimony to the truth of, and by God's grace I never will. If I am imposed upon in any particular relation, I'll do effectual justice to any injured person, of which I shall soon give the world a satisfactory example. From hence I say also, our Scan. Club [4] stories, though they have some mirth in 'em, have all their morals; and this serious sad reflection goes with most of them, that as to vices of every kind, *the Lord have mercy upon the magistrates and clergy of this nation.*

On this score, fewer houses of correction would serve if none of the poor are to be punished till the magistrates and rich people are reformed. Bridewell and New Prison was large enough before, and the usefulness of another house of correction, in Bishopgate Street, remains to be proved.

Vol. III, No. 16 — Tuesday, February 5, 1706

MR. REVIEW DEFENDS THE QUAKERS [1]

I AM NOW called off from my subject upon a new and very unaccountable occasion, in which I must crave leave to be particular. The matter is really very insignificant in itself, but circumstantially considered is not so.

[4] The Scandalous Club, that department of the *Review* dealing with light subjects and answering readers' queries.

[1] From Miscellanea, a section following the main body of the *Review.* Originally

I have often complained of the injury done me by pirate printers in abridging, corrupting, and reprinting, in a less volume and smaller character, everything I write; and, tired with expectation of redress, I had given over the complaint. But I am now dealt with another way, viz., by mobbing me and printing things in my name which I had no concern in. Crying them about [the] street as mine, and in my name; nay, and at last are come to that height of injury as to print my name to every scandalous trifle.

And yet I had took no notice of this had I not once happened to see two gentlemen of quality, strangers to me, run away with the mistake, buy the papers, and read the nauseous ribaldry of a half-penny pirate, as mine. I thought I had no need to tell the world what are and are not my writing; since some would be thought so knowing they pretend they could swear to the style, especially when 'tis to my disadvantage. But above all, I was in hopes I need not defend myself against these single sheets and half-sheets daily cried about the streets, from whence I entreat my friends to observe once for all that whenever they meet with a sheet, or half-sheet, a penny or half-penny paper, sold or cried about streets, they would conclude they are none of mine. I never write penny papers, this excepted; nor ever shall, unless my name is publicly set to them; and I hope this will clear me of the scandal, though it cannot fortify me against the damage.

But I am not only abused in matters of copy, but in subject also, by a person wholly a stranger, who takes the liberty, first, to charge me falsely; and secondly, to personate me, speaking ridiculously, the better to confirm what he pretends to advance, which I take to be one of the worst sorts of forgery. The case is, in short, thus. In *Review*, No. 121, Decemb[er] 13, having occasion to mention the Quakers among the several sorts of Dissenters, I concluded thus: "That I hoped they were all Christians, for I am not so narrow in my charity as not to think the Quakers to be Christians, and many of them better Christians too, than those that pretend to condemn them."

---

headed "Advice from the Scandalous Club," the department was for the first two volumes of the *Review* devoted to lighter subject matter (see above, p. 7); Miscellanea "is graver than the Advice; usually it was only an occasion for changing the subject and introducing a second essay" (A. W. Secord, Introduction to the facsimile edition of Defoe's *Review*, I, xviii).

Upon this note of mine published without any ill design, I am fallen upon by a certain man of volumes, for it seems he has written many, in a penny book entitled *The Quakers Catechism*, to which as a shoeing horn to draw in the people to buy it, is added in the title, *The Shortest Way with Daniel Defoe*, a true printer's cheat, an amusement, that when people were expecting great things, and some new proposal what was to be done with this man, that so many want to be rid of, when they come to look in the book it contained nothing but a long rhapsody of Billingsgate, and raillery against the Quakers, which he must have a great talent of self-denial that can bear the reading of; and at the end a loud challenge upon the poor *Review* for saying he hoped the Quakers were Christians, which he offers at a conference to prove; desiring me to get a deputation from the Quakers to come and meet him and hear him prove this negative.

Indeed this author, whose name it seems is Mr. Bugg, had been answered with silence, the general return I give to such rudenesses, had I not thought it necessary a little to clear up my charity and show the grounds I had for it, which I think every man bound to do; and this not so much for the satisfaction of Mr. Bugg, who, I am informed, may be much sooner confuted than silenced, as for vindicating that true Christian spirit of charity and largeness of principle which I think the laws of God and man oblige me to.

It must not be expected that I shall undertake here to examine or vindicate the principles of the Quakers, when at the same time I do not profess them, nor shall I enter into any of this author's elaborate scandals, who, like Satan, brings a railing accusation. Let him go on with his large folio which he says he is printing; I dare say nobody will give themselves the trouble to reply to him, and not many to read him, who will find it very difficult, as I am told, to print anything he has not printed before, and been answered and answered till he is given over as a lunatic.

But the case here is short; I did not venture to say I thought the Quakers Christians, without giving my reasons for it, which reasons he not only quotes but approves as follows. I say, I am not to debate the fundamentals of any Christians that *profess* to believe in Jesus. Now, replies my author, if to believe in Jesus is the characteristic, and then says he, *I believe it is;* then those who do not believe in Jesus are no Christians; and so he goes on and pretends to prove that the Quakers do not believe in Jesus.

Now I desire any reasonable man to examine with me the foundation of my, and of every true Christian's, charity, and to this end 'tis needful to distinguish here what we mean by a *Christian*, and what by *believing*. I am not so ignorant as not to know that only a true saving faith in Christ, which faith is the gift of God, and wrought by his spirit, can entitle a man to the name of a true Christian; and if Christian be thus understood, I dare not determine where he shall or shall not be found.

But then, as this is hard to be determined, charity dictates that we should judge no man; and our Saviour commands it, that we be not judged, and he that thinks he standeth, take heed lest he fall; and under these dictates of Scripture, I exercise a general charity in calling all those people Christians who *profess* to believe in Jesus. So that in the common estimation, he is a Christian to me that professes to believe, whether he believes savingly in him or no; and how many of all churches do we call Christian who have no more of the faith in Christ than barely that they profess it? Nor is there any farther possible discovering for us to make of a general party than by what they profess; 'tis not whether they live up to that profession or no, for where is that party that does? Nor has my charity anything to do with that, and therefore in the paper I said, "I am not to debate the fundamentals of a man that professes to believe in Jesus." His profession denominates him a Christian, though his faith only can effectually make him so; and who shall debate that in a general appellation?

Upon this head, I have nothing to do with my author and his *Shortest Way* but to prove that the Quakers do profess to believe in Jesus; and if I make out that, though in their practice and doctrine and writings they were never so exceptionable, I think I sufficiently justify my charity to them. And for the proof of this, I satisfy myself to refer to a little tract entitled, *The Christianity of the Quakers Asserted against the Unjust Charge of Their Being No Christians*, wherein is a plain confession of faith of the Quakers, in the form of a catechism, printed the first year after the Revolution,[2] 1689, and given in to the Parliament.

[2] See above, p. 42, n. 7.

Quest. What's your belief concerning the Blessed Trinity, as our term is?

Ans. Our belief is that in the unity of the Godhead, there is Father, Son, and Holy Ghost; being those three divine Witnesses that bear record in Heaven, the Father, the Word, and the Holy Spirit; and that these Three are One, according to Holy Scripture testimony.

Quest. Do you believe the divinity and humanity of Jesus Christ the eternal Son of God, or that Jesus Christ is truly God and Man?

Answ. Yes, we verily believe that Jesus Christ is truly God and Man, according as Holy Scripture testifies of Him; God over all, blessed forever, the true God and eternal life; the One Mediator between God and men, even the Man Christ Jesus.

Quest. Do you believe and expect salvation and justification by the righteousness and merits of Jesus Christ, or by your own righteousness or works?

Answ. By Jesus Christ His righteousness, merits, and works, and not by our own; God is not indebted to us for our deservings, but we to Him for His free grace in Christ Jesus, whereby we are saved through faith in Him (not of ourselves) and by His grace enabled truly and acceptably to serve and follow Him as He requires. He is our All in All, Who worketh all in us that is well pleasing to God.

Quest. Do you believe remission of sins and redemption through the sufferings, death, and blood of Christ?

Answ. Yes, through faith in Him as He suffered and died for all men, gave Himself a ransom for all, and His blood being shed for the remission of sins; so all they who sincerely believe and obey Him receive the benefits and blessed effects of His suffering and dying for them; they by faith in His name receive and partake of that eternal redemption which He hath obtained for us, Who gave Himself for us that he might redeem us from all iniquity; He died for our sins and rose again for our justification; and if we walk in the light, as He is in the light, we have fellowship one with another, and the blood of Jesus Christ his Son cleanseth us from all sin. (I John 1:7.)

Quest. Do you believe and own the Holy Scriptures contained in the books of the Old and New Testament to be given by divine inspiration, and to contain all matters of doctrine and testimony, &c. necessary to be believed and practised in order to salvation and peace with God?

Answ. Yes, we do, and by the assistance of the grace and good spirit of God, which gives the true understanding of the mind of God and meaning of Holy Scripture, we always desire to live in the faith, knowledge, and practice of them in all things appertaining to life and godliness. Holy Scripture, being given by divine inspiration, is profitable for doctrine, correction, and instruction, that the man of God may be perfect, thoroughly furnished unto every good work, able to make the man of God wise unto salvation, through faith in Christ Jesus.

Now lest my cavilling objector should pronounce this modern,[3] and tell me that this Jesus they pretend is nothing but the light within, I refer them to Robert Barclay's *Apology, for the True Christian Divinity of the Quakers*,[4] page 138: "But by this (meaning the light within, of which he is treating) we do not at all pretend to equal ourselves to the Lord Jesus Christ, in whom the fulness of the Godhead dwells bodily; nor do we destroy the reality of His present existence as some have falsely calumniated us." Again, page 139: "We also freely reject the heresy of Apollinarius, who denied Him to have any soul, as also the error of Eutyches, who made the Manhood to be swallowed up of the Godhead; wherefore, as we believe He was true, and real Man, we also believe that He continues so to be glorified in the heavens, in soul and body, by whom God shall judge the world in the great and general day of judgment."

Do these look like the principles of people that are no Christians?

After men shall publicly profess such a belief as this, God forbid I should say they are no Christians; nor is it enough to say they have separate meanings in their words; the profession of a faith in Christ is literal and plain, and so it ought to be taken. This paper will not admit me to enlarge, and religious disputes are foreign to the design. I refer it to Mr. Bugg, who professes himself of the Church of England, and desire him to ask of any orthodox divine of the church whether if a Negro, a Turk, or an Indian came to him and, desiring to be baptised, made such a declaration or profession of his faith in Jesus, he would not admit him to baptism, and own him to be a Christian.

Thus I prove them Christians, and am not at all concerned with Mr. Bugg, or his collections of scandal. What if there have been, or now are men among them that run into extremes! Have not all profes-

[3] Throughout the *Review* Defoe uses the word "modern" as a term of contempt. It is similar to the term as now used when a traditionalist speaks of "modern" music or "modern" art.

[4] Robert Barclay (1648–90), *An Apology for the True Christian Divinity: Being an Explanation and Vindication of the Principles and Doctrines of the People Called Quakers* (1678).

sions such among them, and is there no difference between the Quakers now, and some of those who formerly were called by that name? Nor are private quotations of scandalous things, which this treasure of slander is bringing forth, anything to the purpose. The argument is short: if there be any among the Quakers that do not profess to believe in Jesus, what then? Why then, they are no Christians. And what's all this to the purpose? Neither are they, let them be among what sort of people they will. But such Quakers as agree to the confession of faith above must pass in common charity for Christians, or else I know no rule we have to guide or limit our charity by, and should be glad to find somebody that could inform me.

Vol. VIII, No. 153 Saturday, March 15, 1712

EXIT MOHOCK

IN A NATION and city so well governed as this, I cannot but wonder to see such a consternation among the people about a new gang of rakes and scourers [1] who have lately taken the field, as we may call it, against mankind, and who are very deservedly, whoever gave them that name, called Mohocks. With submission to the ingenious *Spectator*, I must dissent from his opinion, that the Mohocks, from whence these people are surnamed, are a people of India, though the end of the argument is the same; the Mohock, or Mowhawks, are, or rather were, for they are extinct now, or very near it, a small nation of savages in the woods on the back of our two colonies of New England and New York—the same from whence our four pretended Indian kings [2] came lately of their own fool's errand. They were always

[1] A scourer was "one who made a practice of roistering through the streets at night, beating the watch, breaking windows, etc." (*Oxford English Dictionary*).

[2] Four Iroquois chiefs, one of them styled "emperor," were sent to England by British colonists to refute the Jesuit charge that the English were vassals of the French. Queen Anne gave them an audience, the Lord Commissioners of the Admiralty feted

esteemed as the most desperate and most cruel of the natives of North America; and it was a particular barbarity singular to them that when they took any prisoners, either of the English or other natives, they always scalped them, as they called it, viz., pared the skin and hair off from the crown of their heads, and so left the body to lie and languish without any pity, till it died—with several other barbarities peculiar to themselves, which many of our poor English people have felt when they had the misfortune to fall into their hands.

As to the affinity in practice between these and this modern society of rakes which now infest the streets, I shall not say the *Spectator* has, with his usual dexterity, remarked upon them; only one thing I cannot but observe as something astonishing, viz., where the pleasure or satisfaction can lie? What kind of passion, or what humour it gratifies, to murder or wound an unconcerned stranger who has not given the least affront or occasion to the party, and who they not only never saw before but may never hear of again. This is such a committing a crime for the sake of a crime, such a degree above the Devil, that the like of it has not been heard of for some ages in the world; what secret pleasure these people find in it I confess I am at a loss to find out, and cannot imagine what infernal rage it can be said to gratify. But neither is my end here; but my concern is to see people in such a fright about them, as if the gallows, the army, or the navy, would not soon rid us of such a set of bloodhounds as these—for they are no better. And in the mean time, till these places of justice become the lot of the people we speak of, methinks our people should not be at a loss what course to take with them.

I remember in the time of the Popish Plot, when murdering men in the dark was pretty much in fashion, and every honest man walked the streets in danger of his life, a very pretty invention was found out which soon put an end to the doctrine of assassination and the practice too, and cleared our streets of the murdering villains of that day, and this was a Protestant Flail.[3] Now this Protestant Flail is an excellent weapon—a

them, and John Verlest did full-length paintings of them. They returned to Boston in July, 1711. *Tatler*, No. 171, *Spectator*, No. 50, and Swift's *Journal to Stella* have accounts of them.

[3] A state bordering on hysteria swept England during 1679 and 1680, when the Popish Plot, touched off by the notorious Titus Oates, pictured England as about to be taken over by the Catholics. See p. 41, concerning one of the murders here referred

pistol is a fool to it, it laughs at the sword, or the cane, for you know there's no defense against a Flail. For my part, I have frequently walked with one about me in the old Popish days, and though I never set up for a hero, yet when armed with this scourge for a Papist, I remember I feared nothing: so excellent a weapon it is, that really the very apprehension of it soon put an end to the murders and assassinations that then began to be practised in the streets, and otherwise, as upon Godfrey, Arnold, Julian Johnston, and others.[4] I remember I saw an honest stout fellow, who is yet alive, with one of these Protestant instruments exercise seven or eight ruffians in Fleet Street, and drive them all before him, quite from Fleet Bridge into Whitefriars, which was their receptacle, and handled it so decently that you would wonder, when now and then one or two of them came within his reach and got a knock, to see how they would dance; nay, so humble and complaisant were they, that every now and then they would kiss the very ground at his feet, nor would they scruple descending even to the kennel itself if they received but the word of command from this most Protestant utensil.

Now, really, gentlemen, after all that can be said, the *Spectator*, were he to speak like an angel, was he to argue with them to the end of his volume and talk till the seven stars come to be fourteen; should he enlarge upon the ungentleman, the unchristian, the brutish, and the senseless diversion of committing inhumanities and murders in the dark upon people they have no particular quarrel at, it would all signify nothing to a Protestant Flail. He may tell them of the shameless and unsufferable insolence of this, in the face of a Protestant government, of the unfashionable folly of it, and the like. All he says is very true, but when he has said all he can, one Protestant Flail against a hundred of the best *Spectators* he wrote, for any wager of my money, I am persuaded it shall sooner work a cure; and if but half a dozen honest, stout fellows will provide themselves with this happy instrument of reformation, as they promise me they will, and take a turn through the streets now and then in an evening, I would be a volunteer under their

to. "During the panic over the Popish Plot . . . clubs, known as 'Protestant flails,' were carried by alarmed Protestants" (*Encyclopaedia Britannica*, 14th ed., IX, 351).

[4] I cannot identify Arnold or Julian Johnston, but see p. 41 for an account of Godfrey.

command at any time; I dare say they would deliver up to justice every one of these Mohock monsters that dared show their faces, and never make any tumult, shed any blood, or break the peace for the matter; a little Protestant threshing would beat the chaff about presently, and you should soon make it as safe walking the streets of London at midnight as it is at mid-day. It is a strange thing to me, how tame this age is grown to what the last was; bullies range our streets in arms by night, and in print by day; was ever such a passive generation as this! They bear everything, and now they are to be mangled and macerated by a parcel of savages; really, gentlemen, if you will bear this, you will bear the bowstring of Turkey, the smoking of Muscovy, the bastinado of Italy, the galleys of France, and at last, the Inquisition of Spain.

Let the courage you shall assume in defense of your lives against street bullies be a token to the world that you will not bear bullying of any kind, neither French or Popish, neither party bullies at home, or Spanish bullying abroad; neither church bullies, faction bullies, October bullies,[5] Jacobite bullies, or, in short, any bullies at all.

But of these hereafter; in the meantime, pray, gentlemen, begin with these Mohock bullies. I have proposed you an excellent medicine for them, *probatum est*, experience has testified it to be good above thirty year ago; I can assure you, some honest sufferers are furnishing themselves with these Protestant flails for the purpose, and I doubt not, the first Mohock that tastes of this physic is instantly cured; all his barbarity and inhumanity, all his cowardly butcher's nature goes off at once, and though he were my Lord ———'s eldest son, or Sir Tho——'s younger brother, or J——ge ———'s nephew, he shall confess the distemper, however violent, has left him, and be the gentlest civilized quiet gentleman in the place, forever after. The wonderful virtue of a Protestant Flail is not easy to be accounted for; the great regulations it has made in the town, and in public affairs, would fill a large history. Some few that have been exercised with it have been the better for it all their lives after; indeed the discipline of it has been thought severe —but can anything be too severe for a race of men gone mad into such disorders, that no Mahometan nation, no pagan Chinese, indeed, not the native Mohawks of America can be charged with?

[5] A reference to the October Club, a group of extreme Tories in the House of Commons. Defoe flays them in the *Review* of March 13, 1711.

Drunkards will quarrel with any man they meet; envy murders in the dark; revenge will stab at the corner of an alley; lust will provoke to insult one sex, and a bullying temper the other; but nothing but a mad dog bites everybody he meets; and since these mad dogs give themselves such a loose; since blood, murder, stabbing, cutting, mangling, and all sorts of injury is their practise—and this against mere mankind, without enquiring who they are, or what, without provocation, without previous quarrel, without regard to persons, sexes, or circumstances—no measure can be severe to such, nor any remedy that I can think of, is like this Protestant Flail. And let the Mohocks consider of it, for I can assure them, if the few gentlemen, who, as I said above, are providing themselves with these instruments, in order to their correction, meet with them in their walks, no dogs were ever better dressed than they will be. *Exit Mohock.*

Vol. VIII, No. 74 Thursday, September 13, 1711

THE PLAGUE AT ELSENEUR

HE THAT can think on the calamities of his fellow creatures without any concern ought to be very sure the turn shall never be his own. The accounts we have had by every post of the terrible desolations which have been in the great and populous cities of the north, such as Warsaw, Elbing, Danzig, Conningsburgh,[1] Stockholm, and the countries about them, have been very terrible, and have given us matter of sympathetic pity for the poor people for two or three years past; but nothing comes up to the sad accounts we have from Copenhagen, and from the town of Elseneur, and the country thereabouts.[2] To move your thoughts a little in this case, and prepare you in some measure for that which I have long believed, and do still, will

[1] Königsberg, Prussia.

[2] This threat of plague Defoe exploited eleven years later in his *Journal of the Plague Year* (1722).

be your own case ere long, give me leave to abstract to you some accounts which I have had from those parts, relating to the dreadful visitation the kingdoms of Denmark and Sweden are at this very time under the affliction of. The accounts I am to give you the abridgment of come immediately from Copenhagen to Hamburgh, and whether public in Hamburgh or no, I cannot tell.

This was written soon after the defeat of the Danes at Helsinburgh, and from a Danish prisoner in Schonen, to his friend at Copenhagen.

SIR:

You have had too soon the news of our defeat near Helsingburgh, and that our regiment which was on the right was entirely broken by the Swedes. I do myself the honour to give you an account that I am a prisoner in the Swedish army. Your kinsman, Jean Runkle, and my very good friend, receiv'd a shot in his loins, which was not judged mortal; but the prisoners being oblig'd to travel, though they allowed him a sledge, yet the torment of his wound gave him the fever, and he is dead. We cannot say we are very ill handled of the Swedes, but we are reduced here to a miserable condition, in common with our enemies; for the plague which spreads all over the country is in the city where we are, and is among the prisoners; the officers that have the guard of our prison are dead of it, and the soldiers fly from it, so that we may quit our prison when we please, but know not whither to go; the town is desolated by the distemper, and in the villages on the road the dead bodies in many places lie unburied; the people that remain flee away into the woods, where many perish daily with hunger and cold. Our distress is inexpressible, and we expect every day to perish here, either with want, or by the plague; several of our men have died of the plague, others are escaped away; I pray God they do not find means to get passage home, and bring the distemper into our own country.

Your dying friend,

HENRIK BOXTHUYS

From Lunden in Schonen

This account has this in it remarkable, that the thing this gentleman feared, indeed followed; for the Danish prisoners were the very people who brought the plague over from Schonen to Elseneur, where it first broke out. All possible care had been taken to prevent it, and the prisoners who came home were kept at a house a mile's distance, and not suffered to come into the town of Elseneur till they had continued sixty days in that place, yet all was in vain—as by the following letter.

Copenhagen, April 18

SIR:

We are extremely alarmed here, with the plague being broke out at Elseneur, notwithstanding all the means used to prevent it. It is next to impossible to prevent its reaching this place, which if it should do, we shall be in a miserable condition; nor have we the common relief of other places, for this city has been so healthy that although it be the king's residence, here is but one apothecary, and when the king is abroad, not one physician in the city. His Majesty has caused Elseneur to be entirely invested with his cavalry, as if it were to be besieged; they may permit any one to pass thither, but no person of any age or condition can come back. They receive all quantities of provision, as corn and cattle, which being carried to a village within a mile of the place, is set down at the king's charge, and then the persons carrying it retreat, and it is fetched by the inhabitants. The accounts of the misery of the inhabitants is inexpressible, and the dead bodies are frequently found floating in the sea, which it is supposed for want of help to inter them. They write from the guard that invests them that they believe the whole body of inhabitants will die, and that they do not fetch above half the provisions they used to take.

Yours, &c.

It seems, though the inhabitants of Elseneur suffered great hardships by this severe restraint, having not been allowed to flee for the safety of their lives, yet all the caution that was possible to be used could not prevent the spreading the distemper, and it was the general opinion that the very guards of horse that were placed to prevent the people flying into the country brought the distemper with them. Others said that some of the people of Elseneur in their desperation put themselves in a boat, without masts or sails, and put to sea and were after driven on shore at another part of the island of Zeeland, where they all perished except three, nobody daring to relieve them; that these three made their escape incognito, as was thought, to Copenhagen, and could not be found out. Be that as it will, it is certain that about the beginning of May, when the weather began to be hot, the distemper broke out in Copenhagen. The first appearance of it was that abundance of people were found to drop dead suddenly without any notice, at their trades, in their houses, and often in the streets. Then it began with a sudden sickness in the stomach, and a swimming in the head, which was immediately followed with a burning heat, convulsions, and death: of this take the following abstract of a longer account from Hamburgh written to a merchant of Amsterdam.

Hamburgh, August 22

Our accounts from Denmark are amazing and dreadful beyond expression. The distemper broke out at Copenhagen, in the beginning of May. It is not to be described but by themselves; our physicians say it is a new kind of plague which Heaven has sent, differing from what was ever known, that physic may be rendered useless, and the physicians not know what to apply. The people fall dead in the streets and shops without a minute's warning. Others, taken with vomitings, fall into raging madness and convulsions and die, as in a calenture; some with swimming in the head fall down as in vertigos and apoplexies, and with violent pains in the head, attended with a burning fever, die in two or three days. They are in great distress for want of drugs and physicians; some were at first sent from hence by the King of Denmark's procuring, but several of them are dead, and no man will now venture. During the months of May and June, the numbers which died were not great; the principal inhabitants, however, removed to their country seats, and the King being to march on his expedition for Pomeren, the court is removed to Rendsburg,[3] from whence the Queen Dowager is gone to Lübeck, and purposes to remove up the Elbe to Magdeburg. The Queen Regent is going to Glückstadt, this city having excused themselves, &c.

About the beginning of July, the distemper increased to that degree that the principal inhabitants began to flee every way they could, on the 16th of July there died 1,600 in one week, and by the city account, about 9,000 people had been buried in all. From that time it continued to increase to such a height of fury that from the 13th to the 21st of August there died 3,100 people. It is now spread into the villages and towns about, both in the Isle of Funen, as well as that of Zeeland, whither the distressed citizens fleeing for safety carried the distemper with them. And in some villages the whole body of inhabitants are fled away, none being left to bury the dying people they left behind, which still helps to heighten the infection; multitudes fleeing away, and the towns in their way not daring to receive them, die in the fields and in the highways, crying piteously for relief, but none can help them; nor will any venture to carry food to them who are fainting and perishing as well as for want of substance as with the distemper.

The accounts of the numbers already dead in the city amounted August 21st to 19,750 persons, not including the adjacent parts, which it is thought are not many fewer; nor is there yet any visible abatement of its fury; the

[3] "Pomeren" is Pomerania; Rendsburg is Schleswig-Holstein, on what is now the Keil Canal.

last week, having as above buried as many as ever, which considering the abatement of the people, implies that the fury of the distemper rather increases than abates.

The ministers of the several churches do their duty very much to their commendation, not one of them having fled away, and but one of them has died, though they daily visit the people infected, and this is all the consolation the sick can have, for physicians they have none. The poor people flock to the churches every hour, and many are taken up from their knees stone dead, yet they do not refrain their devotions in the public places.

The person who writes the account from Copenhagen concludes with the text which one of the Lutheran ministers preached from, to the people: "Have pity upon me, have pity upon me, O ye my friends, for the hand of the Lord hath touched me."

Vol. V, No. 101 Thursday, November 18, 1708

ENGLAND'S COFFEEHOUSE GENERALS

Review. My Madman, I am very sorry for you.

Madman. For me, sir, pray what am I to be pitied for? I never knew a madman seek anybody's pity.

Review. Why, they say you are to be had up for scandalizing the English nobility.

Madman. When did I scandalize them, I beseech you? I value them as much as any man in my college.

Review. But you told us a rude story, insinuating that the siege of Lisle was retarded and kept back by the treachery of some of the nobility of England who were general officers in the camp and betrayed things to the French; and is not this a scandalous thing of you?

M. You are a strange man. You would not be served so yourself. I never reported it as my own; I only said it as a thing talked of abroad among foreigners.

Rev. Well, but you are satisfied, I hope, it was a scandalous report, are you not?

M. Ay, ay, I am satisfied it is not true, and yet I never heard a word to contradict it in my life.

Rev. This is another mystery. Pray, how come you to be satisfied of that, and yet heard nothing to contradict it?

M. Why, what cannot be true may easily be contradicted, and I am satisfied this cannot be true.

Rev. Why so?

M. Because all the general officers in the army that were English noblemen were absent from the siege, and how could they betray the designs when they were not there?

Rev. That is not a sufficient answer, nor will it bear you harmless upon the matter.

M. What, then, what must I do?

Rev. Why, you must be particular and clear the gentlemen by name; make an acknowledgment one by one that it is not this nor that which you mean.

M. That is very hard; but, however, I am loth to be sued in the *Scan*[*dalous*] *Mag*[*azine*],[1] and therefore if you will begin with the persons of honour you mean, I'll make my public recantation immediately, for I am in a terrible fright at what you say.

Rev. That is very fair and honestly said, and more cannot be expected. Come, begin.

M. Nay, you must begin and name them, for I cannot make an answer without a charge.

Rev. Well, but you must tell us who the five general officers are of the English nobility that were supposed to be charged.

M. No, no, that is to accuse myself; do you name them.

Rev. Nay, I do not know them.

M. No, nor I neither, nor ever a man alive; for except the Duke of Marlborough, the whole peerage of England does not afford one of their body, that I ever heard of, that troubles their head with trenches or sieges, at least now.

Rev. You['re] a great r[ogu]e, I tell you, and you will be trounced

[1] That is, the Scandalous Club, a department in the *Review*, discontinued in Volume II.

for it some time or other. Have we not several noblemen that are generals and lieutenant generals?

M. They are all at home then, I believe, for I meet with none of them in the attacks of Lisle, or relieving the trenches; what you may meet with in the trenches at the coffee houses, chocolate houses, gaming ordinaries, and the like, I have nothing to do with; I am only examining *where they are not*, and this in order to do them service.

Rev. What service do you pretend to do them, I wonder. They will expect but little service from you, I believe. If you please to let them alone, it's the best service you can do them.

M. You mistake very much; I think it is a service sufficient to them to vindicate them from such a scandal as this of betraying things to the enemy, and there can be no better way to prove they were not guilty than to prove they were not there.

Rev. Ay, but you do it by way of banter and slander.

M. You cannot distinguish. Truth may be a scandal, but truth cannot be a slander; and that the thing is but too true, I leave to you to judge. But shall I ask you a question?

Rev. Ay, if you will.

M. Of what nation in the world are there the most noblemen and gentlemen in the armies carrying on the present war?

Rev. I cannot tell. The debate will lie between the Germans and the French. But what is the end of your question?

M. Why, to have an answer; that is the end of all questions, or should be so.

Rev. Ay, but you have some other end in it, I believe.

M. Your charity carries you a great way indeed; but why so hard upon a madman?

Rev. Why, your question points it out; anybody may see it, you would have asked what country in the world has fewest noblemen in the present war.

M. I am very frank in the thing; I would have had you asked me that question if you had pleased; and if you had, I know how I should have answered it.

Rev. You would have said England, I question not.

M. No doubt of it; for name me one nobleman of England that appears in the field, I'll name you ten of any other nation in the world. In all the kingdoms of Europe, in all the armies of the Allies or of their enemies, in the French, in the Swedish, in the Polish, Muscovite, Hungarian, or even the Italian; every nation but England, you have the armies full of princes, dukes, earls, lords, &c. In England nothing like it. Our nobility make their campaigns in chocolate and cold tea, they fight at home and talk of things abroad, they can pass censures, rave at and damn the heroes that act abroad, challenge every man's conduct and find fault with what they cannot mend; but as for campaigns, ask an English nobleman, "My lord, where did your lordship make your last campaign?" "Campaign, sir, d——n ye, sir, I never make campaigns, *I am a person of quality*, sir, it's below my dignity to make campaigns; let the mercenaries go abroad that fight for pay, I scorn the drudgery of the war." Let any man but examine our gentry and nobility: arms and letters are their aversions; the pulpit and the campaign are only for younger brothers, they scorn those employments, and it is below them. It is not to the purpose to tell them that in this it is below them to serve their country, below them to qualify themselves for the public service of God; that learning is below them, honour their aversion, and the character of great and brave, a sham they have no occasion for. That this is a slander, let anybody prove by telling me how many of the English nobility appeared in the field, even when their king was at the head of their armies; and except O——d, R——s, Ess——x, and a few more youths of war and courage, few, if any, of the English nobility have shewn their faces, either with King William or the Duke of Marlborough in the greatest and most honourable war that ever England had; Scotland shames them, and one is apt to blush when we read the gazettes how the Duke of Arg——le, the Earl of Stai——s [2] and other noblemen were as volunteers storming the counter-scarp of Lisle—and not an Englishman of quality to be seen there. It must needs be a slander that English noblemen betrayed us, when not an Englishman of the upper rank has shown his face on that side this summer, neither to honour their generals or the nation.

[2] The incomplete names, as Defoe's readers no doubt could discern immediately, are Oxford, Ross, Essex, Argyle, and Stair.

Vol. V, No. 102 Saturday, November 20, 1708

THE VALOR AND IGNORANCE OF ENGLAND'S GENTRY

MY MADMAN ran a story very high in our last, about English noblemen being general officers, and desires me to explain him a little today. Whether I shall mend the matter or no, I know not; for truth will be truth, though it be opened and explained a hundred times a day. I see but two things need explanation, nor would they need it if this age were accustomed to see with their eyes, or hear with their ears, or judge with their understandings.

1. It is not suggested that there are no English noblemen that can sacrifice their pleasures, and adjourn their soft luxuriant way of living, and serve their country. And yet I have said this, I think, the number is so few I need not name them.

2. Nor is every nobleman that stays at home useless to, or out of the service of, his country.

3. Nor has our Madman's observation of the siege of Lisle any respect to or view of the behaviour of those that are in the service; if there are any who, having commissions to serve abroad, are without just excuse staying at home, let such answer for themselves; I may take some freedoms with their lordships hereafter upon that head, but at present what has been said looks quite another way.

It is certain, and I believe I need make no apology for saying it, that of all the nations now at war, England has the fewest of her nobility and gentry in the field, I mean compared to the great number of gentlemen we have in this nation; and if I make some inquiry into the reasons of it, though it may pinch a little, I cannot but think it necessary to be done on several accounts. The only reason I have found given for it is the riches of our gentry. This has effeminated the spirits of our nation, and taken off the very edge of our genius, either from arms or learning. "A p——x of this Greek and Latin," said an eminent gentleman that I had the honour to know, "they serve to make good priests, but signify nothing to a gentleman; a man of quality ought to speak none of them, it makes him so dull, so stiff, and so formal. The education of a gentleman is above the mechanism of sciences, he learns the language of the field—that's becoming and looks well; any man may know a true-bred gentleman, he always talks dog language, understands a horse, and loves the light saddle."

"Well, but Sir Thomas, what think you of the war? Does not a regiment become a gentleman, and is not the language of the camp a good note of a gentleman?"

"Not at all," says the sportsman. "If you distinguish right, it may do well enough for younger brothers, and men of no fortune; the old song is their motto, 'What cares he to die that can't tell how to live.' But what business has a gentleman of quality and estate to go into the field? No, no, your humble servant; we pay others to fight, there's no occasion for us to go ourselves; they go to get estates, ours are got already; soldiers fight, and scholars read, and parsons preach, 'tis all for money. Now what have we to do to get money? Ours is got to our hand; all our business is to spend our money, hunt, race, game, drink, &c. We do not seek the world, we have it; others pursue, but we enjoy; what have we to do to read or fight? It is none of our business."

"Well, but Sir Thomas, you did go to the army, and made a campaign, and all the world knows you are brave enough; why should you leave it?"

"Ay," says the knight, "that was when I was a younger brother. But as soon as the estate fell, 'Your servant,' said I, 'goodman general.' I faced to the right about, and bid good b'w'ye to guns and swords; let them fight that have nothing to live on. Then for that foppery they call courage, to have a man's head knocked off to be called brave; for my part I believe I have as much courage as a man of two thousand a year ought to have; but I have no occasion to be buried in the ditch of honour. All the world seeks ease, quiet and pleasure, and I have it; what business have I with these sham improvements? my business is done."

This is the true language of our gentry, and this is the true reason why you have few noblemen in the wars, and of inferior gentlemen very, very few that could live without it.

This is quite contrary to the general practice of the rest of Europe;

the French have carried on all the great things they have done in the world by the number of their gentry who universally put themselves in arms, and no greatness of birth or estate excuses them. Who are they that manage the armies of France, who supply their infantry with double the number of officers, who compose their numerous cavalry? It is all their gentry, the eldest sons of their nobility, and indeed all their sons are bred to arms, and it would be a scandal to a gentleman in France not to have made his campaign in the armies of the king. Nor is this the effect of the power and tyranny of the present king; let any man look back to the civil wars of France in the times of Henry IV. They will find him frequently in the field with a body of 6,000 to 8,000 horse, all gentlemen serving at their own charge, or at the charge of such of the nobility as brought them in. Let any man look into Scotland at this time, and in former times yet more—how many noblemen of that nation have we now in the army who at the same time want no estates to live on at home, such as the Duke of Argyle, E[arl] of Orkney, E[arl] of Stair, Marquis of Louthain, E[arl] of Leven, E[arl] of Portmore, and others, that if I mistake not, you have fifteen noblemen, and twenty-three noblemen's sons, of that kingdom now in the field; nor are there many noblemen in that kingdom but what have been bred in the armies.

And let no man wonder why the Scots nobility and gentry obtain so much reputation abroad, at the same time that we endeavour to put so much contempt upon them at home. The reason is plain—they have the true liberal education of a gentleman, they are bred to letters first, and then to arms; the first teaches them to behave, inspires them with generous principles, and true notions of honour; the last gives them opportunity to show it, and makes them terrible in the world. They are first made men of sense, men of letters, and then men of arms; and this I take to be the true reason why there are so few Scots cowards in the world, since 'tis hardly possible for a man of sense to be a coward. And why have we so many people misbehave in the world, especially at sea? The case is plain, they are bred boors, empty and swinish sots and fops, and they are not capable of having a right sense of honour in the world. Nor need we go farther to illustrate this, but to those of our own gentlemen, who by great good fortune had parents of more sense, and that bestowed learning upon them; let any man but view the difference of such when they come abroad, and how they then make the finest gentlemen in the world.

But such is our general disaster that these generally were bred younger brothers. And the best bred gentlemen now in England, I mean of quality and fortunes, are such as were bred so. Is my lord, or is the baronet, a man of letters, a man of reading and study? You need do no more than search, I warrant he was bred a younger brother. The most famous men we have had, Sir Kenelm Digby, Mr. Boyl, the present Earl of Pem[bro]k, and a crowd I could name; almost all your men of value in England were younger brothers. The heir's an ass by birth, and must remain so to entail the family, and continue the race. It's below the dignity of the family to have the eldest son have any education; get him a tutor to carry him about to the taverns, and cover his lewdness; but as for sciences, he is pupil to the groom, and takes his lessons from his father's huntsmen. And this is the reason why a man may venture to say, there perhaps never was a H[ouse] of C[ommon]s in England till now, where there has not been a hundred men could hardly spell their own names, and some that could not write them; and since 'tis better now—it is better. And that is as much as I will say to it.

Vol. IV, 101 Saturday, October 4, 1707

BRIDES BEWARE![1]

It is but seldom that I have taken up any part of this paper with answering questions, and that is now and then to divert you. But I think the following question, as it was most seriously proposed, so it may be of very good service to abundance of good people to have it answered. As to the ladies who are concerned in it, if they are not

[1] From Miscellanea (in the first volume called "Advice from the Scandalous Club"), the section of the *Review* apart from the main body of the issue, often devoted to less serious subjects and to answering correspondence.

pleased I am sorry for it. The question, in short, was not proposed in a letter, but in conversation, and is promised an answer in this paper for the good of others, viz.:

What is the worst sort of husband a sober woman can marry?

I confess this question has led me a long way about, into the great, great variety of bad husbands of the age, with which many a poor lady is intolerably plagued throughout, as the wise man calls it, the years of her pilgrimage under the sun, the best of which kinds are bad enough. As

1. There is the drunken husband, whose picture it would take up a whole volume to describe; his drunken passions, his drunken humours, his drunken smell, his drunken bed-fellowship, and above all, his drunken love. O! An amorous drunkard when he comes home fully gorged and staggers into bed to a modest, a nice, and a virtuous wife must needs have a great many charms in it such as my pen cannot bear the stench of relating.

2. There is the debauched husband who, having a sober, young, pleasant and beautiful wife, slights and abandons her to take up with an ugly, a tawdry, nasty, and noisome strumpet, and convinces the world that lust is blinder than love. This sort of wretch has but one act of kindness to his wife which distinguishes him from other brutes of his kind, and that is that coming home laden with vice and rottenness, he gives his honest wife an ill disease that lifts her out of the world, putting her out of his reach, and out of her torment all together.

3. There is the fighting husband. I confess this is a strange creature that, when anything has put him in a passion abroad, comes and vents his thunder and lightning at home; that having not a heart to fight with a man, for generally speaking such fellows are always cowards, must come home and fight with his wife. These are excellent sort of people, and ought all to come to the same preferment one lately did in these parts who, beating his wife a little too much the poor woman took it so ill that she killed him for it. That is, she died, and he was hanged for the murder, as he deserved.

4. The extravagant husband. This is the *ill husband,* properly so-called, or as the word is generally received. This is a blessed fellow too, and his way is that he spends his money in roaring, gaming, and

drinking, when the poor woman sits quietly at home, waking and sighing for his company. If he is poor, as 'tis a wonder he should be rich, he feasts himself and his gang at the taverns and ale houses while the unhappy wife wants bread at home for his children. If he is an artist, he won't work; if he has a shop, he won't mind it; if business, it runs at random; the sot dreams away his time, ruins himself, and starves his family. The end of this wretch is generally to run away from her into the army or navy, and so dies like a rake, or perhaps takes up his lodgings nearer home in a gaol.

Well, good people, here are four sorts of ill husbands, and take one of them where you will, the best of them is bad enough, and hard is that woman's case, especially if she be a woman of any merit, whose lot it is; but yet I think my first rate is behind still; there is yet a bad husband that is worse than all these, and a woman of sense had better take up with any of these than with him, and that's *a fool husband.*[2] The drunkard, the debauched, the fighting, and the extravagant; these may all have something attendant which in the intervals of their excesses may serve to alleviate and make a little amends to the poor woman, and help her to carry through the afflicting part; but a fool has something always about him that makes him intolerable; he is ever contemptible and uninterruptedly ridiculous—it is like a handsome woman with some deformity about her that makes all the rest be rejected. If he is kind, it is so apish, so below the rate of manhood, so surfeiting, and so disagreeable, that like an ill smell, it makes the face wrinkle at it; if he be froward, he is so unsufferably insolent that there is no bearing it; his passions are all flashes, struck out of him like fire from a flint. If it be anger, 'tis sullen and senseless; if love, 'tis coarse and brutish. He is in good, wavering; in mischief, obstinate; in society, empty; in management, unthinking; in manners, sordid; in error, incorrigible; and in everything ridiculous.

Wherefore upon the whole, my answer is in short, that the worst thing a sober woman can be married to is a FOOL. Of whom whoever has the lot, Lord have mercy, and a cross should be set on the door as of a house infected with the plague.

[2] On this Defoe had not changed his mind seventeen years later, when he wrote *Roxana* (1724).

Vol. I, No. 96 Saturday, February 3, 1705

AN ABUSED WIFE'S APPEAL[1]

THE LAST marriage case the Society spoke to was an unhappy husband, in whose case they were very free with him; and as they purpose to do in all cases which come before them, they endeavoured to answer him as the truth of the case requires, whether it suited his design or no. They are now to present the world with an unhappy wife as a demonstration that there are brutes of both sexes; and though they are unable to give relief in either of these deplorables of human misfortune, yet they cannot but make it public, as a *memento mori* to all those that venture *sans ceremonie de consideration* upon the irrevocable state of matrimony.

GENTLEMEN:

After having been married a year, my spouse, under the supposition of my having money, though I honestly and plainly told before I had him I had none [2] and that I could be no means consent to matrimony if he supposed or believed I had any; but assured him if he would except [accept] of me for a wife he must take me as I then appeared, for I could not deposit any other portion than the duties of love and obedience, and on those terms he accepted; I thought myself no bad match neither. I knew him plentifully stocked with Billingsgate rhetoric of b——ch and wh——re, and full-mouthed oaths, but hoped I might prevail upon him by modest persuasion, and dutiful deportment, to learn him better. But my hopes are vanished, and my endeavours are altogether unsuccessful. Nay, he is arrived to that pitch of unnaturalness, undecent carriage, and incurable obstinacy towards me, that all I can say, or do, though with the greatest sincerity and submissive affection possible, yet he is still worse and worse to me.

Gentlemen, were you sensible what a stock of patience I have almost worn out and spent, you'd scarcely account it a virtue in me to continue so any longer; I am completely miserable and fagged out, and know not which way to act unless I desert him. To maintain myself by an honest servitude

[1] From the department, Advice from the Scandalous Club (later the Miscellanea), designed to divert the reader with social criticism and matters of a light nature.

[2] A parallel to this is found in *Moll Flanders* (1722).

(having really no other dependence) is what I would gladly accept of, and which I count, by many degrees, a heavenly life to that slavish one I now live; yet even this attempt, I know, will be attended with almost insuperable difficulties.

My husband is altogether uncapable of receiving any impressions from sober reasonings, which other rational creatures are bettered by. He governs himself purely by his own absolute arbitrary will. I have often told him the life I now live with him is altogether intolerable and impossible to be continued; I can't bear it much longer. All the answer and relief I can get is this consummate and malicious resolve: that if I leave him, he'll gazette me, cry me down, &c. And if I still continue to bear my burden with him it shall still be heightened in malice, and made still more intolerable by unkind treatment; with much more and worse than I can here relate. I ask him, why I must thus suffer? "D——m ye, it is his pleasure, and he will still plague me."

Gentlemen, I desire the extraordinary favour of your advice: How I shall behave myself to my husband; what course I may and ought to take to defend myself from a mon——r of mankind, and still keep a good conscience and not be guilty of breach of duty. In doing which you'll infinitely oblige a distressed woman, and very near neighbour of Mr. Matthews the printer, and your suppliant.

MRS. MISERABLE

Jan. 27, 1704

P.S. I had a handsome education as most citizens' daughters had; was a widow when my present husband married me; am now 32 years of age; but one happiness I enjoy, I have no offspring by this husband, nor had any child alive when he married me.

The reading of this sensible epistle affected the whole Society; and as it was some while before they recovered themselves, the silence was broke with this melancholy conclusion,

No beast so brutal, as a man depraved.[3]

As to observation and advice, the Society examining into the circumstances, came to sundry resolutions.

1. You may see, madam, how vain the weak things called the charms of your sex are; and how much to blame you were to depend upon them for engaging a man who, it seems, you knew before to be most plentifully stocked will ill manners, foul language, &c.

[3] I am unable to locate the source of this line.

2. As you knew this before, they can go no farther for a reason of all your misfortunes than your own want of caution, and a most absolutely necessary care, which we recommend to all your sex, never to marry an ill husband in hopes of reducing him by goodness and submission, especially when they know him to be such beforehand; and if they do, never to expect to be pitied by us.

As to direction, madam, the first and capital advice they can give you is patience; in the practice of which virtue the sense of your not deserving such treatment will be a special support, and the reflection on your having some reasons beforehand to expect it will move you to the exercise. But your pressing them to advise you what course to take in deserting him, they are sorry for; and 'tis with some difficulty they consent to counsel you in that case; and though at the same time not agreeing that it is lawful for you to leave him, unless he consents or forces you from him, they therefore say farther: if you are resolved to precipitate yourself, they advise you to needful cautions and considerations. *"There's no enduring of this," said the fish when they were put alive into the frying-pan, and away they all jumped into the fire.*

A woman's case can hardly be so bad with a husband but it will be worse with her to leave him. The law gives him great advantages, and custom loads her with numberless difficulties; and amongst the rest, her reputation is aptest to be scandalized and reproached. But if after all, Madam, you will leap out of this intolerable case into a worse, then they advise you:

1. Place double guards upon your reputation, and fix yourself, if possible, in such families, under such conduct, and amongst such people whose unspotted character may screen you from scandal; [4] always taking care to be able to give a punctual, and well attested account of your hours and minutes.

2. Anticipate his publications, and declare in print that nothing but unmanly, unchristian, and intolerable usage has forced you to take shelter with your friends and absent yourself from your husband; and that you declare yourself ready and willing to return to him whenever he shall think fit to make his carriage but commonly tolerable; and that, in the mean time, as you look upon it as your affliction that

[4] This is just what the heroine of Defoe's novel *Roxana* (1724) had in mind when she took modest lodgings with a Quakeress.

he will not suffer you to discharge your duty as a wife, you earnestly invite him to put on the reason and justice of a husband; and till it shall please God to restore him to you, in his senses, and in the temper of a Christian, you resolve to live by yourself; as to the rest, you profess not to bring him into debt, but to do your best endeavour to live without being a charge to him; but that if you cannot, you shall only desire what is reasonable of him, and in such legal method as the laws of English women will oblige him to.

If after this publication, he should pretend to print anything on you, he will stink in the nostrils of all men of sense and manners; and there cannot be an author of any newspaper so much a friend to oppression but what would refuse the advertisement, if it should be offered.

Vol. VI, No. 64 Tuesday, August 30, 1709

IMMORAL AUDIENCE AND MORAL PLAYWRIGHT[1]

THE QUEEN, whose thoughts seem entirely bent to make us happy, among the many other instances Her Majesty has given of her concern for the good of her subjects, and to procure general blessings for them, has shown that it has not been the least of her concern for their reformation, for the suppressing scandalous vices, profane and corrupt practices, and stopping the strong current of the nation's immoralities. That this is one of the best steps to make the nation happy and flourishing I need spend none of your time about, since however God's blessings are not to be expected *for* our reformation, I am sure I see little reason we have to expect them *without* it.

In the prosecution of this blessed purpose of the Queen's, Her Majesty, besides her encouragement of example, and being herself a

[1] The first paragraph has been omitted.

pattern of virtue to her subjects; besides the discouraging immoralities by the royal authority in Her Majesty's household, besides the suppressing vice by proclamation, and forbidding the lewd, riotous meetings of loose people for propagating immoralities, such as at May Fair, &c.,[2] has thought fit to suspend, at least for the present, and we hope it may tend to an entire dissolution of them, those houses of sin and nurseries of vice the theatres or playhouses, of whose practices the nation has so long complained.

I will not deny but public actings and representations may be in themselves lawful, and in some respects beneficial, were some preliminaries adjusted; and therefore, that I may not seem too cynical in my reformation, I shall offer some preliminaries, upon which I might be content to capitulate with them. But I believe when they see them, they will despair of performing; they'll say, as the King of France says of surrendering Spain, that it is not in their power.[3] However, let them give us their two playhouses and their patents, as cautionary towns for security of the performance, and I am for making the treaty with them whenever they please. Some of the preliminaries, on which I would treat about restoring them, should be:

1. That no immodest, indecent words or gestures be used in such representations; no sacred thing jested with, or sacred office ridiculed. That vice be always hissed off the stage, and treated with contempt; all virtuous actions and persons applauded and exalted, and the general beat of the actors be to represent the deformities of crime, and the beauties of a virtuous and upright behaviour.

2. That the taste of the town shall be changed. That the ladies shall

[2] May Fair was held at Brookfield in the parish of St. Martin's, Westminster, on the site of what is now Shepherd Market, from May 1 to May 16. In addition to the usual buying and selling, there were "plays, shews, gaming, music, meetings [and] other disorderly assemblies" (Abel Boyer, *The History of the Reign of Queen Anne* [1703–1713], VIII, 380), which, upon the recommendation of the Grand Juries of late 1708, were prohibited by proclamation of the queen on April 29, 1709. I am unable to find any evidence that suggests that the theaters themselves were threatened with closing.

[3] During May and June of 1709 France entered into peace negotiations with the Confederacy toward ending the War of the Spanish Succession. The Confederates stipulated that Louis XIV recall his grandson from the throne of Spain, where he had placed him (thereby starting the war) and allow Charles III to mount the throne. Louis declared he could not effect this. In a letter to his provincial governors he declared such an act to be "against humanity."

no more love to be made blush in the boxes (for we know blushing has long since been banished from the galleries). That bawdy and blasphemy shall no more please the auditory. That they shall make right judgments of things, and never take profaneness for wit, clap a nasty jest, and like the representations of lewdness under the foppish disguises of love and gallantry. I grant this is a very hard article, but the difficulty has this advantage in it, that while this last article is unreformed—do but secure the players to reform the first, and you effectually suppress the stage, for nobody will give *6d.* to see a play.

I could give you more preliminaries, but I think these sufficient, for either of them obtained will effectually do the work. If you reform the players, I tell you, you undo them; nobody will come to the house. While modesty governs there, they will have no trade; the audience will be so thin it will not pay for snuffing the candles. The authors will be starved, and the poet's third day will not hire him a garret to die in; the effect of which is to make him study for a more honourable place to depart in, I mean the g[allow]s. But of that hereafter. For a poet to write modestly and make a sober play—there will be no wit in it—'twill please nobody; the man will be undone.

> But let him blasphemy and bawdy write,
> The modest and the virtuous all will buy 't;
> The blushing virgin likes and longs to look,
> And plants the poem next her prayer book.[4]

And here by the way, I must do some justice to the actors, and it will help a little to prepare you for the good usage I am proposing for them; and it is nothing but what I have noted formerly in my observations on this subject. As in the common vices of the nation, 'tis not so much the common people, as the gentry, clergy, and magistrates that are the authors of our general debaucheries, by their encouraging the crimes of the meaner sort in their example, so really and honestly (though perhaps you will think it a little too plainly speaking) it is not so much the vicious inclination of the poets that compose, or the actors that represent a comedy, which leads them to the abhorred scenes of lewdness, to the profane ribaldry, the lewd jests, and the long roll of their bantering religion, exposing naked virtue, and debauching by

[4] From Defoe's poem, *Reformation of Manners* (1702).

these things that very language they pretend to refine, as it is the absolute necessity they are in to do thus, or be undone. The vicious appetite of the town is so debauched that nothing else will please them; if you will not provide for them that they may laugh at religion, banter things sacred, and see their Maker insulted; if they cannot have this to laugh at in the play, they laugh at the poet; and if you don't bring them in some bawdy story, expose modesty, and represent a virtuous woman as an unbred thing, dress her up for a country girl that knows nothing, as if our modesty were only the effect of ignorance, and want of breeding—if such things as these do not take up the auditory, they shall have no auditory, they'll hiss a modest play as dull and insipid stuff, not at all entertaining; that has no plot in it, no wit, nor anything that will bear seeing. If it be fulsome in language, vile in design, and beastly in acting, 'tis clapped and applauded and the poet adored. The poor poets and players then are at a pinch; they must please you, or you won't come near them; they must gratify your debauched taste, or you will not taste at all. Like your tailors, they must make your clothes in the fashion or you'll make them pay for the stuff; and thus they are obliged to be wicked to please the wicked inclination of the auditory, and to avoid their own ruin and disgrace.

Now because the mischief lies thus divided between the actors and the audience, I have thought of a medium to correct the mischief in the last by removing the mischief of the first—and yet leave no complainers either on one side or t'other; and this I shall speak to in my next. But before I quit this part of it, I cannot omit speaking to the reason generally given why Her Majesty has thought fit to suspend their acting at this time. And it's plain, in an order on the other side, directing earnest prayers to be made in all churches at the usual times of public prayer, for the success of Her Majesty's arms, and bringing this bloody and dangerous war to a happy conclusion. Now Her Majesty, who never used to trifle with her Maker, and who abhors mocking God, however it is with her less religious people, does not think that plays, comedies, operas and such like divertisements make any harmony with prayers, confession of national crimes, and actions of general humiliation joined with earnest petition, such as those prayers so appointed really import; and has therefore suspended their acting, and in general put down their little depending branches of vice, the common stage players in other places; that nothing might be suffered to hinder the nation's serious application to that great work which appears at this time much more suitable to our circumstances.

This is an eminent instance of the piety and devotion of your Sovereign, and a good example to the whole nation, that as Her Majesty has thought them ill suiting with a time of national judgment, so we might all think them ill suiting with national reformation, and may become humble suitors to Her Majesty, effectually to suppress them in order to remove all the unhappy consequences that have so long been found from them.

If any man enquire what the evil consequences are which attend the playhouses, though such a question would very be needless, I shall take a time to answer it farther.

Vol. III, No. 74 Thursday, June 20, 1706

Hamlet REPAIRS A CHURCH[1]

WE HAVE been told by some people, as is already noted, that the victories of the Duke of Marlborough are good news for the nation, but bad news for the church. Now I'll tell you upon a little news that is good for the church—and as for my text, you shall find it written in the first column on the second side of the *Daily Courant*, No. [1303], June 18, 1706.

Towards the defraying the charge of repairing and fitting up the chapel in Russell Court, at the Theatre Royal in Drury Lane this present Tuesday being the 18th of June, will be presented the tragedy of *Hamlet Prince of Denmark*, with singing by Mr. Hughes, &c. and entertainment of dancing by Monsieur Cherrier, Miss Santlow his scholar, and Mr. Evans. Boxes 5*s*., Pit 3*s*., First Gallery 2*s*., Upper Gallery 1*s*.

From whence I offer this observation to the serious thoughts of those gentlemen who are apprehensive of the church's danger, viz., "If the

[1] The first paragraph has been omitted.

D——l be come over to us, and assists to support the church, the d——l must be in it, if the church be in danger." And here, gentlemen, let us make a few remarks upon this worthy subject.

Certainly you gentlemen of the High Church [2] show very little respect to the church and cannot be such friends to its establishment as you pretend to be; since though you have the house built to your hands, for this chapel was before a Dissenting meeting house, yet you must go a-begging to the playhouse to carry on the work. Or is this a general banter upon the church that people must be invited to go to the brink of the gulf by the religious arguments of its being for the church; as if the lady that now gives 5*s.* towards the repairing [the] church, would not contribute the money unless she could see a play into the bargain? or on the other hand, as if there were not farce enough acted upon that stage, the pulpit, but the hearers must be sent to the theatre to make it up. Some guess rather, this may be a religious wheedle to form an excuse for the ladies, and justify their so frequent visits to the theatre; since the money being thus disposed, they gratify their vanity, and fancy they show their piety both together, please their vice, and smuggle their consciences—something like that old zeal of robbing orphans to build almshouses.

Hard times, gentlemen, hard times these are indeed with the church, to send her to the playhouse to gather pew money. For shame, gentlemen, go to the church and pay your money there; and never let the playhouse have such a claim to its establishment as to say the church is beholden to her. See, *tempora mutantur*, times are finely changed; in the late reigns the church built the playhouses; and now the playhouse builds the church; from whence I cannot but prophesy the time will come, either the church will pull down the playhouse, or the playhouse will pull down the church.

Now, Mr. Lesley,[3] have at the Dissenters; for if they do not come to this play, they are certainly enemies to the church; put their negative upon repairing and fitting up the church, which by Mr. Lesley's usual logic, may easily be proved to be pulling down the church. Now,

[2] Tories and members of the Church of England who were particularly hard upon the dissenters, most of whom were Whigs.

[3] Charles Lesley, or Leslie (1650–1722), non-juror and Jacobite, enemy of Quakers and dissenters, edited the *Rehearsal* from 1704 to 1709. He was a controversialist and a pamphleteer.

Mr. Collier,[4] you are quite aground, and all your sarcasms upon the playhouse, all your satires upon the stage are as so many arrows shot at the church; for every convert of your making, every one you have been the means of keeping from the church has so far lessened the church stock, and tended to let the church fall upon our heads. Never talk of the stage any more; for if the church cannot be repaired nor fitted up without the playhouse, to write against the playhouse is to write against the church; to discourage the playhouse is to weaken the church; and you rob the church of the people's bounty, which is one of the worst sorts of sacrilege.

Nor is it unworthy [of] our remark to see how all hands aloft are zealous in their calling for the church. Can our church be in danger! how is it possible? The whole nation is solicitous and at work for her safety and prosperity; the Parliament address, the Queen consults, the ministry execute, the armies fight, and *all for the church.* But at home we have other heroes that act for the church. Peggy Hughes sings, Monsieur Ramandon plays, Miss Santlow dances, Monsieur Cherrier teaches, and all for the church. Here's heavenly doings! Here's harmony! Your singing of psalms is hurdy gurdy to this music; and all your preaching actors are fools to these. Besides, there's another sort of music here; the case is altered. The clergy preach and read here, &c., and get money for it of the church; but these sing and dance, and act, and talk bawdy, and the church gets money by the bargain; there's the music of it!

But to talk more serious: Pray let us put things a little upon the square; the great law of retaliation comes in here, and as the playhouse owes its original and advancement to our late great champions of High Church, they can do no less than reverence their founders and relieve them in the present straitness of their circumstances. And again in their turn, suppose the playhouse should be burnt down as it once was—the church could not deny to read a brief in every parish for the rebuilding it with a "Pray remember the great loss by fire!" But pray let us inquire here, how comes the chapel in Russell Court to stand in such ill circumstances that the playhouse must be called upon for this

[4] Jeremy Collier (1650–1726) was author of *A Short View of the Immorality and Profaneness of the English Stage* (1698), in which he particularly attacked Congreve and Vanbrugh.

odd, and most unusual, charity; some horrible scandal must lie somewhere. 'Tis plain the chapel was Mr. Daniel Burgess' meeting house [5] before; and as the auditory is large, the persons concerned numerous and able, whence comes this deficiency? It must be from want of sense of the convenience, or want of regard to the church; 'tis a most scandalous contempt of the church. What, send her a-begging to the PLAYHOUSE! of all the churches in the world, I believe none was ever served thus before.

What a reproach is this to the neighbourhood of Russell Court chapel. What, gentlemen, nobody to repair the church for you but those that are every day reproved in it? Must the playhouse boxes build your pews; the playhouse pit raise your gallery? This is the ready way to have the people call them both playhouses, and that, though they have different places to officiate in, they are but the same congregation? Charity would fain crowd in here and say in behalf of this action, that the playhouse is reformed, and that it goes hand in hand with the church, and is a true friend to it, as now appears. I do not know, I confess, but the playhouse may in some things conform to the church, but I hope the church does in nothing go hand in hand with the playhouse. Well, 'tis very unhappy, that no manner of contribution could have been raised but this for the building a church; 'tis like the Italians laying a tax upon their bawdy houses; in short, this contribution is but a civil taking out a license for playhouses; and they may now claim fairly a liberty, and tax you with ingratitude if you refuse them.

It would be worth inquiry now how the play fills. The players are very familiar with their Maker here, methinks, and religion comes in like the poet for a third day. Now 'tis observable that the respect to the poet is shown by the crowds on the poet's day. If there be a full house then, 'tis a signal of his reputation, and tells the world what a value they put upon his performance. The 18th of June is the church's third day at the play. Now, gentlemen, we shall see what reputation religion has among our play hunters, and whether they value her above common poets, or no. I am afraid religion and the church will have

[5] Probably the meeting house in Russell Court, Drury Lane, from which the popular dissenting minister and his flock moved in 1705. His new meeting house in Lincoln's Inn Fields was burned by the Sacheverell mobs on March 1, 1710.

but a poor day of it; on the other hand, here will be room for strange distinctions. First, here you will see who are the best churchmen, High or Low; for, are the players High Church, as most allow if they are of any church at all, then a full or a thin house determines who are best friends to the church. But then here is another misfortune, and I would have the ladies very careful how they brand themselves with this scandal of it: they that go to this play for the sake of the church, certainly never go to the church; if they did, they might find ways to give their money to better hands.

In short, the observations on this most preposterous piece of church work are so many, they cannot come into the compass of this paper. But if the money raised here be employed to re-edify this chapel, I would have it, as is very frequent in like cases, written over the door in CAPITAL LETTERS.

This church was re-edified, Anno 1706, at the expense, and by the charitable contribution, of the enemies of the reformation of our morals, and to the eternal scandal and most just reproach of the Church of England, and the Protestant religion.

Witness our hands,
LUCIFER, *Prince of Darkness*
and
HAMLET, *Prince of Denmark*
} *Church War*

Vol. VI, No. 65 Thursday, September 1, 1709

A PROJECT TO SUPPRESS THE STAGE

IN MY LAST I began to speak a little of a great deal I might say relating to the players. We are at last come to a happy day many a good man has prayed for, and many a ruined family has wished for, when the playhouses (that to us have been nurseries of crime, colleges, or rather universities, of the Devil—Satan's workhouse, where all the manufactures of Hell are propagated) put down, and for a time, *Heaven grant it may be forever,* suppressed.

It has been some ages that we have mourned for this happy time; not all the riots and debaucheries, not the lewdness of the actings, not the worse lewdness of the audience, not the wicked rabbles always attending, not the many murders committed there and about it, could ever bring their just fate upon them before. Indeed, of late years, since the practice and example of the late reigns have generally discouraged our national vices, several attempts have been made to restrain, reclaim, and also to punish the exorbitance of the stage. Our courtiers have been willing to suffer a reformation of them; though at the same time they were loth to part with the beloved charm; the symphony formed between vice and vicious inclinations has been so strong that one could not be touched but the other would [be] found. The fondness of the age of those foster-fathers of their vice still prevented their being totally sunk; many a lame pretense they raised for their preservation—and thus they saved them from destruction in the last reign, contrary to the firm resolution of the late King [1] which was several times fixed for their dissolution.

Presuming upon the conquest they had made over their fate, that the war first having diverted that prince from examining into the mischiefs of their continuance, and death having afterward put a stop to their fears, they not only lifted up their heads in the beginning of this reign, but had the impudence to solicit the nobility and gentry to subscribe to the building a new playhouse, not questioning but as many subscribers as they gained among the great ones for the *playhouse*, so many advocates they should have with their sovereign for the *players*. And here by the way I must note, *and I am sure I do it with a great deal of justice*, that in the first two years of Her Majesty's reign, when the High Flying party [2] had the ascendant over our councils, and High Church principles governed the nation, the kingdom of crime began with them; maypoles and playhouses grew up like churches in the Reformation, and vice began to thrive as a constant contemporary with the party. If any man doubt the truth of fact, let him put me upon the proof of it when he please; and in the mean time let him but observe with me this one thing, that there were more new maypoles erected, and old ones re-edified in that one year, than ever

[1] William III.

[2] Another term for Tories or the High Church party.

were in this nation since Bishop Laud's reformation by the Book of Sports,[3] the year of the Restoration excepted. This gives ground to the story of an old woman, who, having seen the music and dancing about one of their new maypoles on a Sunday, and remembering the blessed time when the Sabbath used to be kept in that manner by authority, brake out in this most pious ejaculation about, "Good Lord, here's the old religion come again!"

This very year the players took heart; they saw their late blessed King William and Queen Mary, who were their terror, both removed by death; they saw the High Church, who were always their friends, got into the administration; and as they knew debauching the people's morals was always a maxim of High Church politics, that tyranny and vice were always brethren and assistants to one another, and that liberty was the friend and foundation of reformation, they made no doubt but as long as High Church kept their seat they should flourish. Hardened with this confidence, they doubled their files, enlarged their territories, increased their numbers, and built their new playhouse at the Haymarket.

But, God be praised, *tempora mutantur*, and the players may say the rest, *the times are changed*. High Church is fallen, and all the encouragements to vice are fallen with them. Her Majesty having dethroned the party, and according to her own constant example being desirous to bring all her subjects to the strictest rules of virtue, modesty, and a Christian behaviour, these nurseries of crime have been brought into remembrance before Her Majesty, as in my last. Now they tell us they are suspended but for a time, during the weight of the war, and while the constant course of our national devotions are employed in addressing Heaven—for its help—and they are then to be restored. And one of our news writers says they have petitioned the Queen in this case and have received a favourable answer, &c.

But now that the resurrection they promise themselves may be effectually prevented, I have an humble proposal to make to all the friends of reformation in this town; and this is the end of my moving it at this time. The players have some dependence upon this work, how-

[3] William Laud (1573–1645), archbishop of Canterbury from 1633, approved the republication by Charles I of the *Declaration of Sports* (1633), which listed Sunday sports permitted to persons who had been to church.

ever wicked; it is their, as they call it, lawful employment; they depend upon it, and they have, at least some of them, families to maintain. Again, there are proprietors or patentees, or what they please to call them, landlords and owners, who have bought properties, shares, &c., in parts of these things; these people plead the ruin and destruction of their families, and will be ever teasing the government to restore them; and the very sound of the word *property* has so much weight in it with me, and is in itself so sacred, that, be the foundation never so rotten, I am for preserving the substance; and therefore to stop the mouths of these people, clinching down the order against them, and preventing the resurrection of vice, I am for making a general collection of charity to raise a sum of money sufficient to make all the players easy, and obtaining their consent to suppress finally the very name of an actor or a stage in this nation.

1. It is to be inquired here, how I would buy them off, and what I would give them?

2. How I would secure the nation from the return?

3. How much money would do it, and how to be raised?

Now, gentlemen, that I may dispatch the case at once, and have time to come back to the affairs of Scotland, and the King of Sweden, I shall speak very short and direct to these three.

1. How I would get the players off from their employ? My answer is: I would raise a sum of money to give every actor in proportion to his or her usual earnings or gains, so as to buy it off at twenty years' purchase. This is an equivalent, for with this money laid out in annuities or other purchase, they may secure the maintenance they received to be constant to their families—and they could have no colour or pretense to complain of hard usage, having a just equivalent in money for what they had quitted.

2. As to the question, How I will secure against the return of the players, I answer: (1) Of the players to whom this money shall be given, I think 'tis but reason to demand some security that they will never act again in the Queen's dominions; this to be by bond, oath, and others bound with them, or otherwise, as may be convenient. (2) That the same fund should purchase the present theatres and demolish them, that is, *as theatres*, and have the patents or licenses for

acting made over to them in order to prevent others being obtained. And lastly, that an humble address be made to Her Majesty that in consideration of this contract, and to encourage the reformation, no other patent, license, or authority may be obtained; but that Her Majesty will be pleased to suppress them by proclamation, and declare that no other patent or license shall be granted for their return.

3. Lastly, I come to the money. And as the sum will be large and extravagant, yet, first, I am for dealing honourably with the gentlemen, the players; they are many of them men of wit and of breeding, and must live something genteelly; I would give every one of them wherewith to buy for themselves and families as much annual rent as they made annual gain of their acting in the best time of those playings; then they could never complain, and I doubt not many of them would be very glad of it.

As to raising the money, which is the last thing; I would raise the money by a voluntary contribution to suppress vice and immoralities in the nation; and if a hundred thousand pound were to be wanted, and much less will not do it, yet I am persuaded it would be obtained. And because I will make no offers to others which are not likely to be done and which I will not endeavour to put forward, I do offer that whenever so good a work shall be set on foot by honest and well directed hands, I will undertake to bring in subscriptions among my own acquaintance, and by my little interest, for at least one thousand pounds of money.

And let no man cavil at going this way to do a work which ought to be done freely by the government. By such delays the thing is neglected, and is not done; I am for buying vice out of the nation if I could, since I cannot get it pulled down any other way. We have bought our liberties, why not our reformation? Our ancestors in the Barons' wars [4] bought their liberties with their blood, the late Long Parliament bought the Habeas Corpus bill, and nobody grudges the money. If the playhouses were effectually suppressed so as to return no more into England, though it cost them an hundred thousand pounds, I believe our posterity would not grudge the money. I wish

[4] Defoe here refers to the Civil War in England between Simon de Montfort and Henry III, 1263–1267.

God would put it into the hearts of some patriots of piety to set this project on foot, in which I dare answer for success, and can promise them very good assistance.

Vol. III, No. 95 Thursday, August 8, 1706

OXFORD REBUKED

IN SEARCHING for lunatics, there happens some occasion to go as far as Oxford to enquire among those gentlemen, of whom perhaps it may be said that too much party learning has made them mad. The happiness of this nation consisting so much in peace and a concord of affection, what pity 'tis it should meet with any interruption, where the foundation of our happiness ought to begin. That our two great and famous universities are allowed to be exemplar in their learning, antiquities, libraries, and rarities, and remarkable for the number and capacities of the men of letters now among them, I readily allow; what pity it is then, that they should not equally flourish in virtue, and how mad must they be that would sacrifice the reputation of their whole body to the pleasure and follies of an interlude!

The matter in short is that, as I am informed, a set of our players of both companies—than whom I need not describe greater patterns of vice, and among them, several who now stand indicted for blasphemy and profaneness—are now gone down to the University of Oxford to assist in the accomplishing, *Anglice,* debauching the morals of the sons of our chief families, and the young generation of the nation's instructors. Blush, ye governors of houses, heads of colleges, and ruling members of the University, when you shall read over your own rules and regulations for the government of the general body in that place, and at the same time are guilty at least of permitting those engines of the Devil who prompt the vanity of our youth to be set openly to work before your faces in your jurisdiction. Nor can it be said this is not a just charge on the University as a body; since 'tis plain no play can be acted in the city of Oxford without license first obtained from the University. How then can the work of reformation of manners go on in England, when the youth of our clergy shall have their minds early made familiar with the profaneness and immoralities constantly acted upon the stage, and introduced under the authority of the University? Nor is it to be concealed that this authority has openly appeared in protecting and encouraging the players—the beadles and officers of the university appearing at the playhouse doors to keep good order and prevent the common people, too justly incensed at the liberty and scandalous crimes of the playhouse, from ill treating the players.

For God's sake, gentlemen, look back upon the gift of your pious founders who built and so plentifully endowed the several colleges and houses that form your university. How do the preambles of their gifts frequently introduce the bounty with these words: "For the honour of God, encouragement of learning, the increase of virtue, piety, and true religion, I give and grant, &c." Pray, gentlemen, which of all these ends of the founders do these comedians answer? What additions do these gentlemen actors make to virtue and true religion? What helps to piety, what design to honour God, in this new addition to study?

I doubt not those gentlemen that charge me with falling upon the church will cease their clamours at this particular. I hope the players are not gone down *at the request of the church.* If they are, no man need say anything more to the church's disadvantage; if it be a dishonour to the church to admit publicly of all the helps to her own destruction; if it be a reproach to her to see some of her reverend clergy preaching against plays, and others crowd the boxes of the theater—with what face can an English clergyman suffer the habit and vestments of a Christian priest, which distinguish him for a person set apart for the service of God, to be seen in the lewd crowd of the admirers of vice? How can ye, gentlemen of the gown, preach against vice, cry down the immoralities of the age, and struggle with the torrent of the nation's crimes? How can you bear testimony for God, and vindicate the church as the bulwark of the Christian religion, while you are seen every day encouraging the interludes and vile representations of the corrupted stage? How can you bear, without indignation, to sit and hear the intolerable scoffs at religion, the banters at your profession, the infamous ridicule put there upon your function? How often do you see the parson made the buffoon of the play, his mere office hissed off the stage, religion itself made the jest of the day, and all the masks of vice put upon virtue? With what patience can you bear to see modesty tossed in a blanket, nature itself worried to death, magistracy hissed out of the world, lewdness and looseness adorning the hero, virtue and manners clothed with contempt? How can you be silent while all manner of morality, whether of the tongue or the gesture, is made the sport of the time; your persons exposed, your constitution bantered, religion made a jest, and your Maker insulted —some of the worst of which is to be seen in the *Spanish Fryar, Recruiting Officer,*[1] and other plays acted already among you?

Nor is it unworthy your consideration how low these things make you in the esteem of wise and virtuous men, you, whose tongues are tipped with eloquence, and whose shining parts adorn the church, unless your shining conversation also adorns the great calling you are placed in; with what awe and reverence to your doctrine, with what respect to your persons, with what attention to the oracles of your mouth, can you expect your auditory should attend your ministry? How can the loose strumpet tremble at the judgment of God, denounced against her sins by the reverend tongue of her minister, when she but yesterday saw the same serious awful countenance that now reproves her, deformed with the smiles of pleasure at the vicious banter of a lewd representation in a bawdy play? How shall that hand extended in laying forth her crimes carry any awe with it, which the day before was lifted up to clap and applaud the vile performance of those sons of Hell, the stage players?

Pardon me, gentlemen of Oxford, if I say you cannot but lessen the esteem the world has of your virtue, whatever it does of your learning, while you invite down such people for your diversion! How can you be diverted with men whose morals are scandalous to the nation, whose persons stand now indicted for blasphemy and bawdy, whose trade it is to laugh at religion, mock their Maker, and banter the nation's virtue? I'll readily allow you the lawfulness of repre-

[1] *The Spanish Fryar,* a comedy by Dryden, was first produced in 1685; *The Recruiting Officer,* a comedy by George Farquhar (1678–1707), was first played in 1706.

sentations, and that plays abstracted from the lewdness and vice of their practice may in themselves be innocent. But, gentlemen, pray be moved by an earnest solicitor for the reputation of English virtue, to consider two things.

1. Circumstances differ, and most evils are so circumstantially rather than naturally. You have placed yourselves in a sphere of opposition to vice; you that are the instructors of youth, the polishers and refiners of manners; you that are forming the genius of those that are to be the instructors of our posterity; you that have the charge of the church's defenders, to whose care the sons of the prophets are committed, and by whose example the conversation of those will be regulated, whose office will be to regulate others; you that are lights set on high places, and of whom every step taken is one way or other exemplar; to you those liberties are not lawful, that men in other capacities might take without sin. What an eternal reproach must it be to the English nation to see the vice-chancellor of an university, the heads of houses, the fellows and graduates going in their formalities to the theatre, adjourning from their prayers to the play, and sometimes adjourning their prayers for the play, to see authority stoop to that vice it ought to trample on? How grievous is it, and how must it wound the thoughts of those pious parents whose children are committed to the tutelage and government of your several colleges, to see their governors lead them to that place which they ought to punish them for approaching? Pray, gentlemen, reflect upon the care of youth under your hands, and what sober parents will ever commit their sons to your charge? I beseech you to reflect upon the scandal to your general character with all the men of virtue and learning abroad; and how it will make you the grief and affliction of all the Protestant churches in Europe, the scoff and derision of the Papists, and the jest of atheists, and men of vice who always act the Devil, first to extenuate, and then [to] accuse.

2. If I should allow the plays to be lawful in themselves, and that abstracted from the vicious representations they are innocent diversions, it would still remain for me to ask: Gentlemen, where's the play, when was it acted, and if such a play was acted who would come to see it? You are too good judges of the taste of the times not to know it would be hissed off the stage; the beaus would damn it for a dull thing, and

the ladies look uneasy at being disappointed of an occasion to blush—in short, the players know better than to act dull sobriety on the stage; abstract the lewd and the profane, there's not a play now will bear acting, and if you should tie them down to do so, they must break and be undone.

On the other hand, you gentlemen of Oxford need neither plays nor actors; you have men of wit to compose, men of humour to present, and the acts and exercises of your own houses are superior diversions in the opinion of men or learning, if they are but men of virtue too, and much more advantageous to the hearers. For this, gentlemen, your theatre was built, this will exalt your character, draw spectators and hearers from all parts of the world; your auditory would then be men of virtue, honour, and learning; the practice would be a reputation to the university, and the university a glory to the nation.

Vol. II, *Little Review*,[1] No. 18 Friday, August 3, 1705

UPON LOVE AND SMOKING

GENTLEMEN:

WITHOUT your immediate advice I am irretrievably lost. It has been my great misfortune some months ago to marry a young gentlewoman against her father's consent, who has not only turned her upon my hands, but swears he will not give me the least penny of that portion he designed her. My circumstances are no way sufficient to support her at the rate she formerly lived at. She is grown very ill natured of late, and what is worse, big with child, and is perpetually slaving me with reproaches as the author of her ruin. Gentlemen, my case is very deplorable

[1] *The Little Review; or, an Inquisition of Scandal; Consisting in Answers of Questions and Doubts, Remarks, Observation and Reflection*, was a separate publication supplanting the Scandalous Club (see above, p. 7), which for the first two volumes was a department of the *Review* itself. The *Little Review* appeared for twenty-three numbers in 1705, published on Wednesdays and Fridays, while the *Review* itself was published on Tuesdays, Thursdays, and Saturdays. Two letters and their answers are here excerpted from the eighteenth issue.

and very little short of distraction, and therefore must desire your speedy assistance how I shall extricate myself out of this gulf of miseries which my own precipitate folly has hurried me into. I am, gentlemen,

Your most unfortunate humble servant,
MISOGAMOS.

July 23, 1705

We think this a most desperate case, and it is easier pitied, or blamed, than remedied! Parents are certainly much in the wrong to force inclinations asunder where they are joined; and children, where they find the aversions of parents, ought to withdraw their affections if possible; and disobedience is there only to be countenanced where love cannot be lessened. But to consider this matter a little.

If you married this lady with her father's consent, 'tis more excusable, because you then had hopes of his proving kind; but if 'twas against his consent, we suppose he told you his mind before, what he intended to do. In this you were to blame to persevere, but we do blame your lady more; for 'tis certain her love was not so great but she might have prevented this chain of afflictions, because that love is now gone. And she may more properly be said to be author of your ruin, than you of hers. Her ingratitude is harder to bear than your own misfortunes.

We add further, that the father is unwise to increase your miseries for a thing now not to be hindred; and it shows as little love for his daughter, as Christianity in him, to continue your misfortunes when he may lessen them. The least he ought to do is to take his daughter and maintain her and the coming child—two things you may wish to be rid of, if she is still so ill humoured. But, however, you need have the patience of a whole sect of philosophers to sustain you; and the only way to put an end to your troubles is to maintain your duty to the old man, and your love to his daughter. If this will not mollify him, and reclaim her, they are fit only for one another; and whatever cares you undergo, think that to have such a father and such a wife still vexing you would make them greater.

GENTLEMEN:

May I desire your opinion without being thought troublesome; whether (now in this age, it being so common for youth under twenty to smoke) it be an unseemly and undecent sight to see a young person, of either sex, take tobacco; and whether it is reasonable to suppose it anyways conducive to intemperate drinking, or inconsistent with sobriety, which is made an argument against the use of it by some people?

June 27, 170[5]

Everybody that smokes (secretly intimating that 'tis no virtue at least) tells you he would not do it but that he has some imperfection, either in his eyes, or teeth, or somewhere else; and what occasion is there of an excuse if there be no fault committed? Truly, we are apt to believe, most that use it have some weakness; the young in their judgments, the old in their nature; but those particularly who take it for diversion. Some use it this hot weather because they find (as they say) a coolness by it; they can't endure the sight of a chimney in a coffee house, but the screens are drawn before them, yet they will have both fire and smoke at their very mouths, and this to cool them. But if they think so, let them enjoy the notion, though we take the reason to be this, that the pipe disposes them to sit very quiet, hardly without any stirring. Now we believe were they to sit so still without a pipe, they would cool as soon.

We conceive it is conducive to intemperate drinking, yet not inconsistent with sobriety; and sure the leaning towards a sin is enough to make a man of sense avoid it, unless he can restrain himself from intemperance.

How odious would the west country ladies appear, should they Cornish a pipe as they do there! But custom makes it tolerable with them; but here such a lady's breath and that of a garlic-eating Spaniard would be equally pleasing.

Vol. I [IX], No. 34 Saturday, November 29, 1712

THE DUEL OF LORD MOHUN AND THE DUKE OF HAMILTON

I HAVE in one *Review* lately taken the liberty to mention that so exploded, rejected thing called peace among ourselves. I confess I see no room to expect good usage among you when I touch so ungrateful a subject, but I look for all sides to fall upon me as upon one prompting them to what they are resolved against.

I look upon the present feuds and outrageous party quarrelling which we are all embarked in to be the worst war we could ever engage in; and I think it was never so lively represented as by the late wretched unhappy duel between the Lord M——n and Duke H——n,[1] wherein, both enraged, both desperately bent to ruin and destroy one another, both draw their swords in an unjust, needless, and dishonourable quarrel, and both die in the engagement. I call the quarrel unjust and dishonourable not as to the cause of quarrel, which I have nothing to do with, but as to the manner by duelling, which I undertake to be unjust and dishonourable, because illegal and unchristian.

I have nothing to do with the duel, or with the persons, nor is this written to reflect on either of their memories; those who are left to do justice are, it seems, fled from justice, and mighty clamour fills our mouths at the dead—a thing that is none of my custom. If I would say anything in it, it should be to adore the justice of God, who retaliates the blood of former days in a most conspicuous manner when others have forgotten it, and shows great men, how high soever they are, or how much soever they may seem to be above the reach of human justice, they are not too great for divine justice. Nor shall I make

[1] The duel took place on November 15, 1712. James Douglas, fourth duke of Hamilton (1658–1712), a member of the Scottish parliament, had been appointed ambassador extraordinary to France following the Treaty of Utrecht when he was fatally wounded in the duel with Mohun. Charles Mohun, fourth baron (1675?–1712), had instigated this duel because of a dispute of some years' standing with Hamilton. Thackeray incorporates the duel between Mohun and Hamilton in *Henry Esmond.*

this a national affair; I abhor the embarking such a quarrel as this with our parties. Murderers (for such duellers are) ought to be accepted or owned by no party; if duelling be a willful premeditated murder in the sight of God, as I believe it is, the two unhappy persons have fallen a righteous sacrifice to divine justice, both for what was past and for the present also. Neither is it a question that deserves, or that will bear, any debate at the enlightened tribunal of God, who, or which of them, sent or received the challenge; but they will both respectively appear convicted murderers at that bar, having each gone out with a premeditated design unlawfully to hazard his own life, and unlawfully to kill his enemy, both of which is murder.

Nothing of purity reaches there; provocation, point of honour, heat of blood, and all the pretenses which fools form to cover themselves with, will argue nothing then; he that needlessly or unjustly puts his own life in hazard is a murderer as much as he that takes his life away; he that foolishly and wickedly exposes his life is a self-murderer as much as he that hangs himself, or cuts his own throat; and in this sense every dueller is a murderer, nay, every duel is a murder whether anyone is killed there or no. But let the miserable rest in their graves; why should the age be duelling every day about who was killed fairly, and who not, or who fought bravest and who not? They either of them wanted grace more than courage, and fear of God as much as the fear of one another; both desperate in this quarrel, both furious, both mad, both dead; they are past pity now, and the action no Christian rules can justify; let the memory of it be buried with them.

Had one of these persons remembered the good advice the Lord High Steward for the day gave him after he was tried by his peers for the death of an innocent,[2] most inoffensive gentleman to this purpose, viz., *That he should be wary how he dipped his hand rashly in blood, for that there was another tribunal where he must be tried after another manner, &c.;* and had he remembered the modest answer he gave there, he would have well considered before he had courted his own destruction as he has now done.

I cannot but observe also what some public papers pretend about His Grace Duke Hamilton, viz., that he spent all the night before

[2] Mohun, around the age of seventeen, had been tried for the murder of the player William Mountfort in 1692. He was acquitted by a vote of 69 to 14.

the action in his closet, retired pensive; and, says another author, in his devotion. I have nothing to say to the fact in this, for I do not believe it to be true. But for the sake of the surviving part of mankind, let us speak to this ridiculous newsmonger a little. Pray, sir, what devotion could you rationally suppose the Duke to be passing the time in? I cannot but think His Grace was a better Christian, at least I am sure he knew better, than to be praying to God for success upon what he was going about; let all the men in England but tell me, what could the Duke say? Could anything of a Christian bring him in saying thus, with his eyes up to heaven: "Lord, thou knowest I will affront thy justice tomorrow by taking my cause into my own hand, and executing that vengeance which thou hast forbid me, and reserved to thyself. Lord, give me thy blessing to this wicked and wilful action, and grant me success that I may kill my enemy, and become a murderer of my neighbour, &c." If he could not say this, let anyone tell me what he could pray. Can they think he would say thus? "Lord, I am going to commit a most grievous wickedness, and I am resolved to do it in spite of its being abhorred and forbidden by thee. But I WILL do it; however, I desire thou wilt pardon the sin and assist me to increase it by my murdering my adversary." This must be the devotion, the wretched devotion of such a retreat, and for that reason I will not so far affront the memory of Duke H——n to say he employed that time in devotion. If I might guess at the perturbation of thoughts which took up those few, or such unhappy hours; I say, if I may guess at them *by my own unhappy experience*, and may appeal to others who know what it is, I am of the opinion such times are taken up in the rolling of the passions, the boiling of the blood, the furious agitation of the animal spirits moved by the violence of the provocation. If conscience presumes to give a pinch in the dark, or put in a word, the inflamed organ answers: "Come what will, I cannot go back, I cannot live; I had better be run a thousand times through the body, I can die but once; but to bear this, is to be stabbed every day, to be insulted at the corner of every street, be posted, caned, and the Devil; I cannot bear it, I cannot help it." If the mind retreats a little and looks in through a very, very little bit, it occurs thus: "You are mad, you give up your reason, you are a murderer if you fall in the action, you are a lost man forever. You know it is not a lawful action." All this is stopped thus: "What! Can I bear to be called COWARD! Had I not better be out of the world! I cannot go off, I must do it, all is at stake, I must, I cannot go from it, die or be damned, or anything is all one, I must do it." And so in the morning away he goes to be undone; goes to lay in a store for repentance, goes to put himself past repentance; goes to take away his neighbour's life, and lay at stake his own, and sometimes, as in this case, to lose both.

Those people who would send the late Duke to his closet to prayers to prepare for his next day's work, I believe know little what fighting a duel is, or what temper the mind is in when such an appointment is upon their hands; I rather believe His Grace was fighting with my Lord M——n all night; many a silent pass was made that night in imagination, I doubt not; not that I believe the Duke was weak enough to act by himself the postures or motions of fighting; but I believe it was impossible to suppose that a mind possessed with such views and such resolutions as he then had could refrain from fixing the ideas of the action itself in its thoughts.

But to talk of devotion, let that jest be laid by. I can take upon me to say, God hears no such prayers, nor can any man who is in his right senses have the face to look up to his Maker in such a case as that was.

Vol. VIII, No. 61 Tuesday, August 14, 1711

A TILT AT PROFANITY[1]

THE *Tatler* and *Spectator*,[2] that happy favourite of the times, has pleased you all; indeed, you were ashamed not to be pleased with so much beauty, strength, and clearness; so much wit, so gentlemanly reproofs, and such neat touches at the vulgar errors of the times. But alas! Are we to be laughed out of our follies? Will

[1] The first three paragraphs have been omitted.

[2] The *Spectator* (1711–12), by Addison and Steele, was successor to the *Tatler* (1709–1711), begun by Steele.

we be rallied out of our dear brutality? Our vices are too deep rooted to be weeded out with a light hand; the soft touches, the fineness of a clean turn, nay, the keenest satire dressed up in and couched under gentle and genteel expressions, has no effect here. That gentleman that has all the art of pleasing may yet complain of the few converts he has made, considering the expense of wit that he has laid out upon them.

Experience tells us this is not the way the temper of this rough and unpolished nation is to be dealt with; to tell the people here that swearing is ungentlemanly, and grows out of fashion, was a pretty thought in the late *Tatler*,[3] and could we say it were true, would, in time, have some effect upon the people so unreasonably affecting that ridiculous as well as abominable eloquence; but what said a proficient in that hellish science when he was reading the *Tatler* on that subject? "Swearing out of fashion! Senseless rascal! G——d damn him, he lies, 'tis not out of fashion, and it shan't be out of fashion, and if it be, I'll bring it into fashion again, by G——d!" Now though the step that author took was certainly right, in a nation where we are so fond of being modish, to persuade us that to swear and blaspheme was quite left off by the quality—yet the truth of fact was so daily contradicted by experience. We hear, even at the doors of our greatest assemblies, under our sacred habits and dignities, the vilest and loudest and professed excesses of this kind, that really we could not join with him, however we desired it, in saying the gentlemen had left it off.

What shall we say then, after so fine a hand has touched them, and they will not reform? They must be spoke to in coarser language and plainer words. And, indeed, if I meddle with them, so they must; as an old poet that had more honesty than wit said of himself,

> Though they're called misses which fond men adore,
> I cannot gild their crimes, a whore's a whore.[4]

When I think of the excess this nation is arrived to in affronting the majesty of their Maker, and when I have wished that the clergy of this nation, whose province and duty no doubt it is, would set themselves effectually to cry it down as a sin against [Him]; it occurs to

[3] The *Tatler*, No. 137, for February 23, 1709/10, states that swearing is "already banished out of the society of well-bred men." Defoe did not agree.

[4] I am unable to locate the source of these lines.

me that it cannot be impertinent to put people in mind how ridiculous, how senseless, how absurd the interlining their speech with oaths is, in the very nature of it; how when men swear they talk nonsense of course, speak without consistency, and in short, make themselves fools. And pardon me, gentlemen, to foul my paper with some of your wise abominations to explain myself.

I have seen two beaux meet in a coffee house, that perhaps had not seen one another for a month or such a matter, who begins thus. "Jack, G——d damme how dost do? Where has thou been all this while by G——d?" The t'other returns the same senseless stuff, I care not to debauch your ears with it. But take them in any other discourse 'tis the same; at play 'tis G——d damn the cards; a-hunting, G——d damn the hounds; they call the dogs sons of whores, and the men sons of bitches. And these are men of wit, gentlemen, men of quality, men of fashion. And what must a man say to them? Say to them! Why, say they are fools. They talk nonsense, and make men of true sense count them ridiculous fellows; in short, it is not wicked only, but senseless, foolish, and ridiculous, and men that pretend to wit ought to be kicked out of company when they swear thus, for talking nonsense. There needs then but one thing for the gentlemen in England to do to banish this folly out of the nation, and that is but to look in the glass and see how simply they look when they swear, I mean in the glass of common sense. I heard a gentleman once, who would have been very angry to be called a fool, accost a lady thus, with a glass [of] wine in his hand. "Madam, my humble service to you, as I hope to be saved." Would any man talk divinity to such a man? Talk divinity, no, tell him he is an ass, and ought to be laughed at for a fool.

Now that this may be a more just and general reproof, I appeal to common observation whether there is one man in twenty who gives himself a loose to this vice, who does not so mix his discourse as to make it most perfect nonsense, if I may be allowed that term. Now really to tell these men of affronting God Almighty, and of provoking their Maker, you had as good talk gospel to a kettle drum; but tell them they are fools, that they talk nonsense, desire them to put their speech into Latin, and shew you which is the principal verb; tell them they are not fit for common conversation, that in common language they cannot be understood. When a man salutes you with "How do you do, G——d damme," and the like, desire him to take a pen and ink and write it down and see how it will read. Ask him if it be sense? If he would have it printed for the test of his eloquence? And desire him to read it over three or four times till the sound grows harsh in his ears, and then give his opinion of it. Had the taste of language any effect upon us, had we any feeling of the music of words, this would appear as the most unharmonious thing in nature, and I believe I may lay it down as a maxim which will be allowed in most cases, that you hardly ever find a man that has any taste of eloquence, any politeness of diction, or regard to cadence in speech, who can be a common swearer.

It is not many years since this vice got so the ascendant of us, that it made two attempts to become universal, but it failed in both; and happy it was for us that it did so, for had it gained the point there, it had obtained by this time to be the essence of speech, and the test of good language among us. These attempts were:

1. To be written in our letters, books, and disputations.
2. To be used by our women.

In the first of these it made some progress, and the *beau monde*, the men of wit and spirit, as they called themselves, began to write as they spake. But the very argument I am upon knocked it on the head, it looked so odd when they came to write it, it made such a jargon, such coarse Billingsgate nonsense when it came to be read, that it lost all the music by that time it had travelled a stage or two with the mail. The first restraint it met with was that it appeared impossible to make it pass in anything but letters of gallantry, as they were called, viz., such as love, raillery, or quarrel; but if they came to write anything grave, or mannerly, it was impracticable. To a superior, it would not do, it was too much freedom; to quality it was arrogant; to a stranger it was an affront, for it presumed he liked and practised it; to an inferior it was making him your equal; so that, in short, the style would not suit one case in fifty that any man had occasion to write upon, and this difficulty sunk the Devil's attempt of introducing it.

Then, as to the ladies, as the Devil never proposed a thing so absurd but some or other would close with it, so here and there one of a coarser breed than ordinary among the ladies came a little into it; but there was something so harsh, so rough, so rude in the thing itself, that shocks the very natural softness of the sex, and it would never go down with them, no, not with the worst of them to this day; drunkenness and swearing will never be called female vices. I remember the late Duchess of Portsmouth, in the time of King Charles II, gave a severe return to one that was praising Nel Gwynn, whom she hated, and with this I shall close this paper. They were talking of her wit and beauty, and how she always diverted the King with her extraordinary repartees; how she had a very fine mien, and appeared as much a lady of quality as anybody. "Yes, Madam," said the Duchess, "but anybody may know she had been an orange wench by her swearing."

Vol. VIII No. 82 Tuesday, October 2, 1711

MR. SPECTATOR DISPUTED

THERE IS NOT a man in this nation that pays a greater veneration to the writings of the inimitable *Spectator* than the author of the *Review;* and that not only for his learning and wit, but especially for his applying that learning and wit to the true ends for which they are given, viz., the establishing virtue *in* and the shaming vice *out* of the world; and I premise this because what I am going to say, which, though it may vary a little, yet is not designed in opposition to what that author has advanced, and I bespeak him not to take it so, I mean in the case of an inexorable father to a repenting but disobedient daughter.

The *Spectator* in his paper, No ——, Sept. ——,[1] gives us a letter from a young lady, which, to make my story more plain, I must abridge thus.

The lady acquaints him that at the age of fifteen she chose for herself, that is, as I think it may be called without justice, married against her father's consent—that till that time her father was exceedingly tender of her,

[1] Defoe has neglected to supply the issue number and date: No. 181, September 27, 1711.

and kind to her; but that this action disobliged him so that he will never be reconciled to her.

To palliate the fact, she says she has the best of husbands, and fine children, which she dwells upon, though that's nothing to the case at all, not much noticing that she disobliged the *best* of fathers, nor setting down any of the circumstances of her behavior in the doing it.

She instances the attempts she has made to obtain his pardon, by tears, casting herself at his feet, &c., but always has been rejected with indignation; that he would not see her, or bear to hear her name mentioned, no, not when he thought himself going out of the world; would not see her little child or give it his blessing; but, in short, has forever irreconcilably renounced her as not worthy to be owned for his child.

I think I have abridged the letter faithfully, and shall make amends if it be thought I have not. Whether the letter be a parable or a history is not material to me; but as the *Spectator* has given his thoughts and told us a story out of Friherus to the purpose,[2] condemning the father, I desire the favour of a word on the other side.

1st. I allow that we are obliged by the Scripture command to forgive the trespasses which others commit against us; and the petition in the Lord's Prayer, "As we forgive those that trespass against us," seems to incapacitate us to pray till we can sincerely do so. Our Saviour also makes it look as an absurd thing that we should pray for forgiveness without it: For if ye forgive not men their trespasses, how shall your heavenly Father forgive you? (Matt. 6:14, 15.)

2. I allow all that the *Spectator* hath said with relation to the generosity and heavenly temper of forgiving, nor will I object, even where I think I might, because I would lessen no man's temper to forgive the offenses and trespasses of others. But I desire, in favour to the case of the parent, to suggest a few things.

1. That there seems to me a manifest difference between the obligation of forgiving the injuries we receive from a neighbour, and the forgiving the breach of relative duties between children and parents. And the severe commands of God upon children with the commination implied in the Fifth Commandment upon the breach of it plainly implies the difference I speak of.

[2] In the *Spectator*, No. 181, for September 27, 1711, Addison tells a story of Eginhart and the princess Imma. He had got it from Bayle's *Dictionary*, which in turn had it out of Marquard Freher (1565–1614), *Rerum Germanicorum scriptores*.

2. That this difference in the case argues strongly that as the offenses of children against their parents are not the same with those of other men; so neither is the obligation to forgive the same. And this is evident from the authority given to the parents in Scripture to bring their disobedient son to public justice, which could not be, if at the same time he was bound to forgive him. It is manifest, the command of Christ to forgive is set forth under the allegory of *our brother,* intimating, as I think, that this was a forgiveness upon an equality of degree. But the disobedience of children to parents, like that of subjects to a prince, remain to be judicially resented; neither does the command of forgiveness take place here, at least the obligation to it cannot be the same. This I give as my opinion, submitting it to the judgment and censure of those who are better skilled in the divinity of the thing.

I come next to the philosophy of it; and I own that without doubt it is a token of a greatness of soul, equal to a hero, so to master our resentment of injuries as to conquer the breaches made upon us in that case; but there is one case which I must always reserve, as a thing perhaps peculiar to our Maker, viz., to forgive the sins against a *superlative affection.* It is because He is God and not man, that sins against the divine love can be forgiven; and 'tis because we are men and not God, that we cannot always forgive the offenses committed against our superior affections. There is no sin so great but God can forgive, because He is infinite; but there are sins so great against man as may be out of his power to forgive because he is not infinite.

The party before us acknowledges the exceeding tenderness of her father before she disobliged him. Pray mark it, proportioned to the greatness of his affection may be the depth of his resentment—as we always say, the highest love turns to the deepest hatred; if his paternal love lay at the bottom of his very soul, the bitterness of the insolence which a rebellion of that nature showed to such an affection, pierced to the same place, and therefore perhaps cannot be rooted out. No, the person himself may not be able to root it out, any more than a man can prevent or conquer natural sympathies and antipathies. For this reason, children who have the tenderest parents should be very wary of effectually disobliging them, because, if once thoroughly offended, suitable to the greatness of the affection will be the resentment; and as it is not a small thing that will wean a powerful affection, so that affection once thoroughly weaned may not be perhaps by the person himself, and if not by him, not by all the world, to be replaced.

Abused love to return! Insulted goodness to flow again! A slighted and rejected tenderness to continue tender! Contemned affections to embrace the object contemning! This is for God to do, whose mercy is infinite above all His works and endures forever. But for men who are finite! who are but men! governed and indeed composed of passions and affections! it cannot be! Some may go higher and be more godlike than another; but there are degrees of provocation which it may be past the power of nature to forgive. Nor will all the submissions, repentings, or returnings of the child move in this case; nature retorts continually the abhorrence of the crime, and like a little water upon a great fire, it makes it burn more fierce.

I cannot say much to the case published; but I could publish some that would make good what I say; as to the particular case, if it be a case, I conceive the parent has not justice in the relation, the several circumstances of the case being left out, as how it was done, with what contempt she might treat her father, what commands he might have laid upon her, and whether he might not have declared to her, perhaps vowed, that if she did so marry, he would never own her again. There also remains some alleviation, as to the thing called forgiveness, and whether a parent may not as a Christian forgive the offense, and yet not as a parent replace her in his affection; the first, I conceive he may do; the last, as above, I believe may be in some cases out of the power of a parent, and to say otherwise would be to make the parent equal with God.

This I have offered with a view to some sad cases within my own knowledge, and cannot but recommend it to those children who have affectionate, tender parents; that they should remember their parents are men, and not gods; and that if by an ungrateful, disobliging behaviour they once wean them, it may not be in the power, no, not of the parents themselves, to be reconciled to them.

Vol. I [IX], No. 53 Saturday, January 31, 1713

THE LUXURY-LOVING MIDDLE CLASS

IT IS a remark of my own, but perhaps too well to be justified by the experience of most who shall read this paper, that though the trade of the nation, by the confession of all men of sense, was *never* more decayed, money *never* scarcer, the number of bankrupts *never* greater, the cries of the poor *never* louder, and the rate of provisions, for some years past one with another, *never* higher; yet the pride, the luxury, the expensive way of living, the costly furniture and ostentation, both in equipage, clothes, feeding, and wearing were never greater in this nation. If any of the temper, which I know some, viz., to cavil at everything, disputes the fact, I could descend to particulars in most undeniable instances. But let the rich coaches, and the extravagance of costly house furniture, even in this city, and among the middling tradesmen of it, speak for what I have advanced.

I will allow, and I'll speak of it fuller in its place, that the usual habits of our people, even of both sexes, are altered from former times, and that to *great advantage;* the ladies never dressed so modest, nor the gentlemen so grave and becoming as they do now; I am no cynic, nor am I finding faults for the pleasure of the complaint. I remember when there was reckoned 70,000 riband weavers in Spittlefields, &c.; and I believe there are not now half so many hundred in England. I remember the naked shoulders and breasts, the monstrous towers of hair, the heads three story high, and the like, of the women; the pantaloons, the shoulder-knots, and the shoulder-belts of the gentlemen. Both sexes have tired themselves of those follies, and I acquit the habits of the age of any part of the antic in the excess I speak of. But I cannot acquit them of the excess in the richness and costliness of clothes, though I acknowledge that is not the thing I am now complaining of in particular.

I remember an accident which gave me a sketch of this very thing, and which I could not avoid taking notice of. Sometime since, being upon business very late in the city, it was my lot to come along the street just as a sudden and terrible fire broke out in a citizen's house, *in none of the wealthiest part of the town neither;* I forbear the place for the sake of the particulars. I could contribute little to the helping the good people in their distress; nor was I very well qualified to carry water, or work an engine; besides, the street was presently full of people for that work. But I placed myself in a convenient corner, near the fire, to look on, and, indeed, the consternation of the poor people was not fruitless of remarks.

And first, I was, I confess, surprised to hear the shrieks and lamentations of the poor ladies, as well in the houses on either side, as opposite to the house that was on fire. After the first fright was expressed with a great deal of noise, terrible gestures and distortions, I observed all hands at work to remove. The chambermaids were hurried down stairs; "Betty, Betty," says a lady, aloud you may be sure, "have you got the plate?"

"Yes, Madam," says Betty. "Here, take the cabinet," says Madam, "run to my mother's. There's all my jewels, have a care of them, Betty." Away runs Betty. This, I think, was about the degree of a fishmonger's lady. At a house that was in great danger they were, like seamen in a storm to lighten the ship, throwing their goods out at window; and, indeed, I think they had as good have let them be burnt. Here I saw, out of a shopkeeper's house, velvet hangings, embroidered chairs, damask curtains, plumes of feathers, and, in short, furniture equal to what, formerly, sufficed the greatest of our nobility, thrown into a street flowing a foot deep with water and mud; trodden underfoot by the crowd, and then carried off piecemeal as well as they could. It was not the fright the people were in, or the error of their destroying their goods in that hurry that was so much matter of observation to me, as to see the furniture that came out of such houses, far better than any removed at the late fire at the French ambassador's.

In the house which I stood nearest to, which was opposite to the fire, and which was in great danger, too, the wind blowing the flame, which was very furious, directly into the windows, the woman, or mistress, or lady, call her as you will, had several small children; her maids, or nurses, or whatever they were, made great diligence to bring the poor children half naked, and asleep, downstairs in their arms; and wrapping them up carefully, run out of the house with them. One of these maids coming again, as if to fetch another, meets her mistress, whose concern, it seems, lay another way, with a great bundle. The mistress screams out to her, "Mary, Mary, take care of my clothes; carry them away; I'll go fetch the rest." The maid, more concerned for the children, than the mother, cries out louder than her mistress, "Lord, Madam, where's Master Tommy? The child will be burned in the bed!" throws down the clothes, and runs upstairs. The mistress, whose fine clothes lay nearer her heart than her child, cries out, "Oh! There's all my clothes!" snatches up the great bundle and runs out of the house half naked, with it, and leaves the wench to go fetch her child, who, poor lamb, was almost suffocated with the smoke and heat.

The mother was back again in an instant, with two or three porters, and some friend's servants which she had got to help her; and away they run upstairs with her, and came down as quickly, loaden with baskets, and bundles of rich goods, and about half an hour after, when the good lady had discharged her passions of those things that lay nearest her heart, and was come a little to her memory, I saw her in dreadful fury, raving and screaming, and tearing her hair for her child. Her child, oh, her child! for the house had taken fire on the top and there was no bearing to be in the rooms; and she remembered the wench had cried out that the child was in its bed, but never saw the maid who had fetched the poor child down, at the hazard of her own life, and had carried it away, and came not back for some time. At last word was brought her that the child was safe.[1]

This scene eased me of the wonder I had been in, to see our citizens who go all day with blue frocks and blue aprons, dirty hands and foul linen, have their chambers hung with velvet, and their wives with jewels. How should it be otherwise, when the ladies love their clothes and furniture so much better than their children, and, no doubt, as much in proportion better than their husbands' prosperity? This costliness in furniture, as the foundation of many fatal disasters to trading people, I shall have much reason to speak to hereafter. And, in the meantime, not so much as to point at particular families and persons, I refer it to those gentlemen who have so often occasion to sit upon commissions in the case of bankrupts. How often have they seized the

[1] In *Moll Flanders* (1722) Defoe has an almost verbatim parallel to this incident.

houses, and sold the furniture of our city trading people which has been as good as, and perhaps better than, in former times had served our princes; where the bankrupt's estate has not divided to his creditors half a crown in the pound!

I think the age was never so madly bent upon these extremes as they are now, when trade is at the lowest ebb imaginable, and this, to me, is a very ill sign; for when trade suffers all imaginable hardships and convulsions, is under general decay, and the scarcity of money is the general grievance of the nation, to have the humour of the town run so excessively upon extravagance, in equipage, furniture, and costly living, I say, it is a plague upon trade, and portends the reducing it to yet greater extremities than ever.

Vol. VIII, No. 75 Saturday, September 15, 1711

GIVE ME NOT POVERTY, LEST I STEAL![1]

THE WORLD has a very unhappy notion of honesty, which they take up to the prejudice of the unhappy. Such a man is a fair merchant, a punctual dealer, an honest man, and a rich man. Ay, says one, that makes him a rich man; God blesses him because he is an honest man. *It's a mistake:* God's blessing is the effect of no man's merit. God's blessing may have made him a rich man—*but why is he an honest man, a fair dealer, a punctual merchant?* The answer is plain: Because he is a rich man. The man's circumstances are easy, his trade answers, his cash flows, and his stock increases; this man cannot be otherwise than honest, he has no occasion to be a knave. Cheating in such a man ought to be felony, and that without the benefit of clergy. He has no temptation, no wretched necessity of shifting and tricking, which another man flies to, to do deliver himself from ruin. The man is not rich because he is honest, but he is honest because he is rich.

Look to the foolish and injurious notion of the age. Men are

[1] The first paragraph has been omitted.

k[nave]s that break, and no doubt many k[nave]s do break. But give me leave to say, men are made k[nave]s by breaking. A certain draper not far from his neighbours had it always in his mouth, such a man was a rogue, such a villain, such a cheat.

"Why, Sir?" says one.

"Why, he can't pay his debts."

If he had said, "won't pay his debts," I had joined with him; but to prevent my asking after his abilities, he always added, every man was a rogue that was a bankrupt. And in six months I found his father's name in the *Gazette*.[2] This made him a little modester, and now he finds as much difficulty to keep his own out as any man in the street has done this seven year. Blessed be God, honesty of principle may remain under deep disasters, all the k[nave]s are not yet broke, some stand behind their counters still and walk the Change still who deserve more the gallows than the miserable that shelter under the fury of creditors; and are only honest now because they are not under the necessity of being otherwise.

And pray, gentlemen, do not vouch too fast for your own honesty; you that have not been tried with distresses and disasters, ye know not what you are yourselves. Many a man that thinks himself as honest as [his] neighbours, will find himself as great a r[ogu]e as any of them all, when he comes to the push. How many honest gentlemen have we in England of good estates and noble circumstances that would be highwaymen and come to the gallows if they were poor? How many rich, current, punctual, fair merchants now walk the Exchange that would be errant knaves if they came to be bankrupt? Poverty makes thieves, as bare walls makes giddy housewives; distress makes k[nave]s of honest men, and the exigencies of tradesmen when in declining circumstances, of which none can judge, and which none can express but those that have felt them, will make honest men do that which at another time their very souls abhor. I own to speak this with sad experience, and am not ashamed to confess myself a penitent. *And let him that thinketh he standeth take heed lest he fall.*[3]

[2] That is, notice of his bankruptcy was printed in the London *Gazette*, then, as now, the official government newspaper. Today it is confined chiefly to announcing official appointments, bankruptcies, and, in war time, casualty lists.

[3] A quotation from I Corinthians 10:12.

Let the honestest man in this town tell me, when he is sinking, when he sees his family's destruction in such an arrest, or such a seizure, and has his friend's money by him, or has his employer's effects in his hands; can he refrain making use of it? Can he forbear any more than a starving man will forbear his neighbour's loaf? Will the honestest man of you all, if ye were drowning in the Thames, refuse to lay hold of your neighbour who is in the same condition, for fear he drown with you? Nay, will you not pull him down by the hair of his head, tread on him with your feet, though you sink him to the bottom, to get yourself out? What shall we say? "Give me not poverty, lest I steal," says the wise man; that is, if I am poor I shall be a thief. I tell you all, gentlemen, in your poverty the best of you all will rob your neighbour; nay, to go farther, as I said once on the like occasion, you will not only rob your neighbour, but if in distress you will EAT your neighbour, ay, and say grace to your meat too. Distress removes from the soul all relation, affection, sense of justice, and all the obligations, either moral or religious, that secure one man against another. Not that I say or suggest the distress makes the violence lawful; but I say it is a trial beyond the ordinary power of human nature to withstand; and therefore that excellent petition of the Lord's Prayer, which I believe is most wanted and the least thought of, ought to be every moment in our thoughts, "Lead us not into temptation."

But to return to my first observation: I am of the opinion that the honour of trade in this nation is the most declined in this age of anything, religion excepted, that can be observed. I believe I need not beg the question; it will be easily granted. Tricking, sharping, shuffling, and all manner of chicane is crept into our commerce more than ever was known. I have hinted above that it is an evident signal of the decay of trade. And the reason is that a decay of trade is naturally the great original and parent of these follies, which if men were thriving, and their affairs easy, they would avoid. Men rob for bread, women whore for bread; necessity is the parent of crime. Ask the worst highwayman in the nation, ask the lewdest strumpet in the town, if they would not willingly leave off the trade if they could live handsomely without it. And I dare say, not one but will acknowledge it.

Vol. VIII, No. 31 Tuesday, June 5, 1711

BARREN BRITAIN

I AM speaking of the native produce of Britain, entirely abstracted from the improvement of commerce or the importations of foreign countries, in defense of the climate and soil of Britain, against what has been printed in the *Spectator*, as quoted from natural historians, viz., that our own country is a barren uncomfortable spot, and that no fruit grows originally among us, besides hips and haws, acorns, and pig-nuts. (*Spectator*, No. 59 [69], May 19, 1711.)

I have instanced in our wool, I have proved that it is a mere birth of Britain, that foreign sheep brought hither improve the fleece, and that our sheep carried abroad lose their wool. But I need not go so far. The wool of this island is so nice in its growth, and so eminently depending upon the soil, that if you carry the breed of our sheep but out of one country into another, they shall with their feeding alter their fleece; I need not give you many instances, but a few are not improper. Herefordshire and the adjacent parts of Wales, mountainous as it is, cold and in some places very barren, produces the finest wool in Britain. Great quantities of sheep are bought about Lemster, and carried yearly into Essex; but keep them in Essex one year, the wool is quite another thing. Lincoln and Leicestershire are the counties of all England for quantities of large sheep and vast heavy fleeces, the wool very fine and the staple long. Go but over the Trent, which parts those countries from Nottinghamshire, Yorkshire, Darby, and Stafford; the sheep are small, their wool coarse, hairy, and short, nor will the sheep of Lincolnshire and Leicestershire live there but their wool shall decay.

If it be said the lands are not rich enough to feed them because they are so large, this grants the argument in part, that 'tis the soil makes the wool. But go on then farther north, and when you come to the North-riding of Yorkshire, the banks of the Tees, and the bishopric of Durham, there you find the sheep vastly large, and yet the wool coarse; this is evidenced by the variety of wool in England, which is fetched and carried this way and that way, as the manufactures direct; Norfolk makes the finest woolen manufactures in England, yet has no fine wool in its own bounds; the worsted-men fetch the fine wool from the clothing parts, the clothiers fetch the long staple wool from the other counties; the Leeds-men fetch long and large fleeced wool from Leicestershire, and coarse harsher wool from Northumberland; the wool circulates before 'tis manufactured, as the manufactures do after it; and all this variety is occasioned by the soil of England—Mr. Spectator's poor barren uncomfortable spot.

From the wool, let us examine three inanimate creatures, the horse, the bulldog, and hound, either these are particular to our climate and soil, or they are not; if you examine the history of these creatures, you will find the breed here is natural, and the kind degenerates if carried into any other countries; the best pack of hounds in England carried abroad lose their noses in two or three year, and their breed in two removes are good for nothing; the best English bulldog . . . carried abroad, loses his courage, and their produce know not a bull from a hedgehog; the generous racer, fleet as the wind, yet strong as the charger, that at Newmarket Heath [1] flies over the four mile course at the rate of a 1,000 guineas a heat, send him abroad, he loses his spirit and his swiftness; and bring the best of his breed hither, after but two years will be distanced by a crimp.

Let any man tell me, are these peculiarities the produce of our soil, and favoured by our clime, or are they not? If not, why are not other nations able to produce the like? Why can nature work these nowhere but in England, poor barren uncomfortable spot!

But to come to the vegetative life, these are more evidently the mere productions of the soil. The simplers [2] are witnesses to the herbage of England, thronged with physical plants, medicinals, restorative and preventive. The surface of the soil is covered with antidotes, with cordials, with healing and comfortable herbs, with noble perfumes, and beautiful flowers, the clothing of a thousand hills: who brought these from beyond seas? They are the mere children of nature, the offspring of mother-soil, not beholden to commerce, but that had their ancient

[1] Still an important English horse-racing center.

[2] "Simple" is a medicinal herb or plant; a simpler would be a compounder of such herbs for medicine.

abode here, beyond the reach of history, and before the island had any people; mere antediluvians, whose families are as old as nature —and which other countries fetch from us, not we from them: I refer to the enlargements or additions to Cambden [3] for the particulars of these natives of Britain, and the several counties they inhabit; it would be endless to enumerate them, there they may be seen.

But we have no plums, no apples, no cherries, but by the assistance of foreign commerce, the utmost produce is a sloe and a crab; though if this were true we might be a very comfortable spot without them, yet every common gardener can detect this fable, when taking the scion of a crab or a wild apple, or the seedling of the same, and by grafting on the pear, or by often transplanting them, they shall daily produce the apple in all its various kinds, without the favour of any foreign importation. The poor cherry is called a foreigner too, and yet I'll produce the right sort, the same we call the Kentish cherry, equal in beauty and taste, though not altogether so large, wild in the woods of Drumulanrich in Scotland, the estate of his Grace the Duke of Queensbury, and in several others, where no hands but those of nature ever planted them; the strawberry and raspberry are to be found wild there also, and the first almost everywhere over the island, even in the very hedges.

Again, honey and beeswax, this is the work of mere nature, the genuine fruit of the soil gathered by the industrious bee; no man will say the little merchant trades beyond sea, and brings home his little freight from foreign countries. The regular insect never strays far from home, never lodges out of his own house or from his wife and children, but keeps good hours, comes home like a good husband every night, and brings what he has gained in the neighbouring gardens or flowery meadows to lay up in his common store for the subsistence of his family. And this supplied us very well without the sugar cane or the limbeck,[4] till luxury increased, and required a greater quantity of sweet than the honey could well answer, and that luxury is supplied by commerce; but sure we lived before very comfortable without it.

Next, let our black cattle bear witness to the soil of England; to

[3] The famous historian and antiquary, William Camden (1551–1623), whose *Britannia* (1580) is his monument.

[4] Alembic, a flask used in distilling.

what a size do they grow, what vast dimensions of fat do they feed to? And this is a testimony to the soil beyond many other nations; not all the kingdoms of France and Spain, empire of Germany, or the rich garden of Europe's delicacies, I mean Italy, can feed a bullock of such dimensions, or to such a degree of fat, as England. If this be the fruit of foreign soil, whence came they, and where are they matched? That it is the peculiarity of our soil is evident from this, that the goodness of land is in some cases and in some parts of England determined by the size of the bullock it will feed. Some land, though the grass is strong, thick, and high, will not fat a bullock at all; others, where the grass seems meaner and is shorter, shall fat a bullock of a great price; some ground will feed an ox of such a price, and so on, and the size of the beef is the test of the land. Alas for England! Poor barren uncomfortable spot! And yet I saw Sir John Fag of Sussex have four bullocks in a small enclosure in his park, which weighed 80 stone per quarter, or each of them 320 stone in the whole, of beef when dressed up, the head and hide taken off, and the entrails and tallow taken out and not reckoned, which bullocks I saw him offered £26 per head for by a butcher. Here's no help of commerce, the Exchange of London has no hand in this; indeed, trade mends the price of beef, but nothing from abroad adds to the bulk. It is fed by the mere grass of the field; no art, no planting or transplanting, grafting or inoculating, but mere English, such as no part of the world can show. Hungaria and Transylvania comes nearest to us, and their cattle are as large, which is owing to the rich soil on the banks of the Danube, the Save, the Tybiscus, but no part of Hungary will feed that large kind to so vast a degree of fat as England. I might read you a lecture of butter and cheese produced by mere nature in this poor barren uncomfortable spot, but the world is so full of witnesses for us to whom we export it, and who can from no part of the world return the like for quality and quantity, that it is needless to name it.

And so much for the barren uncomfortable spot of earth that falls to our share; in which I never saw a man of sense more mistaken than the *Spectator*, who on the contrary ought to have acknowledged his Creator's goodness to England, whose inhabitants may with great justice praise their Maker in the words of David, "The lines are fallen to me in a pleasant place, I have a goodly heritage." . . .[5]

[5] Psalms 16:6.

Index